AF655570

HERMENEUTICS
of Suspicion and Framework for Literary Interpretation

Studies in Language, Metaphor, Time and Narrative

HERMENEUTICS
of Suspicion and Framework for Literary Interpretation

Studies in Language, Metaphor, Time and Narrative

DR. MOHAMMAD TARIQ

AUTHORSPRESS

Worldwide Circulation through Authorspress Global Network
First Published in 2022
by
Authorspress
Q-2A Hauz Khas Enclave, New Delhi-110 016 (India)
Phone: (0) 9818049852
E-mail: authorspressgroup@gmail.com
Website: www.authorspressbooks.com

Hermeneutics of Suspicion
Framework for Literary Interpretation
Studies in Language, Metaphor, Time and Narrative
ISBN 978-93-5529-329-9

Copyright © 2022 Mohammad Tariq

All rights reserved. No part of this book may be reproduced or transmitted in any form or by any means, electronic, mechanical, photocopying, or otherwise, without the express written consent of the author.

Printed in India at Thomson Press (India) Limited

Acknowledgment

This is an honor and privilege to extend my sincere gratitude to my supervisor – Dr. R. B. Sharma who with his exhaustive knowledge, intellectual acumen, perceptive powers, and wealth of insights, has worked as a catalyst. It is true to say that Dr. Sharma has sharpened my epistemic vision. The life-long-lessons taught by him with all possible maxims of politeness have revolutionized my entire life.

I owe a deep and heartfelt gratitude to Prof. Nishi Pandey and special thanks to Prof. SZH Abidi, former Heads, Department of English, University of Lucknow, Lucknow for their encouragement, help and motivation. I am thankful to the Librarian and Staff – Departmental Library; Tagore Library, University of Lucknow; Amiruddaula Public Library, Lucknow; Librarian ICPR, Lucknow; Central Library, BHU, Varanasi; Central Library AMU, Aligarh; and bookfi.org – the, largest free online library for all their help and open access to the catalogues, books, journal and magazines. I owe a special sense of gratitude for all their possible support and assistance – especially to Mr. Vajpei Saheb, a thorough gentleman for his humble, helpful and generous attitude.

This work was submitted as a thesis for the award of the degree of PhD in English. I, therefore, wish to offer my special thanks to the Registrar and Dy. Registrar, Lucknow University (2017) for granting permission for publication of the thesis in book form. I wish to thank Professor Anita Singh, Department of English, BHU and Professor Shankar A. Dutt, Department of English, Patna University for giving their scholarly attention and all the appreciation.

It seems impossible to measure the depth of love, care and concern my parents and siblings have shown, for them, words indeed fail me. What has sustained me so far were their prayers and valuable sacrifices all the time. With a lot of love, I appreciate and acknowledge the academic concerns of my beloved wife, Dr. Afreen Usmani. Without her motivation and encouragement, it almost looked impossible to complete the task of revision and publication.

Dr. Mohammad Tariq (tariq faraz)

Preface

This book sheds light on many of the constantly ignored, forgotten and disregarded aspects of language, hermeneutic principles and praxis. Language, its infinite potentialities and richness had been one of the oldest attractions to me – it was from the days when I used to ask my father many irritating questions about stars and milky ways at night e. g. "How come all this?" "Who created the stars, the flora and fauna in the whole Cosmos?" The reply used to be "the Almighty!" Next, "What was created first?" He would answer – "Pen!" The pen was created at first, then everything else. Next – "What did a pen do?" Answer – "writing!" The pen had got directions to write everything that had to happen in God's created worlds. Next, "How come writing?" and "How come language…...?" No satisfactory reply as yet! My father, Molvies, Pundits, and Masters – best available in the town hired as tutors would all meet their limitations to give any satisfactory answer to the questions.

The same question emerged after my PG Program. The papers i. e. "Structure of English," "Literary Criticism," and "Contemporary Literary Theory" taught by (late) Professor Ashok Kumar; my learned supervisor Dr. R. B. Sharma and Dr. Mirza gave fresh blood to my old and hidden ambitions to understand language and its true nature including the mechanism involved in communication as a whole.

Later, with the discovery of flux in language my curiosity also invited a fine focus on the understanding of time and, therefore, the narratives as well – especially the literary narratives.

Although, the question still remains the same as the assumption /understanding in Islamic theology in which it is generally considered by some scholars that Almighty amongst all his creations –created pen for the first – AND – this constitutes a serious problem! How can a pen be created first if the Almighty has to say "kun" for any creation (as kun faya kun, Arabic: "Be, and it becomes") – or as in the Biblical text "Let there be light…" principle. Which in a way, amongst many interpretations, means that – language is being used for the creation of pen and light...! So the condition for any creation is to name whatever is to be created – then it gets created! Thus, saying pen was created first would be as erroneous as it is in the Bible, in "Genesis" that God created earth one day and sun another day etc. A similar problem arises here – how can earth be created in a day without the creation of a sun? Therefore, how can a pen be created without the creation of language? How can language skills and its writing instruments be created without the creation of language? There can be language without pen but there can never be a pen without language!

If in Lacan's language, naming is time (*Ecrits: A Selection* 172), then to do something with language would be considered doing something *with time* – which means that *language use* and *time* can never be separated from each other. Thus, dimensions of truth or meaning may be revealed only with the appearance of language – and that can only be possible in the strong body of metaphor – metaphor in narratives and narratives in metaphors. Considering all the above problems, the book attempts to understand the nature of language as if it is entirely metaphorical by nature.

The first part "Introduction: A Perspective on Hermeneutics" of the book discusses the research question or establishes the research statement as – "What is language and its nature?" This question comprises half of the research program. The second half deals with the problem of time and narrative with its overall hermeneutics – especially the literary hermeneutics. The "Introduction" dealing with the progress in hermeneutics (principle and praxis) proposes a framework of Hermeneutics – for literary interpretation.

Therefore, Chapter I according to the scheme completely deals with the problematic of metaphor and the nature of language. The chapter consists of two different parts – the first focuses on metaphor and language prior to Ricoeur; and in the second, it presents a critical exploration of Ricoeur's *La Metaphore vive* (1975), (*The Rule of Metaphor* 1977) which successfully and very strongly proves language to be totally and completely metaphorical.

Chapter II after the first one can be said to be a second epic endeavor in the continuation to understand the nature of time and narrative – with special reference to Paul Ricoeur's *Time and Narrative* in three volumes (1981-86). The chapter sheds light on Ricoeur's hermeneutics of threefold mimesis in connection with the three dimensions of time as: prefiguration, configuration and reconfiguration of the temporal aspects of time – and are named at the end as – the aporetics of temporality in the poetics of narrativity. Ricoeur also tells about the narrative identity which is later discussed in the following chapter. In the language of Locke, Paul de Man that narratives are the discourse of the subject, and "we as subjects are explicitly inscribed with the narrative." ("The Epistemology of Metaphor," *Critical Inquiry* 25 – Autumn 1978)

Chapter III explores the old idea of exegesis and Ricoeur's hermeneutics of text.

The chapter strives to understand the existential notion of subject /self and the latent textual being of the text. The problems associated with text are brought into light with special reference to some basics of Ricoeur's hermeneutic corpus i. e. "appreciation" and "distanciation," "explanation," "interpretation," "understanding" and "appropriation" etc.

Chapter IV presents the proposed framework (hermeneutic) for literary interpretation. The fourth chapter may be considered the soul and the heart of the book. It shows how hermeneutics gets freed from the capture of the sacred scriptures to the secular scripture called literature. The framework is presented as *Voice* (human/holy) *IMPACTS* with a channel of hermeneutics and understanding process. At the end, it also shows the subversion of Jakobson's linguistic model of communication into the proposed framework of Ricoeur's practical and subjective hermeneutics.

Chapter V deals with the practical aspects of the framework, it is applied on Salman Rushdie's magnum opus *Midnight's Children.* The text is given a reading following the ways suggested by Ricoeur. The analysis is made in the same fashion as did Ricoeur in his *Time and Narrative.* The analysis is on the basis of the configuration of time with a central focus on the metaphor of midnight. The world of the text meets all aspects of Ricoeur's hermeneutics. The text appears to be half *of* the time and half *about time.* The fusion of history and fiction projects true configuration of time as was observed by Ricoeur in *Time and Narrative.*

In conclusion, a detailed analysis of the entire research is put together including all its success and limitations. The conclusion links all the chapters and suggests further research areas for future researchers.

Mohammad Tariq (tariq faraz)

Foreword

The present work is first-rate academic research in English which combines a wide review of theoretical work, excellent comprehension, a high order of analytical ability and theoretical insight. Popular theory icons: Derrida, Baudrillard and Zizek are often coveted for academic exercises but a valuable work on the unobtrusive, epigenetic brilliant Ricoeur is commendable. The introduction skillfully explains the idea of hermeneutics to discover meaning and the text as a point of initiation to consider the world as textual with human life being expressed through discourses. The significant statement made under 1.3 is that "time in relation to metaphor is the context that creates the possibility of stable meaning," but the fluidity of time itself generates a problematic. The structure of language itself is conflated with sociality and historicity. Citing the works of Schleiermacher, Dilthey, Gadamer and Heidegger, the scholar makes two points, one related to a justful hermeneutics; the other is the crucial understanding of metaphor as ennobling and elevating, an index for the representation, not merely mimesis.

Chapter III explores the subject's authenticity of consciousness that is false consciousness and explains a conceptual understanding of key words in Ricoeur's hermeneutic lexicon. The theoretical propositions are carried forward in the next chapter where hermeneutics is emancipated from the scriptures. In this movement of emancipation, the god/genius axis charts the road toward hermeneutics of suspicion. In an age of freedom, this proposal investigates the symptomatic places exposing its latent content in discovering the interconnectedness between the whole and its constituents involving historical reconstruction and divinatory empathy. The value of connectedness is the understanding of narrative identity, which, the scholar argues, is crucial to understanding literature freed from propaganda and ideologies, so necessary in our times.

The work has been meaningfully structured into seven sections that include a comprehensive introduction and a conclusion that invited further debate and research. In view of the wide reading, comprehension and the scholastic value of the dissertation with careful attention to methodology, it gives me great pleasure to recommend the work to be read by the modern-day academic scholarship.

Prof. Shanker A. Dutt
Department of English
Patna University Paka-800 005

❖❖❖

The work aims at analyzing and exploring Paul Ricoeur's philosophy of language, time and narrative and his hermeneutics of suspicion for the purpose of literary and non-literary interpretations. From scriptural and textual interpretations, the word hermeneutics is now stretched to imply the philosophy of understanding, practice of reading, meaning and interpreting.

The scholar divides his discussion in five chapters. The introduction clearly establishes the aim of the thesis as a study of language and its nature and the problem of time and narrative with its overall hermeneutics. It asserts that the prime source of our understanding is language, literature, morals norms and religion. It further discusses three aspects of hermeneutics laid down by Schleiermacher namely: experience, expressions and understanding. The discussion shows that Gadamer's hermeneutics of tradition and historicity has been rejected by Ricouer for a hermeneutics of suspicion in line with Marx, Freud and Nietzsche.

The first chapter deals with the problematics of metaphor and the nature of language, it establishes Ricoeur's contention that language is purely metaphoric. Chapter two tries to understand the nature of time and narrative, and establish that narratives and metaphor add to language and have a productive circularity. The third chapter attempts to understand the existential notion of the subject/self and the textual being of a text. Chapter four explicates the proposed framework for literary interpretation and concludes by pointing out that in a post-theory period a justful hermeneutics seems to be the most needed approach for the art of interpretation.

The book presents arguments in clear and concise terms about Ricoeur's hermeneutics of suspicion that attempts to find the balance between explanation and understanding, science and art, falls on the side of the perpetual and inescapable open-endedness of art. Additionally, it clears the horizon for a more authentic word, for a new reign of Truth, not only by means of a destructive critique, but by the invention of an art of interpreting. To approach the text with suspicion – to query whether what the text appears to say really does correspond with its true message seems to be both a valid and necessary hermeneutical process. Well-written and conceptualized chapters are supplemented by a comprehensive and well documented bibliography. I wish to congratulate the author on his remarkable scholarly endeavor.

Prof. Anita Singh
Professor, Department of English
Faculty of Arts, Banaras Hindu University
Varanasi 221005 Uttar Pradesh, India

❖❖❖

This book sheds light on many of the constantly ignored, forgotten and disregarded aspects of language, hermeneutic principles and praxis. The book explores the ontological relationship amongst metaphor, time, and literary text. The author has attempted to create a framework of literary hermeneutics by using the conceptual framework of those ideas as given by Paul Ricoeur. It shows how hermeneutics gets freed from the capture of the sacred scriptures to the secular scripture called literature. The book exposes the fashionable none/Sense of THEORY – especially the hypocrisy of theory in English Departments and many other Departments of Humanities. The author argues that Ricoeur's hermeneutics of suspicion are required more than ever before – because today there is always a powerful and panoptic gatekeeper at every door of the textual domain and in every sphere of the modern communication system. The work is well structured and the findings as given by the author add a new dimension to Paul Ricoeur's oeuvre.

Dr. R. B. Sharma
Associate Professor, Department of English and MEL
University Lucknow Lycknow-226007

❖❖❖

Contents

CHAPTER 1

Perspectives on Hermeneutics: Language, Metaphor and Ricoeur

1.1 Is it Possible to Understand the Nature of Language?

We "mortal millions" (Arnold) live in the world of language as Martin Heidegger says that "language is the house of Being." This language-world equally needs the same care and concern as it is with our earthly world. Scientific research and enough scholarship should also be offered as in today's ultramodern world it is given to the study of earth sciences, environment, and all other scientific and physical knowledge to understand and explain the unexplored, unexposed, and all the hidden secrets. In the same fashion, language also needs to be seen and taken as an object of yet unexplored, unexposed and hidden territory which has yet not been disclosed and discovered completely. Language as a tool has been exclusively a human property that has telepathic origins. Biologist defines the modern man as a *"homo sapiens" which* stands in Latin, for *"wise man."* The possession of language defines the animal as *"homo loquens,"* Latin, meaning "talking man," which looks like an appropriate name. "When we study language," says Chomsky," we are approaching what some might call the "human essence", the distinctive qualities of mind that are, so far as we know, "unique to man". This quality is more than any other human attributes that distinguishes human beings from other living animals. This is language which makes man powerful along with all its limitations and complexities.

Human beings are distinct from other beings in the sense that they use language, they make meaning, they interpret meaning, and in other words, they live their life by the meaning that language creates for them. That is why Heidegger became fond of saying – "Man is Language." In another sense human beings' bodies are words if not exaggerated. Language, as a system of relation, resemblance, recognition, reference, and significance or signification makes a connection between thought and reality, self and world, subject and object, ordinary and divine, mortal and immortal, physics and metaphysics. For this connection, one, for the first, must understand the nature of language that makes humans connected.

There is no doubt that language is the source of human life and power, in most of the myths and religions of the world. In Africa, a child who just arrives on the earth is a "Kunta" that is only a "thing" and a "muntu," a "person." There, through the act of learning language-that is "homo loquens," a "talking man," then the child becomes a human being according to this African tradition, the "thing" becomes human because of the possession of one language at least and for them to be human is to be linguistic. Now, curiosity brings nearer to the question: what does it mean to know a language? What is its nature?

1.2 Is Language Metaphorical?

Understanding the nature of language has become one of the most significant topics in the interpretation of human life. In fact, it is not the text that is woven in language, but the human life weaves and is viewed in language. In the later part of the twentieth century, thinkers of language have made radical understandings of the nature of language. Language that is in flux in itself bears the necessity of its own critique, when it is discovered. One of the ways to understand the nature of languages is that it is metaphorical in every sense of the term. Language is metaphorical because it relates itself to the objects that it describes only as an image; the relationship of language with its objects is not syntactical but imaginary.

As a metaphor cannot relate itself in a synthetical manner with the objects that it describes only as an image, the relationship of language with its object is not syntactical, but imaginary. If we assign some concrete meaning to the metaphor, such an attempt is rooted in the ideological thinking of the views of metaphor. Metaphor, in itself, has more than three thousand years' history of its time, and is viewed in various ways; there are various views e. g. the similarity view, the interaction view, the relational view, the pragmatic view, the cognitive view. After twenty-five centuries of rhetorician's attention to the metaphor, philosophers, thinkers, grammarians, and literary theorists and critics are unable to make a general way to identify and recognize a metaphor's nature to understand it. The question arises, what if anything they serve to tell us?

Traditionally the study of language and linguistic meaning takes place within a sub-field called semantics which is also a sub discipline in philosophy where the relationship between meaning and formal logic is emphasized. Semantics and semiotics, the two different branches of language study, deal with the study of meaning that language provides. Semiotics is the study of signs and symbols and how they are used. Semiotics is "a general philosophical theory of signs and symbols that deal especially with their function in both artificially constructed and natural languages and comprise syntactic, semantics, and pragmatics." Semantics is the study of the meanings of words and phrases in language, the meaning of words and phrases in a particular context. It is "the historical and psychological study and the classification of words or forms viewed as factors in linguistic development." Thus, Semantics has two branches; one Lexical Semantics that focuses on the meaning associated with individual Lexical items e. g. words. Second: Provisional or relational semantics, which focuses on those relational meanings that we typically express with a whole of the sentence.

1.3 Metaphor and the Temporality of Time

Is metaphor a semantic innovation or a creation of new semantic pertinence? Or it is a work of resemblance, sense, or reference? Is it affected by the temporality of time? Time in relation to metaphor is the context that creates that possibility of stable meaning. Language being one of the fictional entities, always seeks the support of time to generate stable meaning. However, time itself is slippery and unstable, and very difficult to hold, the future is yet to come, and that will remain forever in future in fact. Language that makes meaning in relation to such temporality is doomed to create unstable meaning. The question of the structure of language naturally remains linked to the question of human sociality and human historicity. This is the place where the problem of language appears in its full shape.

What that metaphor stands for in the semantics of discourse will be the key study of the present endeavor. What is "statement-metaphor" and "word-metaphor"? What is that which makes a word fall in the category of tropes? Is metaphor a sign, a Symbol, a Reference, Resemblance, a Pragmatic entity, an interacting Time, or a Cognitive entity? Is it an existential or structured entity? Does metaphor provide any semantic innovation or creation as a new evolving natural semantic entity? What are the problems that arise when a metaphor travels from a word to sentence, and from sentence to discourse? Is metaphor a "productive imagination"? Does it have any "iconic function"? What if it is a figure of speech? Is there any power to redescribe reality? Does it suggest anything advanced? Does it carry any sort of degree in it? Does it contain any fictitious capacity? Is it transcendental, or of double or multiple allegiance? What is the nature of poetic/ literary metaphor? How does metaphor relate itself to time and narrative? How do metaphorical utterances function in narrative discourse? What is the meaning and its nature that a metaphor serves?

1.4 Origin of Hermeneutics and its Requirement

Generally, a word written or spoken, is treated as a sign in the lexical code of semiotics that passes from semiotics to semantics; and then it turns into discourse. The problem arises in reading, seeing, meaning, explaining, interpreting, appropriating, and finally in understanding. Concisely speaking, the problem that a reader encounters while reading within a literary text is in the unfolding of the metaphors and interpreting it to understand.

In recent years the questions of meaning, interpreting, and understanding have been crucial to the problem of hermeneutics in the very presence of literary and critical theories of reading, writing and understanding from the mid-20th century onwards. Hermeneutics has evolved into its own as a philosophical question on language and to the emerging new interest in human and social sciences in the ultramodern times of globalization.

What does it mean by hermeneutics? What is its origin? Is it a method? Or is it a process of meaning, interpreting and understanding? What are the boundaries and lines it touches? Is it really a modern phenomenon? Is it of any importance and use? If yes, then why is the hermeneutic approach still ignored in the Eastern and Western academia? Why are critical theories and literary theories privileged? In recent times, according to Don Ihade, it seems that in the United States, the impact of hermeneutics has started to be felt, specifically in the philosophy of human and social sciences after the cross-cultural interaction and relations.

According to the folk etymology, the word "hermeneutics" has perhaps two derivations: one is the messenger, Hermes, a Greek deity in Greek mythology, who is an interpreter and translator of Zeus' messages to mankind; he is supposed to be the inventor of language and speech. Second: is the Syncretic Ptolemaic Deity, Hermes Trismegistus, who is supposed to be the representative of hidden, secret and sacred knowledge. Hermeneutics is a wider discipline. The term hermeneutics and exegesis are casually used interchangeably. Though, the word "Hermeneutics" is plural but singular, or plural in construction. According to the dictionary, it contains two different meanings one is of a method and understanding or principle of interpretation; second: is the study of the methodological principles of interpretation and understanding.

Hermeneutics in Talmudic use refers to a process of sacred scriptural interpretation. The earliest and finest example is found in Jewish oral tradition, the summaries of the "principles" by which *Torah* could be interpreted. In this connection, the principles which were set forth in the "Brita" of Rabbi Ishmael are best known. There were different levels of interpretations; some were applied to arrive only at the plain meaning of the text and to expound the laws given in the text; rest were for mystical and secret levels of understanding. Hermeneutics in Vedic approach existed as a kind of *mimamsa* or exegesis of which functions in the classical way, primarily, to interpret the true meaning of the Vedic scriptures. Vedic Hermeneutics involves the oldest sacred text of Sana-tan-Dharma. Mimamsa is the leading school of hermeneutics. The *mimamsa* Sutra of Jamini were used for Vedic interpretations. (3 to 1st BCE)

In the West, hermeneutics is the principle of the interpretation of *Injeel*, now known as the *Bible*. The above discussed, Jewish, Hindu and Christian hermeneutic traditions are distinctly different. The biblical hermeneutics is also known and named as Augustinian hermeneutics which has different tradition e. g.: Biblical hermeneutics in Apostolic Age, in sub-Apostolic period in the age of antiquity, Ante-Nicene period, school of Alexandrine and Antioch, Medieval period, Middle age and Modern Period Biblical hermeneutics. Hermeneutics, therefore, originally discovered and traced the Logos in all the traditions. It was attached only to sacred works. It was only within the boundaries of Sacred and Divine.

But for now hermeneutics in the present times stands for the theory of understanding and interpreting of linguistic and non-linguistic expressions, verbal and non-verbal communication, semiotics of pre-supposition and pre-understanding as well. It is found that Plato used the term hermeneutics in his many of the dialogues contrasting hermeneutic knowledge of the truth-value of the utterance as his Sophia does not involve knowledge of the truth-value of utterance. Aristotle's treatise on logic and semantics, *Peri hermeneias*, translated into Latin as *Deinterpretatione,* also adds to the term hermeneutics. The English version of Aristotle on *Interpretation*, according to R. S. P. Beekes is the first and most well composed work on Hermeneutics in Western traditions. Hermeneutics, for both of them (Plato and Aristotle), is largely on announcement and the art of announcement, expression and the art of expression.

The Medieval Christian biblical interpretation of text incorporates exegesis into a fourfold mode. First, is the literal meaning of scriptures that is what the text states directly? Second, the allegorical sense, that looks at the text in the doctrinal context of Church-dogma; and, the literal meaning having a symbolic one too e. g. typology. Third, is the moral appreciation of the text to the individual readers? The fourth is the implicit allusions which are drawn out of the text. It brings near to the secret, metaphysical, and eschatological knowledge that is concerned with death and judgment in theology and in religion. Such a theory is only to be found in Philo of Alexandria, which has an open and wider effect on allegorical meaning of the Old Testament anticipating the idea that the literal meaning of a text may conceal a deeper non-literal meaning that could only be unfolded and through a systematic interpreting effort. Later, in the expansion of hermeneutic philosophy, hermeneutic view meets another addition: that Scripture has three levels of meaning corresponding to the triangle of body, soul, and spirit. It is Augustine (AD 354-430), who for the first time introduces the universality-claim of hermeneutics. His influence on modern hermeneutics has been acknowledged by a very prominent impact on the development of modern hermeneutics e. g. his notion of 'Being', the problem of hermeneutics has now become a universal issue in modern times.

The word *ta' wil* (تاويل) in Arab-Islamic background is used as equivalent to the term hermeneutics in the same reference. However, Islamic tradition is altogether different from intellectual and philosophical hermeneutics of the Western tradition. Along with the word ta'wil the other equivalent terms for hermeneutics are as: *tafsir*, (تفسير/explanation) *ijtehad* (اجتهاد reasoned opinion) *balaghah* (بلاغه / rhetoric), are expected to reach to a higher level of understanding and reasoning to the study of Al-Qur'an. i. e. the inimitability of the wondrous nature of the Qur'anic text. Some of the major schools of Arab-Islamic hermeneutics are as: Kharijites, Mutazilites, Ash'arites,

Rafidites, Shi' ite, Ismailites, Nusayrites, Qarmatians, Qadarites, Jabri tes, Hanafites, Shafaites, Humblites, and, Malikites, all different Schools. (Ibraheem Nagi Ahmad Tagaddeen)

The famous epithet used by Roland Barthes (1915-80) for Japanese culture as an "empire of signs," also fits equally well with that of China's an "empire of writing and reading." China's hermeneutic tradition is predominantly Confucian in origin, based on both political in-doctrination and on moral education that is commonly called China's politico-ethical-tradition. China's hermeneutics is traced and marked before the fourth century B.C. in the interpretation of classic history, poetry, arts, and metaphysics. The thinkers seem to be very keen to the question: how to read a text adequately and appropriately, and how to fill the gap between language and thought, words and ideas? The early thinkers, Mencius (c.372-289 BC) and Zhuangzi (c.369-286 BC) are considered the pioneers of Chinese hermeneutic tradition.

Mencius' famous notion is "to use one's understanding to trace it back to what was on the mind of the author? That is – how does one grasps the meaning of a text?" Apart from Mencius and Zhuangzi, Shijing and Zbouyi also represent Chinese hermeneutic tradition (Ming Dong Gu 1-50).

1.5 Hermeneutics in Modern Times

It is observed that there has been a constant revolutionary change and shift in the theory and history of hermeneutics. For now, the term hermeneutics can be put in the following categories such as Jewish hermeneutics, Vedic hermeneutics, Biblical hermeneutics, Qur'anic hermeneutics, Chinese hermeneutics, and very recently the Modern hermeneutics. This book, to be very precise, would be an endeavor to focus only on Modern hermeneutics in general and Ricoeurean hermeneutics in particular. Modern hermeneutics consists of three parts: (a) hermeneutic theory, (b) hermeneutic philosophy, and (c) critical hermeneutics. The modern hermeneutics develops a "method," as a science of interpretation and enunciate the theory of interpretation to communicate in general and particular, the modern hermeneutics includes; (i) a theory or philosophy of interpretation of meaning, linguistic or non-linguistic expressions and human actions, and behaviors as well, (ii) theory of religious exegesis, (iii) general philological methodology, (iv) the science of all linguistic understanding, (v) the methodological foundation of

Geisteswissenschaften, (vi) the phenomenology of Dasein, existential and structural understanding, (vii) the systems of interpretation both recollection and iconoclastic, to reach the meaning behind myths and symbols.

Hermeneutics has taken a turn of philosophical approach to the analysis of human understanding and behavior. Hermeneutics today, in postmodern affairs is preoccupied with such questions as; what does it mean when one says that someone "understands" a text?

Does "understanding" mean reproducing and recapitulating exactly what the text says on its own terms and conditions, and interpreting the text in terms of its author's life or its social or historical context? Can understanding and interpreting mean measuring the text against contemporary knowledge and seeing it either wanting or valuable? How can "understanding" overcome the hurdles and obstacles of distance and appropriation of historical time? And, how can understanding be possible in the distance of culture between the text and its reader?

Modern hermeneutics influences both the theory of literature, and literary theory. The former one covers the basic nature and function of literature and the later concerns the aspects of literature i. e. from, genre, style, and technique etc. The renowned modern scholar, who have contributed to the evolutionary process of philosophy of the modern hermeneutics are: Giambattisto Vico (1668-1744), Friedrich Daniel Earnst Schleiremacher (1768-1834), Wilhelm Dilthey (1813-1911), Enrico Betti (1823-1992/1911), Emilio Betti (1890-1968), Martin Heidegger (1889-1979), Hans George Gadamer (1900-2002), Bernard Lonergan (1904-1984), Paul Ricoeur (1913-2005), Karl Max Weber (June-1920), Karl-Otto Apel (March-1922), Jiirgen Hobermas (June-1929), Richard Rorty (1931-2007) Stanley Eugene Fish (April-1938), Andres Ortiz Oses (1943), Maurizio Ferraris (1956), Wolfgang Iser, E.O. Hirsch. The twentieth century interest in the Justinian legal code the Justinian law makes two different classes of obligation, naming as: quasi-dialectic and quasi-contract, generates its own independent hermeneutics of jurisprudence. After Luther, hermeneutics seems to have taken a move in three different directions: the ontological, the phenomenological, and the transcendental.

1.6 Friedrich Daniel Ernst Schleiermacher (1768-1834)

The man responsible for bringing hermeneutics in prominence is said to be Friedrich Daniel Ernst Schleiermacher (1768-1834), commonly known and considered as "father of the modern hermeneutics," who would teach a course on hermeneutics during 1810-1934 in the protestant theology at the University of Berlin. He is all praise for the "divine Plato" and constructs a "religion of art." This German philosopher, theologian and renowned biblical scholar is also known as the "father of modern liberal theology." According to Gadamer, Schleiermacher hermeneutics is "the art of avoiding misunderstanding." Schleiermacher uses hermeneutics for the first time in German theology by framing a "general hermeneutics" in 1819 in a series of lectures, which is also known as "the art of understanding." For him human beings have a "linguistic disposition." Their linguistic competence enables them to understand the utterances of the speakers. In his view, understanding and interpretation always have two aspects, or two components: Grammatical and Psychological. The first corresponds to linguistic aspects of understanding and the later one to divinatory dimensions, which records the individuality and originality of the speaker or the writer. His psychology, or divinatory aspects, take on its basis the phenomenal dualism of the "ego" and the "non-ego" regarding man's life as the interaction of these elements. For him, the "ego" is both body and soul. Man's "organization" or the sense of nature has its intellectual elements and the intellect is "organic," and there is no such thing called "pure-mind" or "pure-soul."

Schleiermacher, having been influenced by Friedrich Schleigal, argues that as every act of a speaker is related to the totality of language that is related to both-the totality of the *language* and the totality of the *speaker's thoughts.* To him thought is essentially dependent on and bound by, or even identical with language. To him, meaning is word usage. Thus, for him, understanding a speech always involves two moments: one, to understand what is said in the *context of the language* with all its possibilities; and second, to understand it as a fact in the *thinking of the speaker.* (*Hermeneutics Reader Compendium,* 74) In Schleiermacher's philosophy, language and persons both exist under existential conditions where psychological and grammatical interpretations are to be understood. There is deep linguistic, conceptual and intellectual difference amongst the people. Schleiermacher does not distinguish between the words, which now turned-terms-*understanding* and *interpretation* clearly. The difference possesses severe challenges to its interpretation. Therefore, to cope with this challenge, is the main task of Schleiermacher's philosophy of hermeneutics. Thus, to cope with this challenge is the main task of Schleiermacher's philosophy of hermeneutics. For Schleiermacher hermeneutics became an art, in his view, every utterance spoken or recorded, in present and in past, can be understood through interpretation. Hermeneutics should be used as a universal discipline which can be applied to all subjects e. g. religion, Bible, law, literature, oral, written or recorded language to modern texts as well as to ancient texts, to the works in one's own languages and to the works in foreign language as well. "Semantic holism" seems to be his most original doctrine in his philosophy of language that is highly relevant in his hermeneutic connection. According to Schleiermacher interpretation is much more difficult task, it must acquire a good knowledge of the text's historical context, keeping in mind that it has two sides-linguistic and psychological dispositions, that have cyclic relationship between the grammatical and psychological interpretations-based on the principles of eternal recurrences. That is why the universal and the particular sustain each other. Schleiermacher says that the author functions as if he himself functions in the language-partly bringing forth new things by his use of language, and, partly retaining qualities of language that he repeats and transmits. In Schleiermacher's corpus, an author does not have any identity except in relation to what he does by writing or recording or in saying or in speaking. His linguistic variety situates him as it links the text with the creator within a geographical locality, having certain peculiar climatic conditions and contexts that on words have the influence on its structure. Thus, Schleiermacher concludes that the divinatory and linguistic, grammatical and psychological effects in the comparative methods cannot be separated from each other. The psychological aspect, which he links to divinatory aspects, helps the interpreter transform himself into the author. Both seek to understand the work as a type, calling the divinatory aspect a "feminine force." and the linguistic "a masculine force" (Schleiermacher, *Hemeneutik,* 1959).

1.7 Wilhelm Dilthey (1833-1911)

It is Wilhelm Dilthey (1833-1911), who actually re-developed Schleiermacher's philosophy in 1890, approximately a century later.

The influential philosopher Dilthey names the "general theory of understanding." of Schleiermacher a "hermeneutic circle" for every form of human sciences to interpret by mutually qualifying the interplay between man's evolving sense of the whole and man's retrospective understanding of the componential parts. The hermeneutic circle is a containment of the verbal part of any linguistic whole that is responsible for the understanding of the determinate meaning. It is taken into account that the parts should be approached with all essential priorities to achieve the meaning of the whole. We, therefore, can only know the meaning of the whole by knowing the constituent linking parts. In this circularity of the interpretive process, there is an application between a single word within a sentence and the sentence as a whole, the magnitude in the Aristotelian term, moreover, an interrelation between all the sentences and the works as a whole.

In Dilthey's views, the hermeneutic circle is not vicious circle, but through it one can achieve a valid interpretation by mutually qualifying interplay between one's evolving sense of the whole and retrospective understanding of its constituent and component parts. Wilhelm Dilthey thus, the author of an influential essay "The Rise of Hermeneutics" (1900) broadens the Schleirmacherian hermeneutics into a universal methodology of human sciences. In his *Introduction to Human Science* (1833), Dilthey argues that humans are a part of nature, but unlike other natural objects like stones, air, trees etc. are imbued with consciousness. Dilthey expands the field of hermeneutics from a study of texts to a study of "life expressions" According to him, the understanding of an expression in life takes place in the medium of *objective mind*. The elementary forms of understanding give rise to the higher form of understanding, though it [understanding] takes place in the medium of "objective mind." The subject matter of understanding is always something individual, the individual not purely as example of a man in general, but man as a "totality in himself." The object of understanding is always a "life-expression," that is in three different classes – a) concepts, judgments and larger thought-structures, b) action from another class of life-expressions, c) the lived experience. In the Hegelian category, the understanding of any expression of life is in the medium of objective mind. Dilthey grapples with the explanation of natural science and understanding with human sciences. He considers that the prime source of understanding arises from language, literature, moral norms, and religion which is the base of man's cultural structure and context. *(The Foundation of Social Research and Perspective in the Research Process 1998)*

In Dilthey's view, texts are expressions of individuals and are constrained by both the values of their period and place reflecting a historical and social context. Hermeneutics for him is the art of understanding objects on which the human spirit or human life leaves its imprint. The objects might be works of art, a law, a judgment, a poem, a sacred text, architecture, dance, that is every form touched and shaped by the human spirit to convey sense or meaning. For Dilthey, hermeneutics should be the methodological foundation for all subjects which fall in humanities as well as the condition of the possibility of understanding and interpreting itself. In conclusion, Dilthey's hermeneutic theory involves three elements: experience (erlebnis), expression (ausdruck), and understanding (verstehen). Dilthey claims that historicity does not mean "tradition-mindedness" or even limitedness to the past traditions, but it affirms the temporality of human experience that is understanding present in relation to past and futures Dilthey's theory of understanding, and his methodology of hermeneutic interpretation seems to have a profound influence in the development of literary theories. In short, it is observed that his categories of "objective mind," and "man as a totality in himself" look analogous to Schleiermacher's division between linguistic and psychological aspects of understanding for both of them, the core issue is that how these two categories of understanding would "appropriate" each other.

1.8 M. H. Abrams' *The Mirror and the Lamp* (1953)

It is observed that after the mid-twentieth century western Literary theories are in a hectic shuffle of a dramatic range of formulations on literature, language, author, text, reader, interpretation, time, history, understanding, reality, and representation. The literary epistemology seems to be a Copernican revolution in the production of meaning and its manifestation. It is M.H. Abrams, who advanced a very influential model of literature in his book *The Mirror and the Lamp* (1953), he sets four essential components of the phenomenon as the Universe, the Work, the Writer, and the Reader. Drawing a triangle with the literary text in the center:

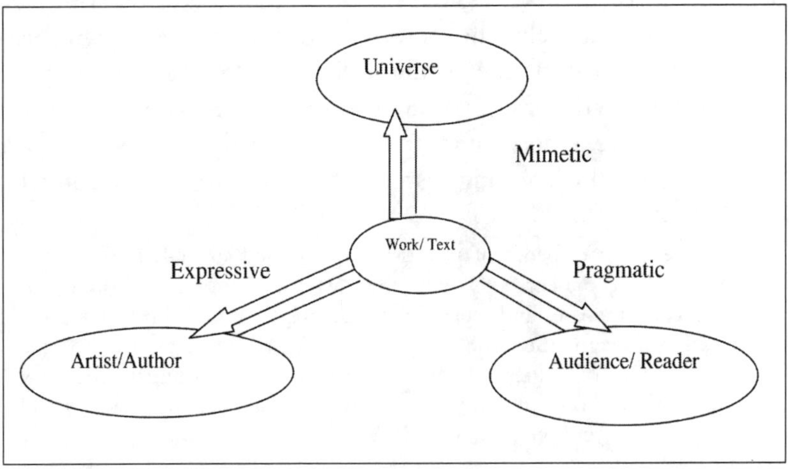

Through this triangle, Abrams represents the ontology of literary text as a reflection of the world, reflection of the author, and its effect on the audience. This representation respectively carries four theories of meaning: (a) the imitative/ mimetic theory, that is universe oriented, (b) the expressive theory that is author oriented, (c) the objective theory, that is work oriented, (d) the pragmatic theory that is reader-oriented. The traditional interest in the development of Western literary theory is an interest in the author's intention. The text is meant merely as a reflection of the author's soul; therefore, the aim of interpretation becomes to recover the original meaning of the text. The authorial meaning of the text, in the history of hermeneutics from Plato, and Aristotle to Schleiermacher and Dilthey give a classic account of such author-oriented hermeneutics. But now, the later twentieth century hermeneutic approaches hold the notion that true meaning of the text is not based on the correspondence between the reader's understanding and the author's intention, and the original audiences' understanding that is *adequate.* True meaning, in a contrasting view, is seen as *aletheia that* is a revelatory insight or un-concealment, found in the reading process rather than in the text.

1.9 Martin Heidegger (1889-1976) and Hans-Georg Gadamer (1900-2002)

In the twentieth century the author-oriented hermeneutic was sharply challenged by Martin Heidegger (1889-1976) and his disciple Hans-Gerog Gadamer (1900-2002). Interpretation, according to them, is not entirely subjective, as the text places limits on how one can understand it. In their views, the historical and linguistic approaches in research would help the reader understand their own biases. Moreover, to an extent the reader will never be able to completely transcend his own biases to understand, to recapitulate and re-experience the text according to the standards of his own time. Commenting on the evolving history of the theory of interpretation, M. H. Abrams says:

> Interest in the theory of interpretation revived strongly in the 1950s and 1960s, concurrently with the turn of Western philosophy to focus on the uses and meanings of language, and the turn of literary criticism-exemplified by the *New Criticism* in America to the conception of a literary work as a linguistic object and to the view that primary task of criticism is to interpret its verbal meanings and their interpretation. (Abrams 135-36).

Abrams further writes that there are two different modes in recent hermeneutics. The first one, is represented by the Italian scholar Emilio Betti (1890-1968) and the American E.D. Hirsch (b-1928). They take off from Dilthey's view that a reader, while reading, is able to get a complete objective interpretation of an author's expressed meaning in the text. Hirsch in his *Validity in Interpretation* (1967), and *The Aims of Interpretation* (1976) argues that "a text means what its author meant," that is the "verbal meaning which an author intends," which goes on to show that each verbal meaning that remains stable through the passage of time, that has the power to be reproduced by all competent readers. He asserts that the author's verbal intention is not, at the time, a state of consciousness while writing, but rather that is in an intention to mean something with the use of pre-existing linguistic convention and existing norms, being actualized in words, is shared by its competent readers in the same system of convention. Hirsch insists that if the text is taken in account independently as a representative of the intentional meaning of its author, it remains indeterminate being capable of an indefinite diversity of meaning. Thus, in conclusion, it seems that Hirsch reformulates Dilthey's hermeneutic circle and is found following traditional hermeneutics while making an essential distinction between a "verbal meaning" and "textual significance." The verbal meaning of a text to Hirsch is the meaning intended by the writer, which is determinate and stable meaning; its significance keeps the text alive and vibrant for different readers of all the period of different times and different readers which meanwhile became indeterminate and ever-changing. In this way the verbal meaning becomes one of the concerns of hermeneutics; and the textual significance in all other various dimensions is one of the concerns of literary criticism, accordingly.

In the same sequence, the second mode mentioned by Abrams, in recent hermeneutics, is the diversion from Dilthey's view that the genuine and the actual understanding of literary and other humanistic texts consists in the reader's re-experience of the "inner-life" expressed in the text. The founding fathers in this mode are Martin Heidegger (1889-1979) and Hans-Georg Gadamer (1900-2002). Heidegger incorporates the act of interpretation into an existential philosophy focusing on his concept of *Dasein*, where he makes an analysis of B/being in his *Being and Time* (1927, trans. 1962). Gadamer, adopting Heidegger's philosophy, constructs an influential theory of hermeneutics for the textual interpretation, concisely called a method, in his book *Truth and Method* (1960, trans. 1975). The modern hermeneutic approaches should be indebted to the works of these two great 20th century philosophers, Martin Heidegger (1889-1976) and his student Hans-Georg Gadamer (1900-2002). Heidegger locates hermeneutics at more fundamental ground of human facticity and Gadamer though slightly diverted in his approach, re-establishes Dilthey's philosophy of hermeneutics and reformulates it. According to Robert C. Holub, they advance and advocate a general paradigm shift in three different ways: i) unlike traditional enlightenment hermeneutics, modern hermeneutics, does not concern itself exclusively simply with understanding and interpreting written, recorded or spoken documents, ii) the purpose of understanding is no more focused on the communication with or the psychology of another person – the author or the speaker, iii) the hermeneutics of Heidegger and Gadamer explores a realm that is prior to, or more fundamental than Dilthey's separation of the natural sciences from the human sciences. (*Twentieth Century Hermeneutics* 382)

In short, it is seen that modern hermeneutics abandons the traditional epistemological domain, and moves into the arena of fundamental ontology and then into the modern semantic epistemology since a man is considered as a time bound linguistic being, which replaces the question of understanding as knowledge about the "world" with the question of being in the world or in this universe. It is Martin Heidegger, a leading exponent of existentialism, who uses Husserl's phenomenology to explore the structure of human beings in his influential book *Being and Time* where he concludes that man is a time bound being. His declared purpose in his arguments is to ask: "What is the meaning of being?" A student of Husserl, and influenced by Kierkegaard, Heidegger discovers the power of negative thinking and projects a general theory of Dasein, which Kant calls, "thinking in itself" Hegel, "being in itself" and he himself, "man being in the world." Following Kierkegaard's existential philosophy, Heidegger tries to recover the ontology of textual being, which is within the metaphoricity of human discourse, and to him, the metaphorical can only exist within the metaphysical. According to him, true metaphors are produced where physics and metaphysics clash. He brings the understanding of the "event" in intentional, phenomenological, historical, existential, ontological, and linguistic contexts. For coming to the birth of an idea and establishing a teleological link between meaning and form is interpretation, and *understanding* is "laying bare" of the text, which was very recently "laying there" and has been "appropriated" now. In his view, there are three kinds of awareness, "fore-having," "fore-sight," and "fore-conception." (Vorhabe, Varschit, Vorgriff) Fore-having is the first interaction to the critic's mobility and unconscious structural grasp of the literary work that is "out there." Fore-seeing or fore-sight, according to Heidegger, is the conscious interpretive grasp, and then linking to fore-having, which was foreign till then and has recently turned conceivable, graspable, known and homelike. Fore conception is for creative writers, who unconsciously get into the hidden semantic meanings. This is pre-reflective and is the subtle invisible agency which transmits and transforms the presentation of the present. Heidegger seems to be trying to break away from the concept of language and brings his hermeneutics with the projection of his analysis of Dasein. Heidegger advocates to renovate, rediscover, reconceive, recapitulate, and retrieve the "being" through language, pronouncing that, "language speaks," and as mentioned in the binging, that "language is the house of Being." Heidegger seems to be taking a sacred turn when he declares that "all being is in Being" (10-25)

A word for Heidegger, has "the emptiest and therefore most comprehensive meaning," that is to widen and deepen the capacities of being to situate it to the Being within itself to create a room for *infinite play*. The first task for Dasein is to have the experience of the Being. Here Heidegger seems to be curious about how the meaning is appropriated by Dasein as being in the world in relation to other similar beings. For him, Dasein exists only through the ontology of understanding in his hermeneutics with "I am," which looks like a fine reversal of Descartes' nation of *Cogito.* His "I am" is the foundation of Being, the Being which makes the "I" think. Thus, Heidegger travels from traditional epistemology to the modern fundamental ontology of understanding. Thus, meaning production and its reception, in communication, occurs in the analysis of the "being there" and the "being-in-the-world." It is found in the conclusion that Heidegger does not develop any methodological device or principle of hermeneutics, but an ontology of understanding, the understanding of being in all its manifestation within the text or outside the text. *(Being and Time,* 1927)

Hans George Gadamer, the student of Martin Heidegger, further develops Dilthey's methodological concerns. He does not develop any new method but insight into his teacher's concept of Dasein and Being. Gadamer is also considered the founding father of the *philosophical hermeneutics* and becomes one of the most eminent thinkers in the twentieth century after the publication of his magnum opus *Truth and Method* (1975) His philosophical hermeneutics presented in this book seems largely to be a "hermeneutics of tradition." Gadamer argues that if the claim of understanding being a category of life is to be taken seriously, then hermeneutics should not be seen only as a methodological tool but as a "universal method." Gadamer translates the hermeneutic circle into a *"metaphor of dialogue and fusion,"* according to him "meaning is an event," "a product of the fusion of horizons," a fusion shared by both the addresser and the addressee in the act of communication. Gadamer simply asks what is understanding, and how is understanding possible? Gadamer traces a fault with both the Enlightenment and Romantic conceptions of understanding-which are based on false opposition between reason and tradition, judgment and prejudice. He rejects the distinction between text's "objective meaning" and its "significance" which looks in direct contrast with E. D. Hirsch's idea of verbal meaning and its significance. Gadamer asserts that there is no possibility of reading simply "what is there," as the text does not have the mode of being of some sort of *neutral object.* The practice of reading a text that claims complete objectivity e. g. Formalist, Structuralist, Marxist, or the Historicist Approaches of reconstruction to see what the text supposingly meant at the time of its real creation, is itself an interpretation and also wide-open to dispute. According to Gadamer, "a person reading a text is himself a part of the meaning he apprehends." In his view, therefore, "a hermeneutics that regarded understanding as reconstructing the original would be no more than recovering a dead meaning." (*TM* 335,160) To Gadamer, hermeneutics comes into existence through the analysis of universal linguisticality, it is the name of a process in understanding that makes the strange familiar and the distant distinct into the space of being, as understanding is the original character of the being of human life. It is a process in which the subject participates. Gadamer seems to be representing Heideggerian mysticism when he says that hermeneutic experience is akin to the experience of *"Thou" in 'I' Thou"* consciousness. In Gadamer's view, it is the "being" that can be understood in language; therefore, the function of hermeneutics is to study being and study language as he says a thought comes through language only. The world does not depend on language as a pre-given intelligible entity, but the world is only that when constituted by the limited sense of linguisticality. Thus, "language has its being only in conversation in the exercise of understanding between people" (*TM* 404).

Gadamer emphasizes on *historicality* in the enfolding nature of understanding which functions within the transcendental application. He tries to think through the historical implication without getting very much into it. Gadamer ponders over the *historicity of language* and rejects the instrumental role of the same. He changes the perspective through *re-birth of self* within the tradition. Another emphasis of Gadamer is to avoid prejudices against prejudices in the attempt to recover the force of tradition in understanding as the essential aim of Gadamer in *Truth and Method* seems to be to recover the validity of tradition in human understanding. He says that prejudice is a big hindrance in understanding Gadamer's canvas of providing criteria of validity that look very broad. The interpretation, in his view, is valid if it helps one to understand, or it makes sense of a text, then that is a valid interpretation and if an interpretation lends itself to an "application," is also a valid one. Gadamer goes beyond the modern methodological self-consciousness prevalent in human sciences explaining how a person comes to understand the meaning of a text. Hermeneutics to Gadamer is "concerned to seek the experience of truth that transcends the sphere of the control of scientific method" (*TM* XXI). Gadamer transcends the method or any science, as it is restricted to certain limitations. He does not provide any method of correct understanding or right interpretation.

For Gadamer, a text does not exist in an independent and in an uninterrupted state, and its meaning cannot be derived through some mechanical and scientific technique or any method. He asserts that a reader is never an independent and autonomous subject who can freely or arbitrarily impose meaning on a text.

In fact, an interpretation always belongs to a communal "tradition" that inculcates the interpreter with certain prejudices, and interests, which, then, are functional consciously or unconsciously. They play an important role in the understanding of any text. According to Gadamer, the community, its traditions, norms and its conventions limit the range of the vision of individuals. The traditions of the interpreter's community and its conventions always help to shape the interpreter's "horizon." For tradition, Gadamer asserts, that human beings are historical beings, who live in a tradition. The tradition, according to him is not the things of post, but something in which people constantly participate in, that takes hold of people thought an interpretive process, it "is not simple a permanent precondition, rather we produce it by ourselves in as much as we understand, participate in the evolution of tradition, and hence further determine it ourselves." To be more precise, in other words, "traditions are constantly evolving, communal, social arrangement, and memories that use, participate in, and live within." (*TM* 282, 293, 461-63)

Through the "hermeneutic circle," Gadamer illuminates the hermeneutic experience which appears in two different modes of interpretations e. g. by tradition the interpreter gets limited as he or she is encountered with the text, the second, on the other hand, in Gadamer's view, it does not exist unless the reader constantly creates and further recreates it through the process of the interpretation. In this way, the reader transforms and reconstructs the tradition. These both sides do not function separately or individually; they are interrelated to each other instead, and thus reading comes into existence with this hermeneutic circle. Emerging from the tradition, according to Gadamer, the text is not merely a historical document, rather something that can be understood since it has historically effected consciousness which allows experiencing the tradition. Here comes another new important word "experience" which has some very unique characteristics, e. g. a particular experience can never occur to a person in the same way again and again. Every new experience challenges the reader, which he already knows. Moreover, in Gadamer's views, the experience which confirms what people already know is not genuine experience, rather, a repetition of previous events (*TM* XXXII 267, 292, 355).

It is suggested by Gadamer that one must not suppose that the reader can have an accurate knowledge of what a text really stood for at the time of its creation. One should respond to a text from its past as in the present time, the reader and the subject matter of the traditional text from the past enter into a unity of play. In this way the subject matter of the text and the interpreting objects are in "Conversation," which creates a circular moment in the expectations of the reader and the meaning existing within the text. The text has, therefore, no fixed or any permanent meaning. The text must be seen within the horizons of historicity in the present. The text might have an absolutely different meaning from the reader's earlier viz-a-vis the future. Gadamer asserts that "every age has to understand a transmitted text in its own way, for the text is part of the whole of the tradition in which the age takes an objective interest and in which it seeks to understand itself." (*TM* 296) The past in Gadamer's view, is not the "no longer." It cannot be reconstructed and also cannot be re-experienced methodologically, rather, the present and the past are constantly mingled in the experience of understanding, and this is what Gadamer calls "effective history." The recollection of the past in order to sustain traditional values is given a fair focus by Gadamer. According to him all understanding is deeply rooted in the historicity and traditionality:

> History does not belong to us; we belong to it. Long before we understand ourselves through the process of self-examination, we understand ourselves in a self-evident way in the family, socially, and state in which we live. The focus of subjectivity is a distorting mirror. The self-awareness of the individual is only a flickering in the closed circuits of historical life. That is why the prejudices of the individual, for more than his judgments constitute the historical reality of his being. (*TM* 278)

In conclusion, it is found that in hermeneutics, there is a moment of "application," which is inherent in all interpretations. In this regard, understanding and interpretation cannot be separated into a sequential moment; the application is not a secondary practical concern, rather an intrinsic component of the one hermeneutic act of understanding, interpretation or application (*TM* 306-08) In this concern Gadamer seems going beyond Romantic or traditional hermeneutics which only referred to interpretation and understanding. Gadamer uses the term "application" as one of the unified processes. He is more concerned with the understanding and application of the text in comparison to its validity. In comparison, the Italian Betti comprises only the term "explanation." Richard Palmer in his *Hermeneutics: Interpretation Theory in Schleiermacher, Dilthey, Heidegger and Gadamer* (1969) makes a fine comparison between Gadamer and Heidegger, with, Betti and Dilthey in which Betti and Gadamer are shown in direct contrast:

> Betti, following Dilthey – wants norms to distinguish right from wrong interpretations, one type of interpretation from another. Gadamer, following Heidegger, asks such questions as: What is the ontological character of understanding? What kind of encounter with beings is involved in the hermeneutical process? How does tradition, the transmitted past, enter into and shape the act of understanding a historical text? (59)

Gadamer seems to be interested in the existential change that arises from the interpretation of the text, as it generally involves "application" in the sense of an assimilation or appropriation to a new-life-context of a work. Although the work would have been created or brought into existence within a very different situation, with the concerns quite unlike, which is now seen with a new approach. In this process the author loses the control over his work-whatever he wrote, progressively acquires its meaning by successive applications to the novel and unanticipated context and situations. In Gadamer's view, the text slips away and escapes from the original zone of its author's intention, and then builds a career of its own. This is what Barthes communicates in his seminal essay "The Death of the Author" (1968). The idea of "application" is that every understanding is at its root, is an application of meaning where one's experience and background are brought together to bear each other. This application is not a conscious procedure. In short, this application is found in Gadamer's most well-known contribution that is – "fusion of horizons." When a text is read, the reader has to project the "past-horizon" in which the text was actually created, and then the text is taken on itself in the "present horizon." Thus, in the process of understanding a real fusion of these horizons occurs. This experience of fusion of horizons differs from one epoch to another, for every fusion carries to a new understanding (*TM* 1960, trans. 1975).

Gadamer's philosophy is further appropriated by a South African scholar, John Henry McDowell in his *Mind and World* (1994). Other scholars who have contributed to this discipline are: Bernard Lonergan (1904-1984), Paul Ricoeur (1913-2005), Karl-Otto Apel (1922), Jurgen Habermas (1929) and Richard Rorty (1931-2007). Lonergan is a Canadian Jesuit, and a philosopher. The "self-appropriation" is the key project to him in his *Insight: A Study of Human Understanding (1957).* That is the self-discovery and personal embrace of the dynamic structure of inquiry, insight, judgment and decision. Apel is a German who has developed a distinct philosophical approach called "transcendental pragmatics" in his *Understanding and Explanation: A Transcendental-Pragmatic Perspective* (1984). Apel reformulates the difference between understanding and explanation that originated in the hermeneutics of Dilthey and the interpretive sociology of Max Weber on the basis of a Persian-inspired transcendental-pragmatic use of language. Rorty, who is an American philosopher, sees the idea of knowledge as a "mirror of nature" in his book *Philosophy and the Mirror of Nature* (1979). He argues that the central problem of modern epistemology depends upon a picture of mind as trying to be faithfully repressive of a mind independent of eternal reality.

1. 10 Jurgen Habermas (b- 1929)

Another contribution to the discipline of hermeneutics is given by another German philosopher, sociologist, and a representative of the Frankfurt School of thought, Jurgen Habermas. His methodological principles show the influence of Marx and Freud. According to him, the methodological structure of Freudian psychoanalysis is paradigmatic for critical sciences. He equates his concept of "depth-hermeneutics" with Freud's psychoanalysis. Habermas uses his "depth-hermeneutics" to present a counter to the Gadamerian concept of philosophical or universal hermeneutics, focusing on the concept of "explanatory understanding" of "systematic distorted expressions." He seems willing to employ his depth-hermeneutics as a source for freeing the discipline from critical sciences. Habermas also asserts to be conscious of the problems of understanding with the Gadamerian hermeneutics.

1.11 Jean Paul Gustavo Ricoeur (1913-2005): Career and his Scholarship

As it was clearly mentioned earlier that a radical departure from the author-oriented views of meaning existed there and had developed in many of the Structuralist and Post-Structuralist theories and philosophies as well. There is a vehement rejection of the reference of an author, or subject and his intention. The scholars of this approach insist that the meaning of a text is rendered unspecified by self-conflicting functions of language itself that is because of the flux in it. The meaning is entirely relative to the particular interpretive theories set to play by the readers e. g. deconstruction and reader-response theories and criticism. Some of the other current theories admit and take the manifest meaning of a text as an intentional meaning of the author. These scholars count such meaning essentially disguised, and displaced from the actual meaning which are present there in the unconscious world of an author. These are the hidden motives and desires which are suppressed social, political, and religious realities. They are suppressed by the power relations of the social structure of a historical era, e. g. Psychoanalytic criticism, Marxist criticism, and New Historicism etc. Some of the 20th century scholars following Marx, Nietzsche, and Freud name such a mode of reading "hermeneutics of suspicion." In this approach "they consider a text as a veiled or mystified set of representations, whose real meaning, or subtext, needs to be deciphered by the knowing reader." (Abrams 135-39)

Jean Paul Gustave Ricoeur is one of the most influential 20th century French philosophers. According to Bengt Kristensson Uggla, "Ricoeur was, for an exceptionally long period, compatible with the contemporary scene of philosophy – and simultaneously starkly ignorant of intellectual fashion." (1) Raised in a family of staunch protestant, a "son of a victim of the First World War," a prisoner of war for more than five years during the Second World War in a Nazi prison camp Paul Ricoeur is remarkably an interdisciplinary thinker and scholar. He is well known as a philosopher of dialogue!

Ricoeur is considered a post-structuralist hermeneutics, who was a part-time professor of philosophical theology at the University of Chicago and an honorary member of the International Institute for Hermeneutics. He is one of the most polyphonic voices of twentieth century philosophical and hermeneutical discourse whose position and status remains highly enigmatic to the modern philosophical arena. Professor Ricoeur, in his college days, became friends with Gabriel Marcel. That is why the existential thought of Marcel and Jasper was one of the major influences on him. He was imprisoned in Germany along with his fellow prisoners Mikael Dufrene during World War II, where he focused on the existential philosophy of Jasper, the phenomenology of Edmund Husserl, and the structural analysis of the language of Saussure. During the imprisonment, Ricoeur translated *Husserl's Ideas I* into French and became one of the leading authorities on Husserl. Ricoeur acknowledges his indebtedness to several key figures e. g. Aristotle, Kant, Hegel, Husserl, Jasper and Heidegger. Ricoeur's multiple manifestations of his philosophy are closely related to questions such as: who am I, how should I live, and what is it that I do...!

Professor Ricoeur is widely viewed as one of the most influential hermeneutics of 20th century philosophy. He devoted his time for over a half century, excessively engaged in reading, writing, lecturing, and teaching. His lectures, articles, essays and books have made an impact on almost all areas of humanities including – history, Christian theology, philosophy, linguistics, and literary studies. Ricoeur also interposed in numerous other disciplines such as neurology, ethics and biblical studies. His works include: *Freedom and Nature: The Voluntary and the Involuntary* (1950, Eng. Trans.1996), *Fallible Man* (1960, Eng. Trans. 1970), a major study of Freud, *Freud and Philosophy: An Essay on Interpretation* (1965, Eng. Trans. 1970), *The Rule of Metaphor: the Creation of Meaning in Language* (1975, Eng. Trans. 1977), *Interpretation Theory: Discourse and Surplus of Meaning* (1976), the three volumes of *Time and Narrative* (1983-85, Eng. Trans. 1984-88), *Lectures on Ideology and Utopia* (1986), *Oneself as Another* (1990, Eng. Trans. 1992), *Memory, History, Forgetting* (2000, Eng. Trans 2004), *The Course of Recognition* (2004, Eng. Trans. 2005).

Apart from these influential works of Ricoeur, there also appear more than 500 essays. Many of the articles and essays appear in the collections: *Phenomenology (1967), The Conflict of Interpretation: Essays in Hermeneutics* (1969, Eng. Trans. 1974), *Political and Social Essays* (1974), *Essays on Biblical Interpretation* (1980), *Hermeneutics and Human Sciences: Essays on Language, Action and Interpretation* (1981), *From Text to Action* (1986, Eng. Trans. 1991), *Figuring the Sacred: Religion, Narrative and Imagination* (1995), *The Just* (1995, Eng. Trans. 2000), *On Translation* (2004, Eng. Trans. 2004), *Reflection on the Just* (2001, Eng. Trans. 2007).

Ricoeur has also been the recipient of many numerous awards which include: Prix Cavallies Award in 1951, Hegel Prize from Stuttgart in 1985, the Karl Jasper Prize from Heidelberg in 1989, the Grand Prize of the French Academy for philosophy in 1987, the Nietzsche Prize from Palermo, Italy, 1987 and the Dante Prize from Florence in 1988. Ricoeur also holds many honorary Doctorates from more than thirty eminently leading academic institutions in thirteen different countries. These prestigious prizes prove Ricoeur's importance and also put a big objectionable question on Vincent Decombes' recording of the same historical period of time in his *Modern French Philosophy* (1979-80) where he apparently disqualifies Ricoeur from possessing any important philosophical and intellectual identity. Nevertheless, Marcelino Agis Villaverde has structured Ricoeur's career and his progressive thought into four stages (i) His education and influences (through 1950), (ii) Ricoeur Phenomenology (1950-1960), (iii) Ricoeurean hermeneutics (1960-1990), and, (iv) Ricoeur's practical philosophy (ethical and political philosophy, 1990-2005).

1. 12 Ricoeur's Corpus of Hermeneutics

Professor Ricoeur reduces the dispute and contradiction about meaning between the subjective intention of the author and the other meaning producing subject of the text as some other entity. The problem of right or actual understanding has yet not been completely solved even after the conscious departure from the intentional meaning of the author until any new present-day perspective or approaches, even, if not exaggerated, the discipline of hermeneutics remains helpless.

Ricoeur starts his intellectual journey by referring to Augustine's and Aristotle's concepts of time, metaphor, mimesis and interpretation. In his initial days Ricoeur was highly curious about existential understandings. He highly refers to Rene Descartes' principle *cogito ergo sum,* Husserl's phenomenological understanding of consciousness, and Heidegger's concepts of *Dasein* and *B/being.* Ricoeur also modifies and adds to traditional hermeneutics and interpretation theory. Thus, Schleiermacher's "general hermeneutics," Dilthey's term "explanation" for natural, and "understanding" for human sciences, Italian Bette's "explanation" to understand in general, Habermas' hermeneutics of "explanatory understanding" and his concept of depth-hermeneutics, Freud's theory of psychoanalysis; and Gadamer's concerns of "historicity," "tradition," "application," and "fusion of horizons." Ricoeur also develops and creates a deep insight in the Swiss Linguist Ferdinand de Saussure's notion of sign and the structural understanding of language, essentially his terminology of language and parole. Ricoeur gives a critique of the prevalent notion of structuralism. After the 1950s, though, the intellectual milieu in Paris changed swiftly. The ideas of Husserl and Heidegger are replaced by those of Freud's and Saussure's. But Ricoeur stands too distant from the new fashions of Paris and does not follow the present trend. Ricoeur continues his scholarship within the existential and phenomenological fields. In fact, later after some times, he could not ignore the change since psychoanalysis and structuralism offered many radical approaches, and in response Ricoeur presents a critique of psychoanalysis in many of his essays more specifically in his *Freud and Philosophy: An Essay on Interpretation.* Ricoeur's collection of essays: *The Conflict of Interpretations: Essays in Hermeneutics* and a collection of his four lectures delved at Texas Christian University and published as *Interpretation Theory: Discourse and the Surplus of Meaning* expose a modern critique of structuralism and Freud's philosophy of psychoanalysis. There, Ricoeur offers a theory of language and a theory of interpretation. It is evident that France as a country has been the center of structural and existential philosophies with its interest and conflicts. "The grooming importance of language in Ricoeur's thought is the stimulus for his critical confrontation with structuralism" (Introduction," *HAHS*, 8).

The term "structuralism" is closely associated with the scholars, namely, Roland Barthes, Claude Levi – Straus, Louis Althusser etc., and the contribution in the structural philosophy of all the scholars with their different approaches are linked and founded on the linguistic model invented by Saussure. Ricoeur, too, is influenced by this model but he takes "more trenchant formulation in the work of the Danish linguist, Louis Hjelmslev." (8) After referring to Hjelmslev *Prolegomena to a Theory of Language* (1961), Don Ihde, one of the editors of Ricoeur's works, writes that language is an institution, an entirely social phenomenon. The structure and logic of language is subterraneously linked to the questions of "sociality and historicity." Thus, Ricoeur criticizes Levi-Straus rigorously but in a friendly way and questions structural linguistics carefully both in terms of operational and foundational presuppositions in the essays:

"Structure and Hermeneutics," and "Structure Word Event." Despite the universality of finite structure of language, according to Ricoeur there exists an infinite power in the dialectic of levels and language at this highest level remains wide open e. g. what we come across to know is that, it "also says" and it also means. This results in a dialectic of "finite-infinite," "closed-open" relations to language and speech. Ihde adds about this finity and infinity of language: There the infinity of "verb," or word act was mediated and located through the finitude of perspective. The significant situation of man is primarily both perception and language as seeing and saying. Now within language itself the finitude of structure mediates the infinity of event (Don Ihde xiii)

Thus, for Ricoeur, a "word" is a system and an act, structure, and history. In this way, the word within itself appears to be polysemic which poses itself with a certain potential for opacity, very difficult to explain and very difficult to understand, he says that is the richness of the "word" and also discusses the problem of the same as:

> The word is much more and much less than the sentence. It is much less, because there is not yet any word before the sentence. What is there before the sentence? Sings, that is, differences in the system, values in the lexicon. [....]. .. the word names at the same time as the sentence says. It is named in sentence position. In the dictionary, there is only the endless round of terms which are defined circularly, which revolves in the closure of the lexicon. But then someone speaks, someone says something. The word leaves the dictionary; it becomes word at the moment when man becomes speech, when speech becomes discourse and discourse a sentence. [......] words are signs in speech position. Words are the points of articulation between semiology and semantics, in every speech event.

Thus, the word is, as it were, a trader between the system and the act, between the structure and the event. On the one hand, it relates to structure, as a differential value, but it is then only a semantic potentiality; on the other hand, it relates to the act and to the event in the fact that it's semantic actuality of the utterance. [....]. The sentence, we have seen, is an event; as such, its actuality is transitory, passing, and ephemeral. But the word survives the sentence. As a displaceable entity, it survives the transitory instance of discourse and holds itself available for new uses. Thus, heavy with a new use-value- as minute as this may be – it returns to the system. And, in returning to the system, it gives it a history. (Ricoeur 92-93)

For the nature of language, meaning and interpretation, action and subjectivity, philosophers, linguists, literary critics and social scientists have been highly engaged throughout the last century with the nature and the problem of language. It has entered into sustained dialogue with the traditions of hermeneutics, the dialogue with this tradition that has focused for centuries on the problem of interpretation. Ricoeur's critique of structuralism proceeds further in the words of Thompson:

> First, structuralism assumes that language is an object that can be investigated scientifically. Second, structuralism distinguishes between a science of states of the systems and a science of changes, and it subordinates the latter to the former. Third, the structuralist model presupposes that in any state of the system there are no absolute terms but only relations of mutual dependence, so that language 'becomes a system of signs defined by their differences done' Forth, structuralism treats the collection of signs as a closed and autonomous system of internal dependencies. It follows from their presuppositions that for structuralism a sign must be defined not in terms of some object for terms of its relation to all other signs of the same level within the systems of which it is part. [...], structural linguistics excludes from consideration a number of important phenomenon. It includes, for instance, the act of speaking, not only as an individual performance but as the free creation of new expression. History is also excluded, for history is more than the passage from one state of a system to another: it is the process whereby human beings produce themselves and their language. Structuralism excludes, moreover, the primary aim or intention of language, which is to say something about something. Language has both an ideal sense, to say something, and a real reference, to say it about something [...]. Language is absolutized as an object and structuralism exceeds the limits of its validity…. (Don Ihde 9-10)

In his *Freud and Philosophy* and in other essays such as "Psychoanalysis and Movement of Contemporary Culture," "A Philosophical Interpretation of Freud," "Consciousness and the Unconscious," and "Art and Freudian Systematic," Ricoeur examines Freud's psychoanalytic technique of interpretation. This technique is a form of hermeneutics which remains only in the verbal and symbolic domain or in the linguistic domain. B. Thompson writes that Ricoeur looks curious about the writing of Freud at the level of philosophical reflection e. g. "(1) how does the mixed discourse of psychoanalysis enter into a reflective philosophy? And (2), what happens to the subject of reflection when the guile of consciousness is taken seriously?" (8)

A dream and a joke are a text in Ricoeurean hermeneutics; later the object of analysis is no longer a text, but a human "Subject." Thus the "subject as text" is a text that is symbolic, becoming a work of deciphering the hidden meaning of the "text-self." Ricoeur admits the novelization of psychoanalytic technique as:

> FOR SOMEONE TRAINED in phenomenology, existential philosophy, linguistic or sociological methods, and the revival of Hegel studies, the encounter with psychoanalysis constitutes a considerable shock, for this discipline affects and questions anew not simple some particular theme within philosophical reflection but the philosophical project as a whole. (Ricoeur 99)

Ricoeur, talking about "the crisis of the notion of consciousness" critiques contemporary culture and discusses "psychoanalysis as a technique of the night." and in the discussion and debate with Freud, he takes on the topics such as: "Language, Symbol, and Interpretation," "Towards a Critique of Symbol," "The Conflict of Interpretation," "The Concept of Interpretation," "Interpretation as Recollection of Meaning," "Interpretation as Exercise of Suspicion," "Hermeneutic Method and Reflective Philosophy," "The Recourse of Symbols to Reflection," "The Recourse of Reflection to Symbols," Reflection and Equivocal Language," and, "Reflection and the Hermeneutic Conflict." The focus on these issues will be taken in detail in the following chapters after the introduction. According to Thompson, the examination and the philosophical operation of Freud's psychoanalysis, the confrontation of Ricoeur with structuralism, and the critique of both, raises many fundamental questions regarding the nature of Language. Therefore, in response, Professor Ricoeur develops a theory of language, which later gets connected to the philosophy of hermeneutics. This theory is originally premised upon a fundamental distinction and division between "system" and "discourse." In Thompson's view, base of this distinction is related to Saussurian dichotomy between *langue* and *parole*, but Ricoeur is primarily indebted to the French linguist Emile Benveniste (1902-1976). For Ricoeur, discourse is an internal dialectic between event and meaning that has an eventful character. There, the notion of meaning is analysed into two basic divisions.

The first one is the "objective aspect" e. g. whatever the sentence means, the second is the "subjective aspect," e. g. whatever the speaker means. Ricoeur further draws the component of the objective aspect into two categories of meaning: the sentence has both – an "*ideal sense*" and at the same time a *"real reference."*

According to Ricoeur, it is on the level of sentence that language can refer to something beyond its usual and functional capacity, that is, in a sense, the "closed universe of signs" can be related to an extra-linguistic world. Thompson adds that this referential relation is a crucial characteristic of discourse. The basic condition of creativity is the intrinsic polysemy of words. The feature that words in natural languages has more than one meaning. The boundaries of polysemy can be understood by semantics of the sign, as the potential uses of a word are accumulated and codified in the lexical system. According to Ricoeur, the actual function of polysemy can be grasped only by semantics of a sentence. The words only have meaning in the relation of the sentence, and the sentences are uttered and inscribed only in the particular Context.

The polysemy of the word brings an additional meaning or a surplus of meaning. Despite the richness of a word, being polygenic which can be deciphered by interpretation, Ricoeur's philosophy of hermeneutics aims at certain "privileged words", the symbolic words. Therefore, the primary task of Ricoeur's hermeneutics is to interpret and investigate those "privileged-symbolic" words having certain types of multiple senses and references attached to them. The surface meaning sometimes hides, conceals, or contains a less obvious depth meaning that can also be a surplus of meaning that is not dependent on the surface of literal meaning. Moreover, Ricoeur's words of symbolic significance take specific shape and get a metaphorical structure. This is the problem of hermeneutics. The task and primary aim of hermeneutics is to unfold the multiple, polysemy/symbolic/metaphoric nature of the word that is implied in the literal meaning. Thus, Don Ihde remarks that this model of hermeneutic task in Ricoeur's thought becomes much more than only a matter of textual interpretation.

The polysemic nature of words provides the basis for the creative extension of meaning through metaphor. Professor Ricoeur, thus, develops his new ideas on metaphor through a detailed analysis of traditional rhetoric where a metaphor is considered and identified as a type of troupe, that is, when a figurative word is substituted for a literal word.

The traditional metaphor never tells us anything new, it is merely a decorative device only for the embellishment of language. Therefore, professor Ricoeur refreshes the current understanding of metaphor and develops a theory and a philosophy of metaphor on his own. Ricoeur refers to some Anglo-Saxon authors such as I. A. Richards, Max Black, and Monroe Beardsley, etc. to give a critique of and reflect on whatever they have thought of. Ricoeur starts looking at metaphors from the Semiotic level to the hermeneutic point of view. Each of them corresponds to each other e. g. the word to semiotics, semiotics to sentence, the sentence to semantics, semantics to discourse, and at the end, the discourse to hermeneutics.

Ricoeur makes an essential distinction between the "rhetoric of metaphor" and "metaphor as figure." According to him, the former one makes the word as its unit of reference, and in the second, metaphor constitutes a displacement with its extended meaning. The explanation of metaphor as a figure is rooted in a theory of the meaning. Ricoeur's analysis is rooted and grounded in the discipline of Rhetoric and poetry. Both of these correspond to specific goals and aims: Rhetoric to persuasion and Poetics to the mimesis of human action, persuasion, in *oral discourse,* and mimesis in tragic *poetry*. For Language, Ricoeur demonstrates further, two major points, first, rhetoric terminates in classification and taxonomy to the point that it focuses on figures of deviation or tropes where the meaning of the word is taken away from its lexically codified usages. For the second, Ricoeur argued that while a taxonomic viewpoint is adequate for a static account of figures, he claims that it fails to explain the production of meaning. In further progression, Ricoeur does not differentiate between the semantic and rhetorical viewpoints until metaphor is transferred into a sentence, not as a deviant denomination, but as an ease of impertinent predication. (*The Rule of Metaphor* 2-7)

"Metaphor and the Semantics of Discourse," a key study of Ricoeur's epoch-making book *The Rule of Metaphor* (1977), *(La Metaphore vive, (*1975). The topic with special reference to metaphor would be the sole subject in the present endeavor. Here, the "statement-metaphor" and the theory of "word-metaphor "is put to observe in extreme radical oppositions. In this concern, the important contributions of three English authors (I.A. Richards, Max Black and Beardsley) are taken up by Ricoeur critically. He delimits the problem which was left unresolved by the English authors. The metaphor is defined as the transposition of the name and tries to integrate the semantics of the word that helps metaphor to be in the category of troupes. Later, Ricoeur focuses on the structural aspect of a sign and shows that linguistics does not make any distinction between the semantics of the word semantics of the sentence. Ricoeur provides new rules of segmentation, identification, and combination of figures of speech. The rhetoric degree zero and the notion of deviation are examined too. Ricoeur exposes a transition from the semantic level to the hermeneutical level. The problem of semantic innovation or semantic creation as a new natural semantic and metaphoric creation is examined in order to resolve the problem that would also be a point of main concern in this book. Ricoeur specifies the problem as:

> The first step is to refute the view (which Roman Jakobson still holds) that the fate of resemblance is linked indissolubly to that of a substitution theory. I try to show that resemblance is no less required in a tension theory, for the semantic innovation through which a previously unnoticed 'proximity' of two ideas is perceived despite their logical distance must in fact be related to the work of resemblance. 'To metaphorize well,' says Aristotle, 'implies an intuitive perception of the similarity in dissimilarity.' Thus, resemblance itself must be understood as a tension between identity and difference in the prediction operation set in motion of semantic innovation. This analysis of the work of resemblance suggests in turn that the notions of 'productive imagination' and 'iconic function' must be re-interpreted. Indeed, imagination must cease being seen as a function of the image, in the quasi-sensorial sense of the word; it consists rather in 'seeing as...' according to a Wittgensteinian expression – a power that is an aspect of the properly semantic operation consisting in seeing the similar in the dissimilar. (4-5)

Ricoeur turns to the hermeneutic point of view, which is the change of the level which corresponds from *sentence to discourse*. This is the point where Ricoeur quotes Aristotle's observation "to metaphorise well implies an intuitive perception of the similarity in dissimilar," that is to "productive imagination" and "iconic function" should be an object of interpretation. For Ricoeur, this problem is no longer the form of metaphor as "a word focused figure of speech," nor the sense of metaphor as a discovery of "new semantic pertinence," but the "reference of metaphorical statement" as the "potential power to re-describe reality." Ricoeur writes about the move from sentence to discourse and "reference" that has potential power:

> The most fundamental support of this transition from semantics to hermeneutics is to be found in the connection in all discourse between sense, which is its internal organisation, and reference, which is its power to refer to a reality outside of language. Accordingly, metaphor represents itself as a strategy of discourse that, preserving

> and developing the creative power of language, preserves and develops the *heuristic* power wielded by *fiction.* (5)

Ricoeur argues that there is a possibility that "metaphorical discourse" suggests something about reality. And the "poetic discourse" in apparent constitution seems to be essentially "non-referential conception of literal reference," that is a must for grasping the power of second-degree reference, that is, a poetic reference. In this way, Ricoeur justifies the concept of "fictional re-description" by developing the theory of the hermeneutics of metaphor. Ricoeur moves to the most important point that "metaphor is the rhetorical process by which discourse unleashes the power those certain fictions have to re-describe reality." When Ricoeur says that the theory of re-describing fiction to Aristotle's theory in his *Poetics* is in the *poicis* of language, which arises from the encounter between *muthos* and *mimesis*, lays foundation of his hermeneutics of fiction and hermeneutics of action. More specifically, for fiction, Ricoeur comes at the end of the present concern of discussion by commenting on the conjunction of fiction and its re-description:

> The 'place' of metaphor, its most intimate and ultimate abode, is neither the name, nor the sentence, nor even discourse, but the copula of the verb *to be.* The metaphorical 'is' at once signifies both 'is not' and 'is like.' If this is really so, we are allowed to speak of metaphorical truth, but in an equally 'tensive' sense of the word 'truth'. (6)

Ricoeur's entire metaphorical and philosophical discourse is essentially to expose the "plurality of modes of discourse" in relation to the "propositions of sense and reference of poetic discourses." The entire course of this dissertation would focus on the issues in detail discussed above. It would progress with the discussion of rhetoric and semantics, from semiotic – the word, to semantics, the sentence, and from the sentence to discourse, then from "textual discourse" to hermeneutics. It is to rectify the injustices and the problem of a double allegiance of meaning with blistering refutation. It is hoped by this endeavor to help reduce the ignorance in the philosophy of language and hermeneutics.

Having discussed about *metaphorical innovation*, *rhetoric of metaphor*, and *metaphor of hermeneutics* in brief, the book would turn towards a discussion of "time" and "narrative" in detail with especial reference to Ricoeur's three volumes of *Time and Narrative*, this would be the point, where this book will reach to its climax of discussion.

Ricoeur mentions that throughout history, for more than 2500 centuries, metaphor traditionally belongs to the theory of tropes or, in other words, to figures of speech; and "narrative" to the theory of literary genres or literary form. The meaning effects produced by both (metaphor and narrative) completely belong to *"semantic innovation."* On the level of discourse, that is, says Ricoeur, equal or higher than the semantics-that is the level of the *acts of language*. The innovation with metaphor is found in the production of "new semantic pertinences" by means of an impertinent attribution. Metaphor thus remains active and alive through the process of novel semantic pertinences. Comparatively, on the other hand writes Ricoeur for narrative:

> The semantic innovation lies in the invention of another work of synbook-a plot. By means of the plot, goals, causes, and chances are brought together within the temporal unity of a *whole* and complete *action*. It is this synbook of heterogeneity that brings narrative close to metaphor-in both cases the new thing-the as yet unsaid, the unwritten-springs up in language. Here a living metaphor, that is, a new pertinence in the predication, there is a feigned plot, that is, a new congruence in the organisation of the events. In both cases the semantic innovation can be carried back to the productive imagination and, more precisely, to the schematics that is its signifying matrix. ("Preface," *Time and Narrative*, Vol-I, IX)

Ricoeur relates his idea of "innovative pertinent" to "imagination," and goes back to refer to Aristotle, saying that being good at making metaphors is equivalent to being perceptive of resemblances. (X). He raises a question: what is it to be perceptive of resemblance? If it is not to bring out the object of similarity that in the beginning seemed there "distant" and all of a sudden becomes very "close." In this connection, Ricoeur writes about the change of distance in logical space:

> It is this change of distance in logical space that is the work of the productive imagination. This consists of schematising the synthetic operation, of figuring the predicative assimilation from which results the semantic innovation. The productive imagination at work in the metaphorical process is this competence for producing new logical species by predicative assimilations, in spite of the resistance of our current categorisations of language. The plot of a narrative is comparable to this predicative assimilation. It "grasps together" and integrates into one whole and complete story multiple and scattered events, thereby schematising the intelligible significance attached to the narrative then as a whole. (X)

Thus, through this process of schematisation, for this, the intelligibility brought here, "is to be distinguished from combinatory nationality put in to play by structural semantics," (X) in the concept of metaphor and the legislating rationality, which is at work in narratology and scholarly history in narrative. According to Ricoeur, this rationality aims at the higher level of a "meta-language" and at the kind of comprehension rooted in the schematisation discussed above.

A hermeneutic framework that is expected to be made through this study is only "to explain more is to understand from human action" whether it is the mechanics of metaphor or the synthetic structure of plot. Ricoeur talks of two different cases of understanding or reading or observing that are in "two different times," that occur in one sequence of time when it passes through the same as what happens in catharsis when it is a play/ drama, and appropriation, in understanding while communicating. For this condition, Ricoeur says that at first the dynamics is grasped through the metaphorical utterance, that is a new "semantic pertinence," and in the second case of understanding, that is to reach to the operation which constitutes magnitude of action, that is formed by circumstances, initiatives, and interaction the reversal of fortune and ends and means.

Pondering over the epistemological problem "posed by metaphor or by narrative," says Ricoeur, "consists in tying the explanation set to work by the semi-linguistic science to the prior understanding resulting from an acquired familiarity with the use of language, be it poetic or narrative." According to professor Ricoeur, the parallel between metaphor and narrative looms large, "the poetic function of language is not limited" because of the referential and sensical function of metaphor that has the potential to re-describe reality, which is difficult to get accessed by direct description.

Referring to Aristotle's theory of 'resemblance," Ricoeur suggests that "seeing-as" through the process of metaphorical power "could be the revealer of a "being –as" on the deepest ontological level". Precisely writing this study would also bring into light the three senses of Ricoeur's concepts of *mimesis*. According to Ricoeur, the mimetic function also poses the same problem, exactly as the "problem of metaphorical references," that we would discuss in detail in the following respective chapters of this study. Ricoeur argues that according to Aristotle, plot is the mimesis of action. For mimesis of action," Ricoeur brings out three senses: the first one is "a reference back to the familiar pre-understanding we have the order of the familiar actions," the second is, "an entry into the realm of poetic composition," and the third, in result is "a new configuration by means of poetic refiguring of pre-understood order of action." In this way, Ricoeur compares both the problem of mimetic function and the problem of metaphorical reference. He concludes that the mimetic function of the plot rejoins metaphorical reference, and the mechanics of "metaphorical description reigns on the field of sensory, emotional, aesthetic and axiological values, which makes the world a habitual world." In Ricoeur's view, on the contrary "the mimetic function of plots takes place by refinement in the field of action and of its tempered values." According to Ricoeur, in his very minute observation, something passes through from the first case of understanding to the second case of understanding equally both in the new metaphorical pertinences and the minute functions of narratives, specifically saying-the plot. In Ricoeur's view, this is the "privileged means," through which "we re-configure our confused, unformed, and at the limit minute temporal experience" (I-XI). To re-configure this "temporal experience" in the capacity of temporal experience, that is, "prey to the aperies of philosophical speculation, resides the referential function of the plot." Thus, professor Ricoeur declares the frontier between these two similar functions – "unstable." He writes in this connection: "In the first place, the plots that configure and transfigure the practical field encompass not just acting but also suffering, hence characters as agents and as victims. Lyric poetry thereby skirts dramatic poetry. Furthermore, the circumstances that, as the word indicate encircle action, and the unintended consequences that make up one part of the tragic aspect of action, also consist of a dimension of passivity accessible through poetic discourse, in particular in the modes of elegy and of lamentation. In this way, metaphorical re-description and mimesis are closely bound up with each other, to the point that we can exchange the two vocabularies and speak of the mimetic value of poetic discourse and the re-descriptive power of narrative fiction." (XI) In this way we find a vast canvas of rhetorical and poetic sphere in the Ricoeurian corpus of his philosophy of language and his hermeneutics. The main interests in this study are the areas such as: the metaphorical utterance and narrative discourse, the configuration of time in the fictional narratives along with the narrated time as well.

CHAPTER 2

The Hermeneutics of Metaphor and the Nature of Language

"Language is *vitally* Metaphorical" – P. B. Shelley.

(Ardent: *Life of the Mind: Volume I*, entitled *Thinking* 102)

The paradox is this: there is no discourse on metaphor that is not stated within a metaphorically engendered conceptual network. There is no non-metaphorical standpoint from which to perceive the order and the demarcation of the metaphorical field. Metaphor is metaphorically stated. The word *metaphor* and the word *figure* alike attest to this recurrence of metaphor. The theory of metaphor returns in a circular manner to the metaphor of theory, which determines the truth of being in terms of presence. If this is so, there can then be no principle for delimiting metaphor, no definition in which the defining does not contain the defined; metaphoricity is absolutely uncontrollable. (*RM* 338-39)

2.1 Perspectives on Metaphors

Even after more than two hundred years of its realisation, metaphor in its complete manifestation remains largely unexplored and unidentified (completely) even in the modern times. This chapter aims at unfolding metaphor in relation to language to the unbelievable possibilities that have not yet been traced because of its constant ignorance. The growing attitudes towards language and its nature in the present-day world is that language is metaphorical rather than a structural system of signs: signifiers and signified, langue and parole. The present world is of the highest uncertain virtual realities human beings have ever seen. Amidst of all, language emerges as one of the most significant sources of all human activities. Naturally human curiosity has an intense engagement to understand the phenomenon of language. John T. Kirby, in his article "Aristotle on Metaphor," therefore, loudly announces that "ours is an age of metaphor." Thus, language is being viewed as if it were metaphorical in every sense of the term. (517)

Metaphor, in general, when it has to do something with meaning in language, is identified as an extension, simply from a literal or standard meaning of present language use. It is a word, when in language it gets used with its temporal beauty in more than one meaning, which is always a conscious and conspicuous departure from its common usage. The meaning arising from this departure becomes metaphoric e. g. 'a dog is man's best friend.' Here the word 'dog' has the commonly understood meaning, simply the animal, 'Romeo was a great lover,' here Romeo is simply to refer to a character in Shakespeare's play who dies for the love of Juliet, 'Monalesa is the greatest portrait, here Monalisa is simply the portrait or painted mysterious character in the art of painting. But if we use the same words in reverse as: 'He is such a dog that I cannot live with,' 'People assumed that he was a roadside Romeo,' and 'Hamlet is the Mona Lisa of literature,' these sentences carry an extended meaning resulting from the same literal words. Here a 'dog' refers to such meaning as: the man is worthless and evil person, notorious or disgraceful, 'roadside Romeo' for a man who has many lovers or, who shows strong feelings of love by doing romantic things, 'Mona Lisa of literature' brings an especial effect for the significance of the Shakespeare's play Hamlet, it begets an analogy between Monalesa and Hamlet, the enigmatic nature, the complexities and aestheticism found in both. Here the extended meaning is that Hamlet is a magnum opus of literature equally as Monalesa in painting. Usually, this extension of meaning in language use is known as metaphoric meaning. Thus, here the extension is a metaphor.

The word 'Metaphor' is Greek in origin, that is 'metapherein' composed of 'meta' means 'beyond' 'after', 'with across,' and 'pherein' refers to 'to carry' and 'to bear' – in this way, metaphor means: a transfer, carrying over, or carrying from one place to another. According to Aristotle in his *Poetics*, 'metaphora is the epiphora of the name (onoma) of something [to something else], both 'metaphora' and 'epiphora' stem from the same root- 'pher/phor' 'to carry'. (Aristotle 21, 1457 b 6-7).

In relation to language, metaphor has been a serious concern to be talked about, that's why to see language as if it is metaphoric is not new. Metaphor has been an object of human curiosity from the time of Heraclitus (535 BC – 475 BC) to the modern world, specifically to

Giambattista Vico's *Nuova Scienza* (1725). Apart from a long tradition and long history of Metaphor, the first clear instance we find regarding it is in Aristotle's *Poetics* (4th century BC) and Roman Quintilian's *Institute of Oratory* (1st century BC).

For Aristotle, Metaphor belongs to one of the sections of six constituents of tragic poetry, that is 'poetic diction' T.S. Dorsch translates Aristotle's concept of Metaphor as "Metaphor is the application to the thing of a name belonging to another thing," he further adds that 'the transference may be from the genus to the species, from the species to genus, or from one species to another, or it may be a matter of analogy'. (61) A.D. Gupta, one of the editors of Aristotle's *Poetics* mentions that 'by a transference from genus to species I mean (e. g.) 'Here stands my ship'; Lying at anchor is one kind of standing' or life's time light' (*Poetics*, Chapter: 22, 1458, 22-25, 34-35, 57B-58A).

It is commonly observed that Aristotle's concept of metaphor is only for the embellishment of language that is for poetic diction in Greek tragic poetry. Aristotle's metaphor is a noun that has obvious extended meaning and has a function to play in poetic diction. The extended meaning that is supposed to be a metaphor is also a beautification of meaning, metaphor adds something special to the meaning expressed that has many dimensions i. e. transference of meaning from a concrete object to an abstract idea, living animals or human beings to non-living object vis-a-vis, animal to human and human to animals, sensory perception to an object, feeling or abstract idea and the extension by magnification. When it is (transference) from concrete to abstract object, the intention is to see and feel the idea clean and clean in a picturesque style to give a word-picture e. g. 'Love is a cream' is a transference from living to nonliving vis-a-vis nonliving to living: 'the head of the pen was nice,' human to animal and animal to humans: 'he is a lion' and 'lion is a king of animal kingdom'. Extension of sensory perception: 'she used the language of loud silence,' magnification: 'the truth was falling from his mouth'.

It is the Roman Quintillion in his *Institute of Oratory*, Book VIII, Chapter VI, where he makes three divisions of Metaphor: (i) Necessity, (ii) to gain increased significance and force, and (iii) ornament. According to M.H. Abrams, after Aristotle, classical rhetoricians gave the fullest and most influential treatment to *The Institute of Oratory*. Since then, the figurative language is after classed in two different ways, as: figure of thought or troupes and figure of speech or rhetorical figure or scheme. Figure of thought or troop is something that turns or twists the meaning, it is "in which words or phrases are used in a way that affects a conspicuous change in what is taken to be their standard meaning. The standard meaning, as opposed to its meaning in the figurative use, is called the literal meaning." (Abrams 101)

The rhetorical figures or figures of speech, or the schemes fall in the same category having slight differences. It is observed that in a way there is no departure from the standard usage of language, primarily in the meaning of the words, rather in the order and syntactical structures of the words and expressions. It is also noted that the above distinction appears invalid in some cases. Sometimes, the most commonly identified tropes are also treated as the most extensively used figure of speech in modern times. It is observed that all tropes can create a twist in meaning but all figures of speech cannot e. g. alliteration and assonance etc. purely remains only a rhetorical device.

It was Giambattista Vico (1668-1744) who is usually credited with being the first to identify Metaphor, Metonymy, Synecdoche and Irony as the four basic tropes to which all others are reducible. This distinction is also seen as having its roots in *The Rhetorics of Peter Ramus* (1515-1572), (Vico, 129-31). This reduction was popularised in the 20th century by the American rhetorician Kenneth Burke (1897-1933) who pronounced these tropes as 'four master tropes of literature' (Metaphor, Metonymy, Synecdoche and Irony). In his book, *A Grammar of Motives* (1945) Kenneth Burke equates Metaphor with 'Perspective,' Met anomy with 'Reduction,' Synecdoche with 'Representation,' and Irony with 'Dialectic'. The primary concern of Burke with these master tropes is rather, with their role in discovering and description of 'truth' instead their purely figurative usage. In *A Map of Misreading* (1975) Harold Blooms adds two more tropes that are: 'hyperbole' and 'metalepsis' to the same class of master tropes.

2.2 Metaphor Prior to Ricoeur

2.2.1 I. A. Richards

Getting back to Aristotle's *Poetics*, it is observed that Metaphor has three-fold dimensions. First is, the 'greatest thing' according to Aristotle, 'is to have a command of Metaphor,' second, 'metaphor is the mark of genius,' and the third is, 'to make good metaphor implies an eye for resemblances.' It is I. A. Richards who for the first-time challenges Aristotle for all the above three assumptions and brings the notion of language as being metaphoric, Richards strongly refutes the assumption that:

> ... "an eye for resemblance" is a gift that some men have but others have not. But we all live, and speak, only through our eye for resemblances...... As individuals we gain our command of metaphor just as we learn wheatear makes us distinctly human. (89)

Throughout the history of Rhetoric, metaphor has been treated as a sort of happy extra trick with words, an opportunity to exploit the accidents of their versatility, something in place occasionally but requiring unusual skill and caution. [.....]. I have just been echoing. Shelley's observation that language is vitally metaphorical...." [...]. Only Dreamy Bentham, as successor to Bacon and Hobbes, insisted – with his technique of archetypation and phraseoplerosis – upon one inference that might be drawn; namely, that the mind and its entire doings are fictions...., namely, that matter and its adventures, and all the derivative objects of contemplation, are fictions too, of varied rank because of varied service. (Richards 89-91)

Thus, Richards prophesied that "a serious study of metaphor may plunge us" and he further adds that, they can carry to "the depths of verbal interaction which give rise to them." For him, metaphor is "the omnipresent principle of language," Richards holds the same notion as Bradley that "doing without metaphor is never more than a bluff waiting to be called." Richards' Metaphor "has two thoughts of different things active together" these two things are supported by "a single word or phrase whose meaning is a resultant of their interaction." According to him, there is an "interaction between co-present thought," which have "immense variety." As opposed to traditional understanding of Metaphor, as: only a verbal matter, that is a shift, implement, transformation, translation or resemblance, Richards says "it is borrowing between and intercourse of thoughts, a transaction between contents." According to him, this thought is, "metaphoric, and proceeds by comparison", thus, it is observed that, this is the point where Richards lays foundation of cognitive and existential view of Metaphor after having discussed the interaction view, for this he asserts as:

> In asking how language works we ask about how thought and feeling and all the other modes of the mind's activity proceed, about how use are about to learn to live and how that "greatest thing of all," a command of metaphor – which is great only because it is a

> command of life – may best, in spite of Aristotle, "be imparted to another." (95)

It is well known that Aristotle refuted strongly but swiftly with Plato, so does Richards with Aristotle's idea when he says that it – "cannot be imported to another." This is the point where he introduces two very technical and very concrete terms in the mechanics of metaphor, the most controversial issue throughout the history of metaphor. Dr. Jonson, mentions Richards, called "[the] two ideas that any metaphor at its simplest gives us. Let me call them the tenor and the vehicle." These two parts or aspects of metaphor have many relations to one another that seem to be quite complex. Richards tries to separate both the parts as: 'The original idea' and 'the borrowed one', "what is really being said or thought of" and 'what it is compared to', 'the underlying idea' and 'the imagined nature', 'the principal subject' and 'what it resembles' or, still more confusing, simply 'the meaning' and 'the metaphor, or 'the idea' and 'its image'. (96) For Richards grounds of metaphor, writes Abrams are some "aspects, properties, or common associations of a vehicle which, in a given context, apply to a tenor." (102)

2.2.2 Max Black

After twenty years it is Max Black, whose most influential essay on metaphor after Richards appears in *Proceeding of the Aristotelian Society* (1954-55) (PP 273-94). In his essay "Metaphor," Max propagates a theory of substitution. For this he says that "a metaphorical expression is used in phrases of some equivalent literal expression; I shall call a Substitution view of metaphor." Max further adds to his substitution view as:

> According to the substitution view, the focus of a metaphor, the word or expression having a distinctively metaphorical use within a literal frame, is used to communicate a meaning that might have been expressed literally. The author substitutes M for L; it is the reader's task to invert the substitution, by using the literal meaning of M as a clue to the intended literal meaning of L. Understanding a metaphor is like deciphering a code or unraveling a riddle. (Max Black, "Metaphor" 280-9)

In this regard, Max seems to refine and expand the then found views on metaphor e. g. I. A. Richards' views on metaphor. In Max's view, there appear two situations: either, "there may, in fact, be no literal equivalent, L, available in the language in question." He further modifies, saying for example "Mathematician spoke of the Leg" of an angle because there was no brief literal expression for a bounding line, thus, according to him metaphor "plugs the gaps" that supplies the want of convenient abbreviations." (280) It is a "use of word in some new sense" that brings very close to the view that metaphor brings creativity. His view of metaphor is stylistic, cathartic, and, moreover, "this is supposed to give pleasure to the reader." He says, when a reader encounters a metaphor "the reader is taken to enjoy problem-solving –or to delight in the author's skill at half-concealing, half-revealing his meaning." (281) for him, "metaphors provide a shock of agreeable surprise" therefore, in this "agreeable surprise" readers "agree in making metaphor a decoration." For him, metaphor is also "a catharsis that remedies some temporary imperfection of literal language," its primary aim is to please and divert. The use of metaphor is deviation in the ways: stylistic and pragmatic both. According to Max, metaphor as a figurative language is a "semantic change" which naturally "consists in some transformation of literal meaning," (282) for example: irony gets the reader to have an opposite meaning and hyperbole brings an exaggerated meaning, both are indifferent from a literal one. Thus, Max's metaphor is a work of detection; it is an "interaction" of two thoughts that are "active together." Max has smartly translated Richards' two component of metaphor: vehicle and tenor, at the conclusion of his essay, he brings Richards very close:

> Let us try, for instance, to think of a metaphor as a filter. Consider the statement, "Man is a wolf." Here, we may say, are two subjects – the principal subject, Man (or: men) and the subsidiary subject, Wolf (or: wolves). Now the metaphorical sentence in question will not convey its intended meaning to a reader sufficiently ignorant about wolves. What is needed so much that the reader shall know the standard dictionary meaning of "wolf" – or be able to use what word in literal sense – as that he shall know what I will call the system of associated commonplaces? (286-7)

Therefore, in the above example of "wolf", in effect, (metaphorically) "is to evoke the wolf-system of related commonplaces," that is the "wolf-language." Here the principal subject is "seen through" the metaphorical expression – or, if we prefer, says Max, the principal subject is "projected upon" the field of the subsidiary subject." (280)

Concluding his views on metaphor, Max distinguishes between interaction and substitution views of Metaphor as: (i) Metaphorical statement has two distinct subject – the 'principal' and 'subsidiary',

(ii) these subjects are systems of things rather than things, (iii) metaphors work through the application of the principal subject to a system of associated implications, that is a characteristic of the subsidiary subject, (iv) the commonly associated implications consist of commonplaces about the subsidiary subject. Though in some cases, there can be a deviant implication on ad hoc produced by the writers, (v) metaphor "selects, emphasises, suppresses, and organises features of the principal subject by implying statement about it," (vi) this act involves shifts in the meaning of the words related to the same system or family as the metaphorical expression. Though some of them can be considered as "metaphorical transfer," (vii) there is no ground for the shift of meaning, nor any blatant reason. This is the reason that some metaphors fail and succeed. (292-294)

It is Soskice who criticizes Blacks views speaking against the "hegemony of the word" that does not take textual context into consideration with the definition of metaphors. According to her, metaphors cannot be identified without application of textual context and particular situations. (21-32)

2.2.3 Donald Davidson

As openly opposed to Black's substitution views, the philosopher Donald Davidson, in his article "What Metaphors Mean" (1978) writes that metaphorisation does not mean to create new meaning. Although he accepts that metaphors have an exotic or artful significance. He associates this idea with an emotion concept. According to Davidson, metaphor is used as any other form of language and it projects its meaning as any other text. In his views, metaphor "nudges" its reader and helps to note similarities between the signified of the signs of metaphors. Davidson seems to be promoting a comparative view of metaphor. To "nudge," according to him, is to find out the same type of meaning similar to that of a simile. For him, the same metaphor "he is green" in which the primary subject "he" and the subsidiary subject "green", the system of associated commonplaces" of green, remolds its reader's understanding of the primary subject, thus a metaphoric meaning is produced. For Davidson, the metaphor "he is green" nudges its reader into noting and finding similarities between the subject one "he" and the subject two "green." This, says Davidson, turns the metaphors into the minds of the readers "he is like green." Davidson's "nudge" to the metaphorical texts does not lie inside of the meaning production of language but an extra-linguistic nudge that is possibly outside of meaning production of language. For a moment, that Language evolved for some practical purposes of good communication (190-211). This view of metaphor puts certain potential questions e. g. will a nudge not establish a more powerful means, quite potential for controlling the meaning production of language? What if it is possible, then, would not then be a part of all languages that seems yet to be defined and discussed?

2.2.4 Beardsley and Paul de Man

Adding to Davidson's theory and modifying his theory of metaphor as a simile, Beardsley discusses that branch of theories of metaphor which claims metaphors to be "elliptical similes" as making the metaphor literal by turning into a simile and finding out the comparison. Beardsley represents a "controversial theory of metaphor" in his *Aesthetics: Problems in the Philosophy of Criticism* (1958), (1988). According to him, metaphors carry something new without its signs, to change their signified. He considers metaphor to instigate a change of focus only within the structure of sign. Following Black, Beardsley does focus on two signs: the subject and the modifier. This pair of subject and modifier constitutes an attribution which implies the textual context for the production of meaning. Beardsley starts with a literal language, the situation that is generally referred to as "self-contradictory attribution." The attribution, within their modifiers, has some connotations that are generally accepted by the subject. The self –contradiction becomes significant, in it, there may appear an indirect self-contradiction. Within a self-contradictory attribution one may not be able to find a connoted meaning from the modifiers that get applied to the subject e. g. "circulars are squares," if the self-contradiction looks directly significant, then it is named oxymoron i. e. "cruel kindness" or "sweet poison" comparatively if this self-contradiction seems to be indirect e. g. "female male" becomes paradox. Beardsley sheds light on the need for the connotation of modifiers to be accepted by a subject as a requirement for the significant and indirect-contradictions to work. Thus, for Beardsley, this self-contradiction is a basis for all metaphors. (134-47)

Paul de Man in his short and crisp essay "The Epistemology of Metaphor" (1978) has a remarkable reflection on the nature of metaphor by subverting Locke's understanding of language which leads him to use a word: tautology. After a meticulous reading, it appears that like the other authors reflecting on metaphor, Paul de Man does not land his readers to any clear conclusions on metaphor – or even if it does, it only justifies the title of his essay and drives himself to think on different lines i. e. comparison between literature and philosophy. But this is to be noted that he ends up with some other interesting problems to be pondered over by the scholars of metaphor as he writes at the end of the essay that rhetoric falls in the epistemological discipline, he adds that:

> ...possibility arises those temporal articulations, such as narratives or histories, are a correlative of rhetoric and not the reverse. One would then have to conceive of rhetoric of history prior to attempting a history of rhetoric or of literature or of literary criticism... patterns of historical periodisation are at the same time as productive as heuristic devices yet so demonstratively aberrant." (*Critical Inquiry*, 30)

2.3 Paul Ricoeur

2.3.1 Paul Ricoeur's *La Metaphore vive:* A Counter

In modern times, it is only Paul Ricoeur who has made an attempt to explore the concept of metaphor in all its manifestations in his *La Metaphore vive* (1975), translated as *The Rule of Metaphor* (1977), a very detailed and highly systematic study on Metaphor ever done by any author in modern times. Here Reoccur refutes with Aristotle, I. A. Richards, Max Black and Monroe Beardsley etc. making novel arguments and associating metaphor with the basic nature of language.

La Metaphore Vive is a Ricoeurean reflection on metaphor and language in eight detailed studies beginning from Aristotle's rhetoric to poetics, to metaphor and philosophical discourse. It includes metaphor and semantic of discourse, semantics of the word, decline of Rhetoric and the new Rhetoric, metaphor and the work of resemblance metaphor and reference. Here "some of the decisive doctrines are taken from English-Language Literature and some from the French." Ricoeur says that "this is an expression of double allegiance of my research as well as my teaching." Thus, through this double allegiance he hopes by this "to help reduce the mutual ignorance that persists among specialists in these two linguistic and cultural worlds." (7)

Ricoeur claims that the English-language authors always take two ideas to make a metaphor. If it is the case to "affect just one word, the metaphor has to disturb the whole network by means of an aberrant attribution." (23) The mechanism which is found in the representation of English authors and the representation of two ideas together is questioned by Ricoeur who also questions the relationship of both the ideas which remain puzzled at a time:

> At the same time, the idea of categorical transgression allows us to fill out that of deviation, which seemed to be implied in the transposition process. 'Deviation' appeared to belong to a purely lexical order, but now it is linked to a kind of deviance that threatens classification itself. What remains to be puzzled out is the relationship between the two sides of the phenomenon, between logical deviation and the production of meaning that Aristotle calls *epiphora.* This problem will be solved in a satisfactory manner only when the statement-character of metaphor is fully recognised. The name-related aspects of metaphor can then become fully attached to a discursive structure. (23)

Here the idea of the categorical transgression looks interesting only because it creates meaning. Ricoeur suggests that metaphor destroys an order only to create or invent another, it "bears information" because they "re-describe reality," it also "belongs to a heuristic of through." (24) Ricoeur develops his ideas by refuting Aristotle's views on metaphor first with the pains to examine each view with proper methodology to reach the analysis of the phenomenon. One of the observations made by Aristotle is that "it is a great thing, indeed, to make a proper use of the poetical forms [...]. But the greatest thing by far is to be a master of metaphor [literally: to be metaphorical, to metaphoric on ennui]." (25) This is the thing that Aristotle declares, "that cannot be learnt from others; and it is also a sign of genius [euphorias], since a good metaphor [literally to metaphorise well, eu metapherien] implies an intuitive perception of the similarity." (25-26, *Poetics*, 1459 a 3-8)

Ricoeur asserts that there are many notable aspects in Aristotle's definition. The word that Aristotle calls a ***noun*** later becomes a verb [as it is to metaphorize]. Thus, Aristotle's view "to metaphorize well" brings up the problem of usage that is too "appropriate" which is a "process of lexis." In this connection, one has to metaphorize well, that is to be appropriated the "greatest thing" that is to be metaphorical. It cannot be taught as it is a "gift of genius, of nature." In this regard, Ricoeur questions the view given by Aristotle:

> Are we not now back at the level of finding or inventing that heuristic that we said violates an order only to create another, that dismantles only to redescribe function? All of modern creativity

> theory confirms that there are no rules for innovation, no recipes for the concoction of good hypotheses, only rules for the validation of the hypotheses [...]. But why can we not learn to "be metaphorical" if to "metaphorize well" is to "see resemblance?" (25)

Ricoeur unites the concept of "mimesis" that has been remarkably narrowed down translating it with the word imitation from Plato to Aristotle. According to him, the very general relationship between something that it resembles is the only reliable thing. The latter may be good, bad or apparent. But the "reference to ideal models merely allows the construction of a scale of resemblance marking the degree to which this or that appearance approximates being." (42) Ricoeur makes a possible objection by saying that though *Poetics* uses the concept of imitation, it does not define it clearly. Ricoeur asks whether if the function of imitation is to provide pleasure, if yes then of what sort of pleasure? The tragic variant of the pleasure that is associated with imitation is – 'Katharsis' (Catharsis), though not a "part" as such, in the sixth constituent parts of the Greek tragic poetry. It is only linked with the effect or experience of the audience. The term is "less dependent on the spectators' psychology than on the intelligible composition of the tragedy." (43)

Ricoeur concludes that imitation is a process of forming each of the six constituent parts of the tragedy: muthos, ethos, dianoia, [As the object of imitation], melos-lexis [As means of imitation], and opsis [As the manner or medium of imitation]). Here Ricoeur seems busy in focusing on the logical construction of imitation. He asks the ordering function; the pleasure which imitation puts forward. This is a variety of pleasure that is also found in learning and knowing. It is the pleasure of imitation which is found in tragedy at the end that is called 'tragic – knowledge.' In tragedy the imitation of action is the one which magnifies and ennobles. (But Ricoeur asks-to whom?) Here he relates the understanding of the cathartic experience with that of metaphor. Ricoeur confesses that this is the key point to understanding the function of metaphor, he adds that "metaphor ceases to be arbitrary and trivial" and becomes more complex if it is taken from ordinary language. If metaphor is conceived merely as "a fact or element of language, it could be taken for a mere deviation in relation to ordinary language," which includes "the rose word, the newly coined, the lengthened, abbreviated and altered" words.

Ricoeur puts another aspect stating that "the subordination of *lexis* to *muthos* already puts metaphor at the service of "saying", of poetizing." At this point metaphor belongs no longer to the level of the words it rather reaches "at the level of poem as a whole." The subordination of muthos over lexis provides "the stylistic process a global aim" which is from the "rhetoric intention to pursued." Here, this metaphor taken as a deviation gives nothing but a twist, turn, and a difference in the meaning. Metaphor that is related to the imitation of our action gets attached with "double tension that characterises this imitation," the first one is the "submission to reality" and the second that is the "fabulous invention" that un-alters representation and enabling elevation. According to Ricoeur, this double tension "constitutes the referential function of metaphor in poetry." Thus, being abstracted from the referential function, substitution gets itself out in ornamentation, allows running free and finally "loses itself in language games." Ricoeur mentions that according to Aristotle lexis is rooted in mimesis and "through mimesis metaphor's deviations from normal lexis belong to the great enterprise of "saying what is." Metaphor relates and makes one see things as in Aristotle's view, it "represents things as in a state of activity." (14 11-b 24-5, 44-48)

Commenting on the poetic language, Ricoeur writes that "a poetic composition that is at once clear and base is precisely one that employs only the most familiar vocabulary in its most common usage." This is the exact time for deviation where "two standards meet," the first is "the strange" and the second is "the noble." Ricoeur, therefore, asks – "if the strange" and the 'noble' meet in the 'good' metaphor, is it not because the nobility of such language befits the grandeur of the actions being depicted?" In this connection Ricoeur admits that:

> [T]his interpretation goes beyond Aristotle's intentions, but it is permissible in terms of his text and arose from my reading of it. In any case, if this interpretation is valid, we are forced to ask whether the secret of metaphor, as a displacement of meaning at the level of words, does not rest in the elevation of meaning of the level of muthos. And if this proposal is acceptable then metaphor would not only be a deviation in halation to ordinary usage, but also, by means of this deviation, the privileges instrument in that up word motion of meaning promoted by *mimesis*. (46)

In conclusion, Ricoeur declares that mimesis does not embody only the referential function or signify the discourse in the world but "Being *mimesis phases*, it connects this referential function to the revelation of the real as Act." He says the "concept of mimesis serves an index of the discourse situation. It brings us close to the point that "no discourse ever suspends our belonging to a world," all the concepts of mimesis "take place within the horizons of a being-in-the-world." Ricoeur now moves from rhetoric to semantics and from semantics to the end discussing the conflict of the idea and word, in this connection observes that "the priory of the word does not abolish the bipolar organisation. But every time the examples seem to put discourse above the word." (48-58)

Ricoeur at the end of the second study, of *The Rule of Metaphor*, refers to Fontanier's comparative analysis of figure and catachresis. Focusing on the importance of catachresis constitutes "a foundation for our entire topological system." (213, 71). Supporting Mountaineer's view, he continues arguing that the fact of language which is-this that some ideas lack proper signs, as catachresis stands for-a situation – which is with a sign already having one idea, is also made associated and attached to a temporary new idea. Therefore, all the troupes which create the extended meaning are only a result of catachrestic cases.

Ricoeur draws attention to the "figure-trope" which has a remarkable characteristic of being free. The newly invented metaphors thus, "confirm a close relationship between the trope and the living event of actual speech." The first quality of being free "applies to usage, all usage tends to become habitual, and metaphors tends to resemble catachresis." (11-2) This is the point where metaphor seems clearly a "part of the foundation of language" later, it, being more prevalent, "starts calling like a literal meaning." (71)

2.3.2 Metaphor and the Semantics of Discourse

Ricoeur moving to the next study "Metaphor and the Semantics of Discourse, in which he investigates" the interpretation ship of meaning that gives rise to this transposition of the name which according to him emphasizes to open the frame of reference "determined by the word and a portion that is determined by the name or noun." For Ricoeur this is the very point which "imposes the statement as the sole contextual milieu within which the transposition of meaning takes place." Therefore, at this point Ricoeur looks strong to the "direct examination of the role of the statement" supposing as if it carries complete and dependent autonomous meaning what he calls "metaphorical statement." For

Ricoeur, metaphor as "transposition" is nominal only and not real "which in return only allows us to identify something" in the same manner as Aristotle and Fontanier have assigned meanings to metaphor. Keeping all these aspects in view "a theory of the metaphorical statement will be a theory of the production of metaphorical meaning." (74-5)

In this connection Ricoeur promises to establish a relationship between semantics and semiotics of metaphor by making extremely minute observations especially "in the English-language tradition of linguistic analysis." Ricoeur claims that theory of discourse has not been developed by linguists, but rather by some Logicians and epistemologists who hardly paid any attention to it; sometimes they seem to be engaged with literary criticism to some extent. But this remains ambiguous, as he does not specify any author. But Ricoeur attacks the ambition of the linguistic discourse, writing "as one cannot any longer simply disregard the relationship between discourse and language." In this regard Ricoeur compares English-language linguistic analysis with the work of Emile Benveniste (1902-1976) focusing on the distinction between semantics and semiotics. Ricoeur calls him a "great French Sanskritist" who has taken fundamental aspects of language and discourse, signs and sentences. According to Ricoeur, the first one is associated with the lower land and the second one with the higher level. Benveniste (1902-76) names these two levels semiotics and semantics.

Before plunging into this debate, a short view on semiotics and semiology seems to be relevant. It was pointed out by M. H. Abrams that Charles Sanders Peirce (1839-1914) an American philosopher proposed a study called "semiotic" at one hand and the Swiss linguist, Ferdinand de Saussure proposed a similar science in his lectures called semiology. Thus, semiotics and semiology become a common alternative name for the systematic study of "sign" and in this way sign is not seen limited to explicit systems of communication such as language. It is observed that Ricoeur might have ignored its expansion crossing the boundaries of language. This is, Ricoeur quotes Benveniste's view of sign as something of a "lower level" as a form of signifying system. C. S. Peirce distinguishes their categories of sign to its object, a relation between a signifying item and something that it signified: (i) Icon, (ii) Index, and (iii) Symbol. According to Pierce, *icon* functions as a sign by means of inherent attributes e. g. similarity of a portrait to the person it exposes and the similarity of a map to a place it stands for. The *index* is something which bears a natural relation of cause or effect to whatever it signifies e. g. smock to fire. The *symbol* which he names a "sign proper" here the reaction is not natural or artificial but entirely a matter of social connection." This is a fact that structuralism developed in France under the aegis of de Saussure. To a great extent the semioticians, too, appear to be Structuralist. All of them, therefore, deal with any set of social or cultural phenomena or any social or cultural production as TEXT. Text as an object of research will be taken in the second half of this study in detailed description.

Moving back to Ricoeur, it is observed that he is getting critical of de Saussure's and all semiotic notions of sign in relation to language – as language for him is a "system of signs." Ricoeur thinks that to characterise language as a system of sign is just one of its aspects and not in its totality. This definition ignores the utterance, statement or sentence in relation to semantics of language which stands equally functional as a sign at a larger scope. The following diagram will reflect this case as:

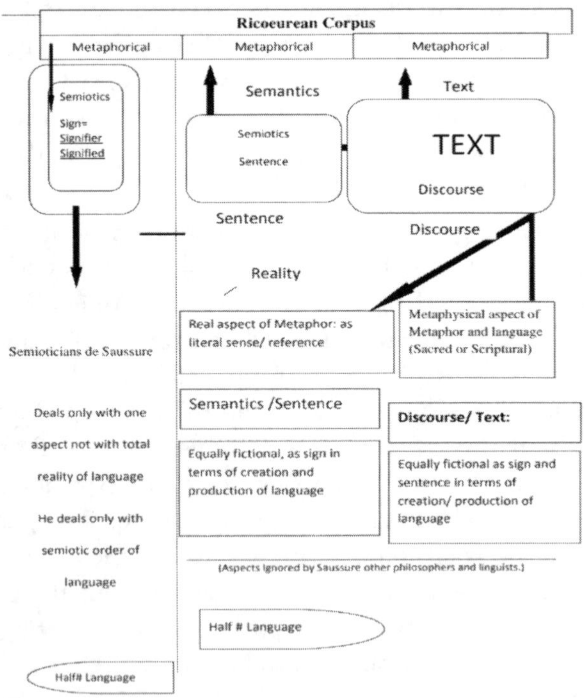

Thus, circumscribed in this manner Ricoeur writes that "sign leaves out the order of discourse." In this connection he offers some following enumeration for the "distinctive traits of discourse" in pairs, which projects discourse as if it is of dialectical character having a requirement of methodology which is "different from that which applies to the operations of segmentation of distribution appropriate to a purely taxonomic conception of language." (77-80) Ricoeur writes in pairs about the distinctive traits of discourse, beginning to believe for a while in "a purely taxonomic conception of language":

(i) Discourse occurs as an event, but is to be understood as meaning.
(ii) Distinguishing between identifying functions of predicative functions.
(iii) Structure of act of discourse.
(iv) Sense and reference.
(v) Reference and reality from reference to the speaker.
(vi) Important for the understanding of the nature of language and metaphor, that is the "redescription of the spheres of the paradigmatic and syntagmatic, which is the distinction between semiology and semantics brought along with it." (80-87)

According to Ricoeur, "the process of interpretation takes place at the level of modes of existing." Here Ricoeur seems to be asserting that if one believes that metaphor consists in talking "about one thing in terms of another," it also consists in perceiving, thinking – as he writes "seeing one thing in terms of another." (96)

One of the finest observations made by Ricoeur in his book is that "metaphor does not represent some additional power, but the constitutive form of language." He argues that only restricting itself to the description of the ornament of language, rhetoric condemned itself to treating nothing but superficial problems where a metaphor penetrates to the very depths of verbal interaction." (92) In this connection, discussing the nature of language of metaphor as and the nature of metaphor as if a constitutive part, Ricoeur writes:

> This pervading presence of metaphor results from the 'context theorem of meaning.' If the word substitutes for a combination of aspects that are themselves the missing parts of their diverse contexts, the principle of metaphor derives from this constitution of

> words. According to one elementary formulation, metaphor holds two thoughts of different things together in simultaneous performance upon the stage of a word or a simple expression, whose meaning is the result of their interaction. Or, to bring this description and the theorem of meaning into accord, we can say that the metaphor holds together within one simple meaning two different missing parts of different contexts of this meaning. Thus, we are not dealing any longer with a simple transfer of words, but with commerce between thoughts, that is, a transaction between contexts. If metaphor is a competence, a talent, then it is a talent of thinking. Rhetoric is just the reflection and the translation of this talent into a distinct body of knowledge. (92)

Thus, Ricoeur gets back to conclude the "contrasting pair," that is the distinction between metaphor of statement and metaphor of the word. According to him, in the metaphorical statement the "contextual action creates the new meaning" and this meaning, according to him, has a truly "status of event since it exists only in the present context." (115) Moving further, in the same context Ricoeur observes that it can also be re-identified as the same meaning and its construction can equally be repeated. Thus, in between the rediscovery or re-identification, writes Ricoeur, "the innovation of an emergent meaning can be taken as a linguistic creation." And possibly if this newly created linguistic meaning gets adopted by the "significant part of the linguistic community gets the impetus to become a common meaning which can add to the Polysemy of lexical entices." In this way "it contributes to the history of language as code or system." At its final stage this aspect of metaphor increases Polysemy – though at the final stage, it becomes a dead metaphor, but Ricoeur adds that "[one] authentic metaphor, that is, living metaphors are at once meaning and event." (114)

2.3.3 Monism of the Sign and Primacy of the Word (Polysemy Synonymy, Homonymy)

Now dwelling on to "The necessity of the sense-reference polarity for metaphor" questioning the use of such a language that "satisfies the two principles of congruence and plenitude." (115) In the fourth study of metaphor Ricoeur starts with a detailed description of monism of the sign and primacy of the word. Referring back to Saussure's views, especially when he talks of "the fundamental units that characterise various levels of organisation in language are homogenous and they all come under a single science, the science of signs or semiotics," therefore, for Ricoeur, the homogeneity in the organisation of language and the "fundamental orientation towards semiotic monism is most decisive reason for the divergence in the explanation of metaphor." Putting together those two major tendencies: monism of sign and primacy of word, Ricoeur observes that there is a "metaphorical crisis," which is found in the context of the word. This is the point which shows, in Ricoeur's word an "abyss," a constant ignorance with 'sentence' the first dichotomy between language and speech as the message always remains with sentence. This is the course in which lexical semantics becomes the linguistics of language focusing only on the general semantics with lexical semantics which Ricoeur names as Pleonasm.

The word is at the level of "connective layer" between Phoneme and Syntagma. The distinctive level of first side of the word (phone) "presupposes the significant units of the lexical level," therefore in this connection "the test of communication cannot be used if a phonematic change does not lead to a change in the semantic of a word," this is the only reason that phonology is always semantically conditioned. With Syntagma, the second side of the word remains the same. The lexicology and semantics do not coincide with each other. But in a way respond to two different disciplines: for its form and its meaning. It is seen that the lexical semantics contrasts with lexical morphology, composition, derivation, fusion, suffixation etc. in Ricoeur's views. In this regard, the important thing is that the syntax itself provides a morphology and semantics; here he stands astonished when he brings some points in his derivation of different aspects of lexical semantics, its changing and its transforming nature. Ricoeur writes about this surprising nature as:

> … the decision that the adjective-turned substantive, '*the* semantics,' should be called on to designate, through abbreviation, lexical semantics alone, that is the theory of the meaning of words. As for metaphor, it remains classed among the changes of meaning. It will be recalled that this was the place assigned to it by Aristotle when he defined metaphor as *epiphora of the name*. Thus, the most explicit aspect of the Aristotelian definition is taken up by the 'semantics of the word.' (121)

2.3.4 Logical-linguistic Treatment of Metaphorical Dimension

Now Ricoeur turns to logical-linguistic treatment of metaphorical dimension where he analyses the French-language work which for more than twenty years, according to a critic, has just been considered the best work on metaphor. This is the study done by Hedwig

Conrad. His work is based on the description of Metaphor explained as "a modality of denomination" based on the logical-linguistic consideration. Therefore, Ricoeur dwells on "metaphor as change of meaning" rather than sticking to logical-linguistic consideration of metaphor.

Having been influenced by the semantics of Stephen Ullmann, Ricoeur links his discussion with one of the key phenomena of the entire semantics of the word, he calls it *Polysemy* as it has been defined previously as something "established base of name-sense relation." The present work at this point also includes the issues related to synonymy, homonymy and homonymy. Discussing one of the very general characteristics of language, namely called vagueness. Ricoeur commenting on this aspect of language [vagueness] writes:

> Vagueness is to be understood not exactly as that abstraction which is itself a phenomenon of order, a taxonomic feature, but in the 'generic' sense, that of not ordered, indefinite, and imprecise, which always demands that a further discrimination be made on the basis of actual context. (132)

Moving to the phenomena of synonymy in language, that is one of the subjects of polysemy which has potential to be a general reflection of systematic and non-systematic features of language. This in Ricoeur's words, "implies partial semantic identity" and it also "points to overlapping of semantic fields." At the end it's the acceptance of a word which is synonymous with an acceptance of another word. Words, thus according to Ricoeur "are not just distinctive from one another," moreover, he observes that they "trespass on one another"' as the very act of communication hugely depends on distinguished synonyms and using them with all appropriateness and with required and needed adequacy as well within the desired and targeted contexts. This contextual discrimination "pre-supposes just this phenomenon of synonymy, as a descriptive trait of natural languages." (133) He defines such synonymy as "the possibility of substituting words in given contexts without altering the objective and effective meaning." (133) In his view synonymy confines the "possibility of providing synonyms for various acceptations of a single word." (133)

Thus, synonyms, say Ricoeur, "play two roles at once," one, they offer a "stylistic resource for fine distinctions," and second, they are also useful for "emphasis," "reinforcement," and "filing on." Here opens another similar association: Polysemy and homonymy in the same connection which "rest on the same principle of the combination of a single signifier with more than one signified." (133) This aspect with a slight difference "homonymy applies to a difference between two words, and between two words, and between them entire semantic fields, Polysemy takes place within a single word whose several acceptations it distinguishes." (133) According to Ricoeur "the central phenomena of disruptive semantics are Polysemy." (134) He mentions that "I also called it a lexical ambiguity," in connection with polysemy he writes:

> A language without Polysemy would violate the principle of economy, for it would extend its vocabulary infinitely. Furthermore, it would violate the rule of communication, because it would multiply its designations as often as, in principle, the diversity of subjects of experience demanded. We need an economical system that is economical, flexible, and sensitive to context in order to express the spectrum of human experience. It is the task of contexts to shift the variations of appropriate meanings and with the help of Polysemy words to devise discourse that is seen as relatively universal – that is giving rise to just one interpretation that which the speaker intended to bestow on his words. (134)

Therefore, similar is the case of metaphor in language and "a word," says Ricoeur "should have several acceptances at a given moment in a state of a system that is variant belonging to several classes". It should also be able to acquire a new meaning without losing its earlier meaning. He suggests that "this cumulative capability" is important for the understanding of metaphor where there is a potential possibility of "double or stereoscopic vision." For Ricoeur this cumulative character of the word opens language to innovation. (136)

However, coming back to the understanding of Polysemy specifically in relation to the understanding of metaphor in a parallel order it "attests to the quality of openness in the texture of the word," the word that has the potential of having several meanings and also being of acquiring many more. This with a critical view is the "descriptive trait of meaning" which carries to the theory of chance of meaning as if there is more than one name for one sense and more than one sense for one name.

This is to get back to the previous discussions where Ricoeur refers to the view of Saussure, Ullmann, Esnant and Leonce Roudit and also adds that a "psychological mechanics regulates semantic innovations and that principle is *association*". With this explanation

Ricoeur exposes the theory of *resemblance* and the associations of *similarities.* "Association," for Ricoeur, "is still the guiding thread of the innumerable borrowings that metaphor brings into play." In this connection the psychology of association becomes very crucial for the production of meaning. When one figures out that a sentence or a word has the potential of more than one possible semantic meaning, the words start getting "new values."

Ricoeur turns critical having discussed Ullman's semantic theory centered on Synonymy, Homonymy Polysemy, important aspects of language. He moves to Ferdinand de Saussure and his theory of semantics in relation with metaphor. More specifically, the view about language as a system of sign: signifier and signified being referential and arbitrary. Ricoeur criticises this view and this notion of understanding of language as only a referential play ending with the aporia results. He seems disappointed and disturbed with this narrow semiotic horizon of linguistic dimension in relation with language.

Ricoeur appears to be helpless to write "nothing would be more accurate than to say that Saussurean dichotomies create as many problems as they solve." (144) For his Saussure "contrasted the relation between signifier and signified with the external sign-thing relation, which he repudiated," here we see that "The thing is excluded from the factors involved in meaning." According to Ricoeur for Saussure a "sign does not unite a thing and a name, but a concept and an *acoustic image.*" Therefore, the discourse through this sign system, the so-called referential play, ends with an *Apria.* This is because discourse through its referential function sets signs completely into relation with things. Denotation is in this connection a sign-thing relation, whereas signification is a relation between signifier and signified. Whatever it leads to is an ambiguity with Saussurean understanding as:

> Signified meaning is nothing other than the counterpart of signifier, what defines one defines the other as both sides of a sheet of paper are cut by the same motion of the scissors. But in relation to the reality denoted, meaning stands as mediator between works and things, i. e. it is through which words relate to things. (144)

It becomes very difficult to understand the nature of language as a sign rather than a denotative function of language where we find a semantic innovation. This sort of the understanding of the function of language "allows one to interrelate at work in metaphor and predicative operation that gives it the framework of discourse." (146)

Ricoeur makes haste to conclude this debate in this study regarding sign, semantic innovation and discourse as:

> The word preserves the semantic capital constituted by these contextual values deposited in its semantic treasury. What it brings to the sentence is a potential for meaning. This potential is not formless: the word does have an identity. Certainly, this is a plural identity, an open texture, as we said; but this identity is nevertheless sufficient for it to be identified and re – identified as the same in different contexts. The game of naming discussed just above is possible only because the semantic 'diversity' that the word consists of endures as a limited, rule-governed, and hierarchical heterogeneity. Polysemy is not homonymy. But this plural *identity* is also a *plural* identity. This is why, in the game of the word and of the sentence, the 'Initiative of meaning,' as it were, passes over again to the sentence. The passage from the potential to the actual meaning of a word requires the mediation of a new sentence, just as the potential meaning issues from the sedimentation and institutionalisation of previous contextual values. (152)

For Ricoeur, the word gets "the determination that reduces its imprecision" from the context. This, in a way, is also applicable even with the proper names. Referring to Ullmann, Ricoeur notes that the name "Queen Victoria" as women, at the same time was also found at the time of Boer War. These two women of the similar name need a context to refer to each one separately. The proper name can indicate only one person, only if there is any instance of some "inferior descriptions" that may be within the given context. It is applicable for both verbal and non-verbal communication in which the name is mentioned. Ricoeur intuitively confesses that "action of the context-sentence, discourse, work, discourse situation" is a problem some to reduce Polysemy attached with them is the key problem that has motivated this work on language, metaphor and its function. He says "[if] it is true that metaphor adds to Polysemy then the operation of discourse set in motion by metaphor is the inverse" that he has described. At the end Ricoeur adds that "[for] a sentence to make sense it is necessary that all the acceptations of the semantic potential of the words under consideration be eliminated except one, that which is compatible with the itself appropriately reduced, of the other word of the sentence." (153) In the same way, with metaphor, all the acceptations already codified are fairly suitable. Even though it seems important to retain all the acceptations allowed plus one – the one which will "rescue the meaning of entire statement." The statement and the word metaphor both look equally compatible. The metaphorical statement gets its statement of meaning by means of an epiphora of the word.

Thus the "analogical" and contextual aspect of word and metaphor are compatible with each other to the level of complete perception of language. Here it is also realised that metaphor "is the outcome of a debate between predication and naming; its place in languages between words and sentences." (150-156)

The fifth study of Ricoeur in *The Rule of Metaphor* does not reflect much on the present problem that we have with specific limits. Nevertheless, he does talk about metaphor at the closure of this part explicitly by taking in account all the aspects of deviation in language – referring to the discussion of Rhetoric and new-Rhetoric that we are not taking in account in detail. He concludes that if "edition is only the impact on that of semantic phenomena that connects the entire statement, then one must call 'metaphor' the entire statement with its new meaning," the meaning taken on ad hoc basis which is not supposed to be a paradigmatic deviation which "focuses the mutation of meaning of the whole statement on one word." (200-3)

2.3.5 The Works of Resemblance

Turning to the sixth study "The Works of Resemblance" of *The Rule of Metaphor,* it is found that it is devoted to the examination of a problem, the problem which creates the nation of resemblance in the understating of metaphor. Ricoeur proposes here to dissociate "the fate of resemblance from that of the substitution theory of interaction." (204) In one of the sub-sections of the same study, Ricoeur writes that in "substitution and Resemblance" the role and place metaphor in classical rhetoric is assigned among the "figure of significations" in its explanation of resemblance and is found in the "transference from initial idea to new idea." Therefore, metaphor then, was a troop of resemblance something *par excellence*. Critiquing the above discussed definition of metaphor Ricoeur writes:

> Metaphor is the trope of resemblance *par excellence*. This pact with resemblance is not just an isolated trait; in the model underlying the theory of classical rhetoric, it is intimately connected to the primacy of naming or denomination and to the other traits that follow from this primacy. Now resemblance operates first between the ideas named by words. Subsequently, in the model, the theme of resemblance is closely united with those of borrowing, deviation, substitution, and exhaustive paraphrase. Indeed, resemblance first of all motivates the borrowing; next, it is the positive side of the process

> whose negative side is deviation; further, it is the internal link within the sphere of substitution; finally, it guides the paraphrase that annuls the trope by restoring the proper meaning. To the extent that the postulate of substitution can be taken to be representative of the whole chain of postulates, resemblance is the foundation of the substitution that is set in motion in the metaphorical transposition of names and, more generally, of words. (205)

Ricoeur expresses his gratitude towards the famous linguist appreciating his famous and well-known article, "Two Aspects of Language and two Types of Aphasic Disturbances." (1953) Here the complying for metaphor and Metonymy is associated with Roman Jacobson. Where it is considered to have "connected this properly topological and rhetorical duality with a more fundamental polarity that concerns the very functioning of language." This is not only for figurative use as observed by Ricoeur. Furthermore, it is also announced that "metaphor and Metonymy do not merely define figures and troops; they define the general process of language." This is that language metaphorical by nature is at risk to successfully prove that this is a natural process of language. The famous linguist, according to Ricoeur, has made the idea, the idea of substitution and of resemblance "are two inseparable concepts, since they rule together over processes that work on numerous levels at which language is affected." (206)

After these numerous levels, Ricoeur moves to another discussion of metaphor and language, he recalls Saussure and Roman Jacobson "on a distinction between two ways in which signs are arranged – combination and signs are arranged-combination and selection." For Ricoeur the "primary mode of arrangement unites in preventing two or more terms in absentia in a virtual mnemonic series," therefore, "this concerns entities associated in the code but not in the given in the message." (205-6) There is always a possibility of substitution if there is a selection between the alternative terms, there is a possibility for one which looks equivalent to the first at one level and also different from the in another angle aspect. For him, [selection] and substitution, accordingly, are the "two fares of a single operation," (207) and all that is left, according to Jacobson, is to concept properly, the combination and contiguity, substitution and similarity as well. In this connection Ricoeur opens up as:

> Indeed, contiguity and similarity characterise the status of the constituents, in the context of a message on the one hand, within a substitution group on the other. From this point on, the correlation

> with tropes presents no difficulty, if it is granted that metonymy rests on contiguity and metaphor on resemblance. Thanks to this series of correlations, one can for short call combination itself the metonymic pole and selection the metaphoric pole of linguistic operations. These operations can be represented only with the help of orthogonal axes of which only one, that of combination, corresponds to the linearity of the signifier. (207)

Dwelling upon this point (combination and selection) which is borrowed from Jakobson, Ricoeur ponders over here for a while that Jakobson's analysis bypasses the distinction made by Benveniste that is between semiotics and semantics, between sign and sentence. Ricoeur remarks on this as "[this] monism of sign is characteristic of a purely semantic linguistics." (207) He confirms the hypothesis of his work that "the model to which a substitution theory of metaphor belongs is one that ignores the difference between semiotics and semantics and takes the word and not the sentence as the basic unit of topology." (207) It is to draw attention to the possibility of 'Superimposing' the pair syntax-semantics onto the other pair combination selection, as is the same with contiguity-similarity and so also onto "the pair comprising the autonomic and metaphorical poles." (208)

The difference which results from the 'cleft' between discourse and the sign in the entities of linguistic literacy "are equivocation affecting the concept of combination as much as selection." (211) Thus, the notion of metaphorical process is only equivocal in Ricoeur's view and in this sense, it is too wide. It is too wide only "when one considers the heterogeneity of substitution and selection operation level from one level to another." (211) The metaphorical process is also "cut off paradoxically from an essential trait-so that, despite its extremely general character it remains too narrow," (211) Ricoeur thinks that the notion of metaphorical process "is ever more emphatically to narrow" only if one believes that there is no room for the concept-*interaction*-specifically the metaphorical statements. It is "in the orbit of selection-substitution phenomena." At the end, the predicative character of metaphor is left out. Coming to the fundamental problem of the difference between newly invented metaphors in common use Ricoeur writes: that: "[it] appears to be very difficult to do justice to this important difference if one cannot contrast phenomena of discourse with phenomena of language." (212) He indicates at the solution that it is "indeed, catachresis is ultimately an extension of denomination." Thus the catachresis is a natural phenomenon in terms of its evolution. Metaphor and the newly invented metaphors and a "phenomenon of discourse" this is what Ricoeur names as "unusual attribution." (213)

The further development of the convening model of Jakobson and the critique of Jakobson done by Michael Le Govern and his reformulation, Ricoeur intends a systematic analysis of this aspect. The model already discussed above selection and combination is the present concern for the reinterpretation of the very definition. If the one model is based on an *'internal'* relation, and the second on 'external' relations, then the first one should be understood in the sense of *inter-linguistic* order of reality and the second as an *extra-linguistic* order Ricoeur argues that if it is so, then "it is possible to superimpose a Foregone distinction between *sense* and *reference* on the distinction borrowed from Jakobson, between selection-substitution and combination structure." (213) Thus, in this light metaphor is set to be understood as "The *substance* of language, i. e. meaning (sense) relation, while metonymy modifies the referential relation itself." (213) This argument brings the two most important metaphorical functions i. e. sense and reference. The analysis given by Le Guern clarifies that "metaphor is just a phenomenon of abstraction." (215) In this relation, Ricoeur concludes that there is no metaphor if there is no deviation detection "between the figurative meaning of a word and the isotropy of the context." (215)

Therefore, for interpreting a metaphor, suggests Ricoeur one should be able to image triggering that is "incompatible with the context." (216) Referring to the suggestion of Le Guerin, Ricoeur moves to the "[extension] nuclear analysis of *noun-metaphor* to the *adjective – metaphor* and *verb-metaphor*." The verb-metaphor Ricoeur writes "heralds the first consideration of context even in the production of figure." (216) It is impossible to bring metaphor and comparison in discussion without coming close to the role of *isotropy* of the context into play. The comparison is totally "based on the isotropy of the context". Which is like the qualities comparison (simile) projects the deviation with regard to the same isotropy as does metaphor. In Ricoeur's eyes the role of isotropy is quite fundamental. Ricoeur again refers to Le Goren and his addition to Jacobson's thesis that begets the final conclusion for the "incorporating change of isotropy into the divination of metaphor" specifically focusing on the relation between denotation. According to Le Goren, mentions Ricoeur, that "metaphor combines a purely denotative aspect of connotation, which is external to the properly logical or informative function of the statement." (217)

2.3.6 The 'Iconic' Moment of Metaphor

One of the subsections of current study "The 'Iconic' Moment of Metaphor" seems to be quite important and interesting as well. It is observed that through the history of rhetoric, the relation between substitution and resemblance has not been possible to dissociate, nevertheless Ricoeur writes that this notion seems to be broken within the span of a brief history by Pail Henley. The author is influenced by Charles Sander and borrows the concept of icon from him. Ricoeur attempts to analyse it, he writes that the "essential role of the icon is to contain an internal duality that at the same time is to overcome," this may surprise many that Ricoeur quotes from Keats's verses "When by my solitary hearth I sit, and hateful thought enwrap my soul in gloom," here the metaphorical expression "enwrap consists in presenting sorrow as if enveloping the soul in a cloak." (223) According to Henley, says Ricoeur, we are moved by figurative discourse to think of or thinking by the consideration of something that is like the iconic pattern of signification. Therefore, metaphor is analysed "in accordance with two modalities of semantic relationship," this iconic understanding in Ricoeur's view "harbors the power to elaborate, to extend the parallel structure." (244) This is to note here that how Ricoeur in this connection describes resemblance in this paragraph:

> It is resemblance that allows us to function in new situations. If metaphor adds nothing to the description of the world, at least it adds to the ways in which we perceive; and this is the poetic function of metaphor. This still rests upon resemblance, but at the level of feelings. In symbolising one situation by means of another, metaphor 'infuses' the feelings attached to the symbolising situation into the heart of the situation that is symbolised. In this 'transference of feelings,' the similarity between feelings is induced by the resemblance of situations. In its poetic function, therefore, metaphor extends the power of double meaning from the cognitive realm to the affective. (224)

Ricoeur projects all the related problems associated with the view-called resemblance. He stands defending the resemblance view as "the factor of resemblance is of even greater necessity in a tension theory than in a substitution theory." Ricoeur considers it a mistake on the part of the reason, on the logical status of metaphor that is "to believe that the notion of tension, interaction and logical contradiction makes every possible role of resemblance superfluous." (229) Talking about the strategy of language at work, in a metaphorical expression specifically with an example of oxymoron as: "bitter truth" and "obscure clarity," says Ricoeur that in a literal sense these expressions hit us to an enigma – a problem to understand it in common sense. This is what Ricoeur says one way call a *"semantic challenge"* or *"semantic impertinent"* in Jean Cohen's language. According to Ricoeur here this metaphorical meaning is not a semantic class rather it is a new pertinence but provides the meaning and this challenge is silenced only with a metaphorical meaning – that is a new pertinence in the present semantics.

Going back to Beardsley's model of metaphor where "the metaphor is what forms a meaningful self-contradictory statement from a self-destructive and self-contradictory statement." Thus, in this way the substitution view of metaphor appears to be limiting and narrowing the horizons of metaphor. As it is "purely semantic in character." (229) For Ricoeur if resemblance serves any purpose in metaphor, it "must be a characteristic of the attribution of predicates and not of the substitution of name." Thus, a new pertinence is called by Ricoeur "kind of semantic 'proximity'." Metaphor thus is something which is between the terms. Despite being the distance apart and which for a moment before which seems for apart but also of a suddenly appearance, closely related as Aristotle himself said it as something alike about metaphor and its predicative effect of resemblance when he tells the virtue of a good metaphor: being its "appropriate" and "harmonious." (230)

Ricoeur answers the second objection as "resemblance is not a good candidate to serve as the reason or cause of the new pertinence, because it is what results from the statement and from the rapprochement it affects." (230) Ricoeur gives the reference of *Metaphor and Reality* of Wheel/Wright, that according to him appear very close where he distinguishes between epiphora and diaphor, the terms given by Aristotle Ricoeur calls it "transposition" and "transference" which occurs between "alien ideas," The ideas that are distant from one another. Such uniting processes, writes Ricoeur, results from an "apperception", something that is related to the "order of seeing" and "insight." This is what Aristotle had already pointed to this "apperception" when he says that to metaphoric well is to see, to have a right eye for the similar – is it not resemblance? For Ricoeur, "there is no epiphor without diaphor, no intuition without construction" it is, he calls, "the intuitive process, bringing together what is disparate, contains an irreducibly discursive moment." Ricoeur writes that Aristotle himself who might have contemplated on the view of "similar" "is also the theoretician of what proportional metaphor in which resemblance is more constructed than seen." (231) Ricoeur admits that it is Max Black who captures this discursive moment when the predicate "[choose] and organises certain aspects of the principal subject." Here he finds it in zero contradiction in the understanding of the language of apperception on account of "vision and then the language of construction." Thus, for him, it "is at once the gift of genius" and the skill of the geometer, who sees the point in the "ratio of proportion." (231) Now it seems visible as he answers the objections that were put against Aristotle by Richards, a common language philosopher. Ricoeur defends Aristotle as if he is defending a messenger or a prophet of metaphor.

The aspects discussed above, observes Ricoeur that "this constitutes a divorce from semantics and this constitutes a psychology." (231) For this the "gestalt psychology" in this respect seems to be very instructive while dealing with the phenomena of *invention*, where the change of structure "passes through a moment of sudden intuition in which the new structure emerges from the obliteration and modification of the prior configuration." (231) According to Ricoeur the paradox of psychological attraction, that is between genius and calculation, between intuition and construction – is a pure semantic paradox which in his eyes "has to do with the unseal character of allocation of predicates in the instance of discourse." (231)

Moving his attention to the objection made for the "logical status of resemblance," he argues that "we know that anything resembles anything else… except for a certain difference!" Ricoeur mentions that last paradox discussed just above as the key reply to the objection. To be more concise, this is to understand that "to sameness in what is different," in this case the very similar is quite dissimilar being similar on the other side. It is not to see the similarities. Therefore, Ricoeur writes that:

> Metaphor reveals the logical structure of 'the similar' because, in the metaphorical statement, 'The similar' is perceived *despite* difference, *in spite of* contradiction. Resemblance, therefore, is the logical category corresponding to the predicative operation in which 'approximation' (bringing close) meets the resistance of 'being distant.' In other

> words, metaphor displays the work of resemblance because the literal contradiction preserves difference within the metaphorical statement; 'same' and 'different' are not just mixed together, they also remain opposed. Through this specific trait, enigma lives on in the heart of metaphor. In metaphor, 'the same' operates *in spite of* 'the different.' (232)

Ricoeur mentions Turbine and his *The Myth of Metaphor* in which he is comparable with that of Gilbert Ryle's – "Category Mistake." Ricoeur adds that this definition of metaphor does not differ radically from that of his. Therefore, obviously consists in "[speaking] of one thing in terms of another that resembles." Ricoeur claims that "it is tempting to say that metaphor is a planned category mistake." This can well be applied with that of Aristotle as a concept of metaphor. The idea of category mistake brings Ricoeur near to his field, when he notes that the "strategy of language at work in metaphor consists in obliterating the logical and established frontiers of language, in order to bring to light new resemblances, the previous classification kept us from seeing." (233) Thus metaphor, in Ricoeur's view, would be to overtake an old categorisation, simply in order to establish a new logical frontier within the process when language is at work. This is the point where language being quite metaphorical starts evolving on its own metaphorical structures.

The fourth objection that Ricoeur takes on here is "whether the iconic moment of metaphor stands concerned the status of resemblance as a figurative presentation" – that is an image showing abstract relationships. This problem arises from the remark given by Aristotle when he adds something to metaphor as– "set before the eyes" and the concept of "associated image" given by Michael Le Guern Ricoeur is more afraid of the surrender of semantic analysis to a logical grammar that is "the greater its reluctance to return to the notion of image." This in Ricoeur's words "is considered too as a schema," which is in his view "the matrix of the category, the icon is the matrix of the new semantic pertinence that is born out of the dismantling of semantic networks caused by the shock of contradiction." (235) The iconic moment involves a verbal aspect – it is openly suggested by Ricoeur that it constitutes the grasping identity within differences," although having all the difference; it is based on a preconception pattern. This is the point where Ricoeur seems less confident and clear about the semantic structure and its identity enmeshed with bad psychology. The question of imagination has something to do with the conflict between identity and difference.

Ricoeur writes that in "non-verbal kernel of imagination" imagery is understood in the – quasi-visual, quasi-auditory, quasi-tactile and quasi olfactory sense. According to Ricoeur with the perspective of semantic theory, on a verbal plan and to start with "productive imagination" and set off from the reproductive imagination/images to the extent it is possible. For Ricoeur "the image presents a verbal dimension" being treated as schematism in which the metaphorical attribution is produced. This metaphorical schematisation moves imagination into the place where the figurative meaning arises in the "interplay of identity and difference." Thus metaphor, in discourse is the place where this iconic schematism is visible. It's quite clear that identity and difference actually do not sit together rather confront each other. Here at this point Ricoeur admits and confesses the same what we reflected earlier. He focuses on "the frontier between semantics and psychology" where there is the function of verbal and non-verbal over the iconic and imagery attached with the concept of metaphor. It is also observed the Ricoeur processes to clear certain things in the following parts of present discussion. Never less, Ricoeur writes that Aristotle's remark "to see the similar" is the representation of the same iconic moments" and also clarifies the Kantian schema, that is to teach the genus, "to grasp the relatedness of terms that are for apart" and to "bring them before the eyes." In the same fashion, metaphor too "is established as the information not to incorporate and consider the image into the semantic theory of metaphor of metaphorical discourse." (236)

2.3.7 Psycholinguistics of Metaphor

In the fifth section of the sixth study of the book *The Rule of Metaphor* that is "Psycholinguistics of Metaphor" followed by the sixth sub-section "Icons and Image." Advancing on the concept psychoanalytic of metaphor, Ricoeur starts exploring "the frontier between semantics and psychology," that he sets it up as psycholinguistics, in this connection opening it as:

> A radical way of exploring the frontier between semantics and psychology is to set up a combined discipline, *psycholinguistics*, at that boundary. The need for this move is not shown only by the concern that the image be incorporated into the properly semantic operation of metaphor. The very notion of transposition, the constant theme of a theory of tropes, brings operations into play that legitimate a mixed approach involving psychology *and* linguistics. We will deal with this motif in the present section, leaving till later the psycholinguistic consideration of the *image* itself. (237)

Ricoeur at this point suggests that the principle of a psycholinguistic approach is quite a new and recognised approach that is involved in the operation of metaphor deserves to be examined. It does not encounter the paralinguistic part strictly. Its aim is in fact to introduce a new semantic field. Concentrating on some related figures, Ricoeur writes that it is Gaston Esnault who sees "the operations brought into play by reducing the capacity to increase or restrict extension or comprehension." (237) According to Ricoeur synecdoche is nothing but "a modification of extension, and metaphor and metonymy," Ricoeur writes that "it follows the order and proceeds analytically," while on the other hand metaphor "plays on comprehension by means of a reaction that begins and ends in imagination." (237)

This is to conclude present discussion after all "neither 'is,' nor 'to call,' nor 'to name,' nor 'to do' nor 'to name in the place,' nor 'to stand for' is an identification" of metaphor. For Ricoeur, the nature of these above-mentioned relations is that of "Copula," something that connects as the connecting link between the subject and predicate of a proposition, more clearly the linking edge. Ricoeur ends the section mentioning the problems of metaphor depicted by Hence who sees three aspects in the central problem of metaphoric expression: first is the double metonymic operation, second identification and third the imaginative illusion.

The very hypothesis about the psycholinguistics in relation to metaphor is challenged by Ricoeur himself as: "Is a psycholinguistics of imaginative illusion possible?" and furthermore he doubles that "could psycholinguistics perhaps crossover this line and join the properly sensual aspect of image to a semantic theory of metaphor?" Dealing with the problem, Ricoeur proposes to write on this problem in the light of Marcus B. Hester's contribution. The problem projected here is "the intersection between 'saying' and 'seeing as.'" Ricoeur gets a step back and reverse what he did in his third study for the orientation of present exploration to that of a semantic theory, in this connection he opens up as:

> That theory opposed not only any reduction of metaphor to mental imagery, but also any intrusion of the image, considered as a psychological factor, into a semantic theory Conceived as logical grammar. This was the price for containing the interplay of resemblance within the limits of the predicative operation, and therefore of discourse. But, ruling out a passage from the imaginary to discourse, the question remains whether one cannot or ought not

> to attempt the reverse, and *proclaim the image to be the final moment of a semantic theory* that objected to it as a starting point. (245)

Ricoeur does not hesitate to admit that his plea "on the behalf of resemblance ended with certain rehabilitation of the iconic moment of metaphor." (246) This is the most honest admission done by Ricoeur. Nevertheless, he does believe that "certain concepts of imagination return with iconic moments," therefore, metaphoric alterations do not seem to relate "the boundaries of a semantic theory." (246)

According to Ricoeur, on the other hand the semantic attribution constitutes "the point on the frontier of semantic and point on the frontier of semantic and psychology where the imaginary is anchored in a semantic theory of metaphor." Ricoeur, thus, strengthens his argument with that of Marcus B. Hester which is related to English Language Literary Criticism, and is rather applauded to poetic language in general and also to metaphor in particular. (247)

2.3.8 Poetic Language

Ricoeur mentions that Hester presents three principles of the understanding of poetic language, (a) poetic language projects certain fusion between meaning and senses. This trait distinguishes poetic and the common language use and in non-poetic language use as in non-poetic language. "The arbitrary and connotational nature of sign separates meaning from the sensible as much as possible," (b) the second trait is that in poetic language "the passing of sense and the sense tends to produce an object closed in on itself." This is something in a constant contrast with an ordinary referential quality. According to Hester, the sign in poetic language is not looked "through" but rather as "looked at," that is the language being as a medium or "route crossed on the way to reality" in the process of communication. Language itself appears as some stuff like the marble of a sculpture that is somehow looks similar to that of Jakobson's "poetic function" where for him, the poetic function consists essentially in accentuating the message as such at the expense of the referential function," (c) the third dimension of poetic language is that it "allows to articulate a fictional experience" in the language of Susanne Langer too "an experience of virtual life." Thus, Ricoeur comments at the conclusion that these three traits: (i) Fusion of sense and senses (ii) the intermingled form of language that appears as some 'stuff' or the 'marble.' (iii) Functionality or "vitality of the experience articulated by ties non-referential language" is quite akin to that of the notion of icon, but this iconic consists of "sense and the sensible." Ricoeur also overuses that it is like a hard object which is that of "similar to a sculpture" – it is that language itself becomes "stripped of its referential function and reduced to its *opaque* appearance." This is the time where Ricoeur seems turning something to the transformation that has to take apart after language is used. Ricoeur turns to the process of the interpretation of the 'stuff.' as Hester, says Ricoeur who lodges the notion of the sensible strongly with the meaning of an image or imagery. Ricoeur accepts that this notion of conception is quite a new one for the conception of 'reading' to the concept of *epoché* (a Husserlan concept). For him a poem is a "real object." 'Reading' to him, is "*a suspension of all reality and an active openness to the text.*" Thus, the concept of 'reading' as suspension and openness introduces a "*complete arrangement of previous themes.*" (247-48)

Thinking on the first theme, Ricoeur observes that "the essential trait of poetic language is not the fusion of sense with sound, but the fusion of sense with a wave of evoked or aroused images." This fusion constitutes the true "iconicity of sense." Ricoeur adds Hester's acceptance of the same phenomena of the "understanding of images as sensorial impressions evoked in memory," and the Welker and Warren's concepts of 'vestigial representations of sensations.' Thus, in Wittgenstein's term poetic language is a game of words which evokes and arouses images. Sense and sound do function ironically with each other, Ricoeur says that "sense itself is iconic through this power of developing images." (248) The other two themes of reading suspension and openness, says Ricoeur, reflect the same iconicity. Advancing the concept of image, Ricoeur writes about its status as:

> On the one hand, the image is the achievement *par excellence* of neutralisation of natural reality; on the other hand, the deployment of images is something that 'occurs' and towards which the sense opens indefinitely, giving unlimited scope to interpretation. One can say truly, in connection with the flux of imagery, that to read is to grant original right to all the data. In poetry, openness to the text is openness to the imagery as liberated by the senses. (249)

Thus, for Ricoeur a metaphor can be identified with what is called iconic which can also be interpreted as "fictive." Moreover, adds Ricoeur that this is epoché "the suspension proper to the imaginary" which brings all the references back "to empirical reality from the verbal icon." (249) Observing on the problem of 'sense' and 'reference,' especially the problem of meaning to the exclusion of the problem of truth. Ricoeur writes that the schema and the verbal icon are methods for constructive images. Here Ricoeur puts the idea of Kant and of Husserl forward to strengthen his argument. In this fashion, the poet can be considered, suggests Ricoeur, the "artisan who sustains and shapes imagery using no means other than language." (250)

Thus "seeing as" in his view "proffers the missing link in the claim of explanation," it is a "sensible aspect of poetic language." It is the intuitive relationship, writes Ricoeur, that "holds sense and image together" the phenomena "Seeing as" is an experience and act" at the same moment. Therefore, it is to think that the mass of images that may occur all of a sudden voluntarily has no such disciplined rule; there is no such provision so that they could be controlled. However, there is no rule to be learned to do so. This is the reason that "one sees, or one does not see," the intuitive mode cannot be taught, but assisted as one someone helps to see. So, seeing *as* is an act – 'understanding' also is equal to doing something. As Ricoeur writes "the image is not seen but tied and in effect, 'seeing as' orders the flux and governs iconic deployment" at this process "the experience act of 'seeing as' ensures that imagery is implicated in metaphorical significance – the same image that occurs also means." The "seeing as" that is activated in reading, according to Ricoeur, does join the verbal meaning with all its "imagistic fullness" that is all within the shape of language. These conjunctions just reflect the relationship of both within the linguistic domain. (252)

Thus, the notion of 'seeing as' is a founding ground for what we call 'resemblance.' This is not the resemblance of two ideas rather is "what results from the experience – act of 'seeing as." The 'seeing as' phenomena project the resemblance "not the reverse." The act of "seeing as" plays the rule of schema. According to Ricoeur it "unites the empty concept and the blind impression." Through the character the "half thought" and "half experience" this joins the "light of sense with the fullness of the image." Ricoeur observes that this is the point where the verbal and the non-verbal are naturally merged "at the core of the imaging function of language." For Ricoeur if this is so, "then 'seeing as' designates the non-verbal mediation of metaphorical statement." In his eyes the "semantics finds its frontier; and in so doing, it accomplishes its task." (253-54)

Gaston Bachelerd mentions Ricoeur, who has taught that "the image is not a residue of impression, but a surrounding speech" as when he writes that the poetic image places us at the origin of the speaking being. For Gaston the poem begets the poetic image that appears as a "new being in our language" which puts our expression. Thus, this expression creates a being. Ricoeur tenaciously proves that the "phenomenology of imagination" surely intends beyond "psycholinguistics" and beyond "The description of seeing as" because of the reason that if it "follows the path of the 'reverberation' of the poetic image into the depth of existence." The poetic image according to Bachelor is "a source of psychic activity." Thus, the new being that is in language passes an "increment to consciousness" that is what Ricoeur calls "a growth of being". (254)

2.3.9 Metaphor and Reference

The seventh study "Metaphor and Reference" of the book *The Rule of Metaphor* is inclusively devoted to the general question that Ricoeur puts in the very bringing as "What does the metaphorical statement say about reality?" This question diverts our attention from the problem of sense to the problem of reference: The reference of discourse and the problem of reference is projected on two different levels: (i) semantic and (ii) hermeneutic levels.

The first belongs to the order of the sentence and the second to the structure that is larger than the sentence. At this point writes Ricoeur, where the problem reaches into a very crucial condition. The "postulate of semantics" says Ricoeur, belongs to the same distinction of semiotics and semantics which has already been discussed, regarding this semantic problem he further adds:

> … this distinction first sets in relief the essentially synthetic character of predication, the central operation of discourse, and opposes this operation to the mere interplay of differences and oppositions among signifiers and among the signified in the phonological code and in the lexical code of a given language. Moreover, it means that what is *intended* by discourse [l'*intenté*], the correlate of the entire sentence, is irreducible to what semiotics calls the signified, which is nothing but the counterpart of the signifier of a sign within the language code. The third implication of the distinction between semiotics and semantics that concerns us here is the following: grounded on the predicative act, what is intended by discourse [*l'intenté*] points to an extra-linguistic reality which is its referent. Whereas the sign points back only to other signs immanent within a system, discourse is about things. Sign differs from sign, discourse

> refers to the world. Difference is semiotic, reference is semantic: 'One is never concerned in semiotics with the relation between the sign and the things denoted, nor with relationships between language and the world.' (255-56)

In this connection Ricoeur says that one must proceed beyond semiotics and semantics. For him, semantics is "an abstraction from semantics, which relates the internal constitution of the sign to the transcendent aims of reference." (256) For him, there are approximately two concepts of reference i. e. *complementary* and *reciprocal.* Irrespective of each whether they emerge from synthetic composition from the proper name toward that related proposition or released by the "analytic dissociation from the sentence down to the semantic unit of the word." (258)

Referring to Wittgenstein's *Tractatus Logical Philosophicus* sternson and Fregean views about the subject and the character of reference is related to the "function of singular identification" which is carried by the logically proper name. For Ricoeur, the "postulate of reference" needs a complete independent discussion with a separate section when it gets close to the "particular entities of discourse." This is what he calls text, which is a more extensive composition than the sentence." Ricoeur observes that the problem of reference is more related to the context of hermeneutics rather than the "text is a complex entity of discourse." He considers discourses as a work, as the word implies with the work "new categories enter the field of discourse." These categories according to him are "the pragmatic categories," or in other words, the "categories of production and labor." Discourse for Ricoeur is an arena of work of composition and arrangement" or a disposition in other words. This is something that makes "a poem in a novel a totality irreducible to a simple sum of sentences." (259) This 'disposition,' 'composition' or 'arrangement' "obeys formal rules," this he calls "a codification "belongs no longer to language but to discourse," the code is that one of the literary genres which "regulates the praxis of the text," here this codified production ends in a particular work – "this poem or that novel." Thus, there comes a third stage which he calls style – a fashion in which it is understood – something that "makes the work a singular, individual thing." Thus for him the labour is the labour of interpretation, the text taken as a work and categories belongs to genus, that is an achievement in a particular style, there are the proper categories. According to Ricoeur to the production of discourse – he calls – "a work."

The specific realisation of discourse, says Ricoeur, needs an "appropriate reformation of the postulate of reference." Referring to the Fregean concept, Ricoeur offers that if one says that he is not satisfied with the sense and thinks to pre-suppose reference besides, if one is not satisfied with the structure of the work. Ricoeur says that the "structure of the work is in fact its sense, and the world of the work and its reference." (260)

At this point Ricoeur moves to define his theory of hermeneutics for the concept of discourse that he has been in defining and discussing, for him hermeneutics is "the theory that regulates the transition from structure of the work to the world of the work." Therefore, in his view, 'to interpret a work is to display the world to which it refers by virtue of its arrangement.' its genes and its 'style'." At this point of the understanding of hermeneutics, we get very close to Derrida's concept of 'deconstruction.' This is not the right place and time to devote and spend much energy on this comparison as there is a lot to cover which still remains untouched yet in. The works that are usually called 'literary', Ricoeur suggests that, it requires a distinct postulate, because of its specific nature. For him, "the production of discourse as 'literature' signifies very precisely that the suspended, " literature is a kind of discourse that has no denotation, but only connotations can be well rejected not only by an "internal examination of the literary work" and by Frege's own theory of denotation, adds Ricoeur here ends his debate saying that in contract of the scientific inspection keeping the view of Frege, the artistic pleasure seems to be linked to our senses without having any reference Ricoeur thinks that and appropriate distinct discussion to the "literary work" and the "formulation of the postulate of reference" where it is shown that "every sense calls for reference or denotation." Thus, discourse in literary work, writes Ricoeur "sets out its denotation as a second-level-denotation" and this is in his view "by means of the suspension of the first level denotation of discourse." This postulation brings back the same problem of metaphorical statement is, precisely the one that joins out most clearly this relationship between suspended reference and displayed reference." It is similar to that of the metaphorical statement which captures its sense within the ruins of a literal sense and a reference within the sense of its literal reference in a symmetrical fashion.

Ricoeur claims that "if it is true that literal sense and metaphorical sense are distinguished and articulated within an interpretation, so too it is." Laying emphasis on this point, "within an interpretation that a second-level reference, which is properly the metaphorical reference, is set free by means of the suspension of the first-level reference" Bracketing the discussing of "reality of the world and of truth" for the last study of *The Rule of Metaphor*, Ricoeur emphatically poses as "[do] we actually know what 'reality,' 'world,' and 'truth' signify?" at the end of the second last study of his work. (260-61)

Writing about the status of the discipline called *Literary Criticism* where discourse is "realised as a work." Ricoeur remarks that the Literary Criticism is purely influenced by "linguistic analysis of poetic function." In this strong linguistic structure, the poetic function is presented by Roman Jakobson in a more general and specific way in his framework of linguistic communication. Ricoeur admits and accepts the validity and vitality of this powerful framework. It is an openly known fact that this is the most "powerful synthetic exactitude to embrace the totality of linguistic phenomena" that is in six factors where each of them contributes to the entire process of verbal communication e. g.:

	Context	
Addressor	Message	Addressee
	Contact	
	Code	

Thus, each factor has a function to play:

1	Addressor	Emotive Function
2	Addressee	Connotative function
3	Context	Referential function
4	Message	Poetic function
5	Contact	Phatic function
6	Code	Para lingual function

Thus, amongst the six factors any one of them may predominate at any point of time. The verbal structure of the message depends primarily on the predominant function. The emotive function corresponds to the Addressee. The conative function is to the addressee, the phatic function to contact the meta-lingual or meta-linguistic function to the code, the referential function to the context and poetic function to the message, or it may be to the 'pleasure' indicated in Aristotle's *Poetics*, or to some aesthetics pleasure in a possible sense of understanding. The poetic function is productive in nature, it results in the very essence of creativity and making. To some extent the last point made by Jakobson does not seem agreeable by Ricoeur because he points that the view of poetic function of language is "in opposition to the referential function through which the message is oriented towards the non-linguistic context." For this Ricoeur projects two ideas in this connection: (a) the analysis concerns only the 'poetic function' of language, it does not shed any light on "poem" as a literary genre. This one will not be able to identify a poem with "the poetic" in light of Jakobson's concepts. But on the other hand, Ricoeur also adds and appreciates as well– that the linguistics of Roman Jakobson does present "a second analytical instrument." This view is related to the theory of the poetic function to that of the strategy of discourse which is proper to the poem. Ricoeur relates Jakobson's concept of 'split reference' to the metaphorical truth and also with the wonderful expression. "It was and it was not," quoting from Jakobson's as "the conversion of a message into an enduring thing." He observes that the domain of American and European literary criticism does not have the concept of split-reference in mind, rather the destruction in mind. To the idea of "an enduring thing," Ricoeur suggests that it may serve "as the subtitle of a whole series of works on poetics for which the essence of the strategy of discourse in poetry is the attainment of the meaning within the haven of sound." Ricoeur accepts that this idea is an old one that has already been given by Alexander Pope in his expression "the sound must seem an echo to the senses." Therefore, for Valery writes Ricoeur, *Dance* is the *model of poetic act*, and for a "reflecting poet" poem is "a prolonged oscillation between sense and sound", similarly, the Sculptor, who converts the thing called as 'poetic' from language into matter. To understand the imitation of language, Ricoeur refers to Wimsatt, who has forged a very agreeable suggestion – that is of *verbal-icon*. This, writes Ricoeur, recalls not only Peirce but also the Byzantine tradition for which the "icon is a thing." Thus, a poem is not a sign but an icon to him which has an "iconic solidity." (262-65)

So, for Ricoeur, "language takes on the thickness of material or a medium" something generally called as "the sensible," "sensual plenitude of a poem" which is more like that of the sculptural and painted from as mentioned above "the combination of sensual and logical ensures that expression and impression coalesce within the poetic thing," something that is commonly called a poem. (265)

According to Ricoeur "the fusion of sense and sound" is not only, in his opinion, against the concept of reference in poetry, rather "radical attack" which lies in "the fusion of sense and image." Ricoeur appreciates this image-dimension that he had bestowed on in his previous section of the study for the combination of metaphorical meaning in language where the concept of reference is at issue. According to Hester, poetic language is the language in which sense and sound usually function in an iconic structure where the fusion of sense and 'sensa' is created, for this conception of sense Ricoeur adds:

> These 'sensa' are, essentially, the ebb and flow of images allowed to be by the *epoché* of the referential relation. Therefore, the fusion of sense and sound is no longer the central phenomenon, but an occasion for an unfolding of the imaginary that is bound to the sense. Now with the image comes the fundamental moment of 'suspension,' of *epoché*, Husserl's notion borrowed by Hester and applied to the non-referential interplay of imagery in poetic strategy. The abolition of reference, which belongs to the achievement of poetic sense, is thus *par excellence* the work of the *epoché* that makes the iconic functioning of sense and of sensa possible, itself achieved by the iconic functioning of sense and sound. (266)

It should be appreciated here when Ricoeur mentions the valuable contribution of Northrop Frye, who in Ricoeur's words "approaches the limit most radically." The limit that shows the paragraph quoted above, the aspect of understanding of the concept of "reference" which seemed extremely deemed there. Here again, it is clearly mentioned that the referential types of discourse can be opposed to information or didactic discourse. Frye thinks that the information or didactic discourse, the symbol is taken as a sign that it 'stands for' something, 'points to' something or it represents something whereas in the literary discourse it represents, stands and points nothing outside of itself. Symbol in literary discourse links and connects the parts to the whole of it within the framework it is located. It locates the stylistic structure of season and his generic framework with the symbols and myths taken by Frye. Ricoeur appreciating Frye's contribution grafts his further reflection on the subject more especially his view about the unity of a poem. According to Frye, the "unity of a poem" is accordingly a "unity of mood, and considers this mood, the poem. Ricoeur thus adds that "[all] literary structure is ironic in this sense," the poetic structure, mentions Ricoeur, is "a self-contained" texture. Here Ricoeur slackens his interests in this case against the notion of reference without leading it to the "epistemological argument." Nevertheless, Ricoeur indicates that Jakobson's linguistic ideas and Frye's literary criticism at one point of time reveal their pre-supposition. Which is hidden and disguised, as he remarks: "Critiques shaped by the school of logical positivism state that all language that is not descriptive, in the sense of giving information about facts, must be emotional." Ricoeur suggests that whatever is 'emotional' is always "sensed purely 'within' the subject and is not related in any way whatsoever to anything outside the subject." Ricoeur openly declares that "[emotion] is an effect which has only an inside, and not an outside." He seems to be putting his concept of 'sense' with 'connotative' in opposition to cognitive and denotative as these two represent something outside not inside as in 'reference.' There comes an idea of 'discourse of reference', 'discourse without reference', 'discourse of sense' and 'discourse without sense' as if only 'referential' or only 'sensical.' Ricoeur concludes that thus the "semiotic selection is assigned to denotation," and on other hand, "the associated image arises from communication." Ricoeur also proposes "[a] general theory is denotation." Ricoeur discovers that after the analysis of Jakobson's and Frye he sees some clues denoted to the poetic function in general which are "quite apart from the particular role of metaphor." (270)

Ricoeur takes on Frye's idea of 'hypothetical' where he thinks that the poem is 'neither true nor false' rather hypothetical. This hypothesis is unlike that of mathematical one, the poetic hypothesis is a suggestion, proposal in an imaginative and fictive mode of a world. Therefore, "suspension of real reference is the condition of access to the virtual mode of reference." The major problem that arises here is that of the understanding of a virtual life. Thus, what is a virtual life, a question remains in the centre of this investigation. Ricoeur questions that "[is] it not the function of poetry to establish another world – another world that corresponds to other possibilities of existence, to possibilities that would be most deeply our own?" Taking help from Heidegger's contribution of "finding on self among things," Ricoeur writes that the "epoché of natural reality is the condition that allows poetry to develop a world on the basis of the mood that the poet articulates." Thus, it is the task of 'interpretation' to decipher and "elaborate the design of a world" which is liberated by suspension from descriptive reference. In this way the creation of poems, the concrete object which "cuts language off from the function of sign." Although at the same point of time, the poem "opens up access to reality in the mode of fiction and feeling." (271) For Ricoeur in this may the language of art, he strongly "links verbal metaphor and non-verbal metaphorical expression to the plane of reference." (281) It is Goodman, mentions Ricoeur, who has arranged growing categories, in an order i. e.

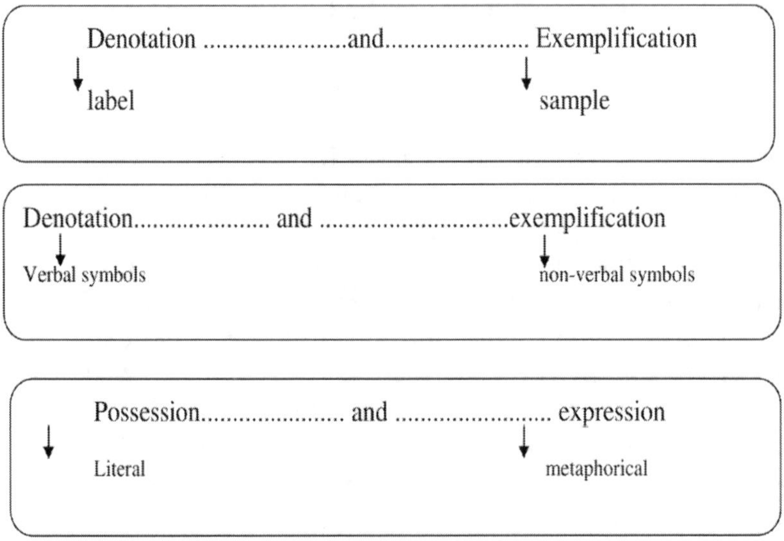

Thus, at the end of the third section of his seventh study, Ricoeur suggests that the inter connection of three themes at first in "the metaphorical discourse of poetry, referential power is linked to the eclipse of ordinary reference" and the second adds Ricoeur is "the creation of heuristic function is the road to re-description" and the third is the "reality brought to language unites manifestation and creation." (283)

The fourth section is devoted to "Model and Metaphor" ; the seventh study focuses on the importance of models with reference to Max Black's essay "Models and Archetypes." Ricoeur writes "with respect to the relation to reality metaphor to scientific language," therefore, in scientific language, the model which is essential is "a heuristic instrument" which seeks "by means of fiction to break down an inadequate interpretation and to lay the way for a new more adequate interpretation." Throughout the section Ricoeur tries to establish relation between metaphor and model and finally ends up with one of the important questions of metaphorical truth – as the very meaning of truth is false in question. The aforesaid comparison shows the direction "as the conjunction of fiction and description suggests, poetic feeling itself also develops an experience of reality in which invention and discovery cease being opposed and where creation and revelation coincide." Here Curiosity makes Ricoeur ask... what does this reality mean then? (291) Left unanswered!

2.3.10 Towards the Concept of Metaphorical Truth

The last section of the seventh study, "Towards the Concept of Metaphorical Truth," seems to be essential to the present quest of "Metaphor and Reference." In the present section, Ricoeur's conclusion is as follows: the "poetic function" and the "referential function" can be hardly distinguished without the "conjunction between fiction and redescription is brought to light." (291) The poetic and rhetoric function appears to be each other's "inverse." The rhetoric function aims to "persuade us by adoring discourse with pleasing ornament." The poetic function aims to "redescribe reality by the roundabout route of heuristic fiction." Thus metaphor "in service to the poetic function" is the "strategy of discourse by which language diverts itself of its function of direct description in order to reach the mythic level where its function of discovery is set free." Ricoeur allows to "presume to speak of metaphorical truth in order to designate the realistic intention" which belong to the "descriptive power of poetic language." This idea, writes Ricoeur "implies the theory of tension, "or in other words called the theory of 'controversion' "might be extended to the referential relationship of the metaphorical statement to reality." Therefore, Ricoeur tells us that there are three applications which have been devoted to the idea of tension: (i) the first one is the "tension within the statement," that is between tenor and vehicle, focus and frame, principal subject and secondary subject. (ii) Second is the "tension between two interpretations: between the literal interpretation that perishes at the hands of semantic impertinence and a metaphorical interpretation whose sense emerges through non-sense." The third application to the idea of tension is the tension in the "relational function of the copula" of "being as" that is between "identity and difference in the interplay of resemblance." This ends the seventh study with this powerful observation. (292-99)

The last study "Metaphor and Philosophical Discourse" dedicated to Jean Ladriere belongs to the "philosophical confines of investigation." This study has its "character of gravity shifts from rhetoric to semantics, from problem of sense to the problem of reference" and finally moves its passage to the plane of hermeneutics by Ricoeur. He puts forward "the semantic and the hermeneutic postulate functioning in the theory of metaphorical reference." The hypothesis of this study is to show that in what way "the concepts of truth and reality, and ultimately the concept of being have to be remarked in order to respond to the semantic claim of metaphorical utterance." (301-306)

Ricoeur distinguishes between speculative discourse and poetic discourse and says that "on one hand, speculative discourse has its condition of possibility in the semantic dynamism of metaphorical utterance discourse has its necessity in itself." (349-50) Ricoeur gives a gentle reminder of third and seventh study where he emphasized that the reference of any "metaphorical statement" could be positively considered as a "split reference," according to him "[for] a split sense one might say, a split reference" (351). Thus, the concept of *speculation* seems to be difficult to understand. To this problem replies Ricoeur as:

> ... speculative discourse is the discourse that establishes the primary notions, the principles, that articulate primordially the space of the concept. Concepts in scientific language as well as in ordinary language can never actually be derived from perception or from images, because the discontinuity of the levels of discourse is founded, at least virtually, by the very structure of the conceptual space in which meanings are inscribed when they draw away from the metaphorical process, which can be said to generate all semantic fields. It is in this sense that the speculative is the condition of the possibility of the conceptual. It expresses the systematic character of the conceptual in a second-order discourse. If, in the order of discovery, the speculative surfaces as a second level discourse – as meta-language, if one prefers – in relation to the discourse articulated at the conceptual level, it is indeed first discourse in the order of grounding. This discourse is at work in all the speculative attempts to order the 'great genera,' the 'categories of being,' the 'categories of understanding,' 'philosophical logic,' the 'principal elements of representation,' or however one wants to express it. (355)

Ricoeur glorifies the concept of attraction of the speculative discourse which in his opinion on metaphorical discourses, results in the process of interpretation in return. The "interpretation" is something which can be understood as "a work of elucidation," and "a struggle for univocity" in the Hesserlian sense. Here the second in metaphorical utterance is left in suspension and the reference does not take any direct pretension according to Ricoeur. For him "interpretation is necessary a realisation that at its limit eliminates the experience that comes to language through the metaphorical process." At the end of the present section, Ricoeur sheds light on his own notice of "living metaphor." For him metaphor does not only live to the level of unifying "a constituted language" but also "living virtue of the fact that it introduces the spark of imagination into a "think more" kind of process. The struggle that is "to think more" is "guided by the vivifying principle" and that becomes the 'soul' of interpretation. (358)

It was promised in the beginning to concentrate on the central problem that is the understanding of the relation of language with reality and the meaning that is created there. This quest seems to be a philosophical one in relation to language. It concerns the conditions of reference in general and to the meaning of language as a whole. In this connection Ricoeur rightly claims that "semantics can only allege the relation of language to reality but cannot think of this relation as such." To be more specific as "positing language as whole" and a mediation that is between man and his world, "between man and man," something that is "within the self itself." (359) Thus, for him language appears to be something that "raises the experience of the world to its articulation in discourse, "something which lays the foundation, the act of communication puts "the advent of man as speaking subject." (359) At this point Ricoeur ponders over the relationship between being and something which is "being said." He mentions the possible objection as there is an absence, adds Ricoeur "it is and has always been in language that men claim to speak about language." And he admits that yes, it is true. Nevertheless, he tells that, even though speculative discourse is possible:

> Because language possesses the *reflective* capacity to place itself at a distance and to consider itself, as such and in its entirety, as related to the totality of what is. Language designates itself and its others. This reflective character extends what linguistics calls meta-linguistic functioning, but articulates it in another discourse, speculative discourse. It is then no longer a function that can be opposed to

> other functions, in particular to the referential function; for it is the knowledge that accompanies the referential function itself, *the knowledge of its being-related to being.* (359)

This "reflective knowledge" adds Ricoeur "allows language to know that it is installed in being." There is a reversal between the relationship of language and its referent. It is language which becomes "aware of itself in the self-articulation of the being" as what it is all about in terms of meaning. For him "this reflective consciousness is the very consciousness of its openness" too. This is something which implies "the possibility of stating propositions regarding what is said and of saying that this is brought to language in our saying it." Thus, he says that this is the knowledge which "articulates the reference postulates in a discourse other than semantics, even the latter is distinguished from semantics," when one speaks, he knows that throughout this process-or act something is brought to language." (360) This signifies the knowledge of extra – linguistic and not the inter linguistic knowledge. For Ricoeur "it moves from being to being said at the very time that language itself moves from sense to reference." Here modifying Kant's statement – "something must be for something to appear" as "something must be for something to be said." Ricoeur also gives a fine emphasis on the secondary reference in language. But that is something which is in constant suspension. Therefore, it seems similar to that of polysemy in language – there is also a polysemy of being. This is what signifies "the ultimate meaning of the reference of poetic discourse is articulated in speculative discourse." It appears to be "discourse on being" in fact. This process of operation signifies that the "semantic aim of metaphorical utterance does intersect most decisively with the aim of ontological discourse." This is not, adds Ricoeur, "at the point where the reference of metaphorical utterance being as actuality and as potentiality into play." This power is stated as a power to project things as in "a state of activity." The ontology of power and 'act' links to Aristotle. Through this idea Ricoeur discusses the concept of "signifying things in act" with all its manifestation. (363) Ricoeur locates us by saying that this "may mean seeing things as actions." e. g. in tragedy men are projected "as acting", in in act. Actions for sure have special significance and place, "the act inherent entirely in the agent as vision does in the one who sees, life in the soul, and contemplation in the mind." He affirms that "seeing all things in act" would be like "seeing them as naturally blooming." This is blooming fourth, not only becoming a novel realisation, similar to the notion as nothing is, but rather becoming in a way. The "signifying thing in act" would also be "signifying potency" which looks like controlling attraction for all the productions of the novel's meaning. With this reference, Ricoeur questions whether the poet, in this way, be the one who could perceive "power as act and act as power." For him, the poet perceives these things "as a promise of newness." (364) Thus, the task of speculative discourse according to Ricoeur is:

> ... the task of speculative discourse to seek after the place where appearance signifies 'generating what grows.' As this sense is no longer to be sought in the region of objects occupied by physical bodies and living organisms, it indeed seems to be at the level of appearance as a whole and as such that the poetic verb 'signifies things in act.' In relation to this open and unlimited acceptance, signifying actions, signifying artifice, and signifying movement are already determinations, that is to say, limitations and restrictions that miss something of what is indicated in the expression 'signifying the blossoming of appearing.' If there is a point in our experience where living expression states living existence, it is where our movement up the entropic slope of language encounters the movement by which we come back to this side of the distinctions between actuality, action, production, motion. (365)

In conclusion, Ricoeur states that "poetry in itself and by itself, sketches a 'tensional' conception of truth of thought." This is to sum up all the tensional aspects which are brought close to semantics. The tension that is between subject and predicate, literal and metaphorical, metaphysical, identical, and interpretational and referential seems existing in the theory of split-reference and turns to be completed as in "the paradox of copula, where being as stands being and not being. Therefore, "poetry in combination with other modes of discourse articulates and preserves the experience of belonging that places man in discourse and discourse in being." For Ricoeur the speculative thought founds its work "upon the dynamism of metaphorical utterance, which it construes according to its own spheres of meaning". Here at the end of the book Ricoeur uses one of his key terms called 'distanciation' as the speculative discourse is potential to respond only on the basis that distanciation develops the critical moment "is contemporaneous with the experience of belonging that is opened or recovered by poetic discourse." This is because discourse as text and as work "prefigures the distinction that speculative thought carries to its highest point of reflection." (370)

In this way, the "splitting of reference" and "description of reality" are attached to the "imaginative variation of fiction." This, adds Ricoeur, "strikes us as specific figures of distanciation, when they are reflected and rearticulated by speculative discourse." Thus, the motion of 'tensional' truth which in Ricoeur's view is "most primordial" and the "most hidden dialectic," a governing factor "between the experience of belonging as a whole and the power of distanciation that opens up the space of speculative thought." It is observed that Ricoeur emphasises on the specific issues e. g. realisation of language as discourse, the same later as a structural work, realisation of speaking to writing in the discourse analysis, the work of discourse as the projection of a world, and finally he concludes with the understanding of discourse as "the meditation of self-understanding" all these aspects finally "constitute the criteria of textuality." (371)

Any reference to reality, any function to redescription and the act of distanciation will be bound to the understanding of the tense and the time. The following chapter fulfills the desired and required thrust dealing with time and narrative in a broad and detailed way.

CHAPTER 3

Hermeneutics of Time: Three-fold *Mimesis* and the Aporetics of Temporality in the Poetics of Narrativity

My name is Nikita Sergeyevich Khrushchev. I have to come take things in hand here. This city is not Kursk nor is it Kiev, nor Minsk. This city is Stalingrad. Stalingrad! This city bears the name of the boss. It's more than a city, it's a symbol. If the Germans capture this city, the entire country will collapse.

Now, I want our boys to raise their heads. I want them to act like they have balls.

I want them to stop shitting their pants. That's your job.

As political officers, I'm counting on you. You, what's your suggestion?

"Shoot all the other generals who have retreated and their chiefs of staff, too."

"Make some examples. Deport the families of the desserts… That's all been done."

"Give them hope. Here the men's only choice is between German bullets and ours. But there's another way, a way of courage. A way of the love of the motherland…. We must publish the army newspaper again, we must tell magnificent stories, stories that exalt sacrifice, bravery. We must make them believe in a victory. We must give them hope, pride, and desire to fight. Yes. We need to make examples but examples to follow. What we need are heroes."

Do you know any heroes around here?

Yes, Comrade. I know one.

(25:35 – 26:36, Film: *Enemy at the Gates,* 2001)

3.1 The Phenomenology of Time

At the end of the 20th century, it was David Wood who had predicted that in the next coming century human attention will cross over the *linguistic turn* to the phenomenon known as *time* – which will become the central focus and horizon of human thought and experience. This proposition seems to be true when Tony Roark pondering over the same problem in 2011writes that "time arises from the language we frame the propositions of speech and thought." (11) Time at once, is quite an abstract and fundamental concept. According to Aristotle it's a matter of perception – the perception of motion. In recent times Tony Roark confirms Wood's prediction by saying that "the philosophy of time is enjoying a good deal of attention." (3) This can be traced back to Ricoeur's *Time and Narrative* in three volumes which deal with time in relation to time and time in relation to narrative. These volumes are followed by *The Rule of Metaphor* which in Ricoeur's words, were conceived together. In both the works it is observed that one of the central themes of his philosophy is the creative capacity of language – both in metaphor and narrative.

The creative language may have novel and unexplored aspects of reality which would not be the case with ordinary language as there are some aspects that always remain hidden. According to Ricoeur, metaphor and narrative open new ways to understand the world and therefore metaphor and narrative unite other novel, strange and yet ignored aspects of the world and reality in front of us to be explained, interpreted and understood. At this point the gravity of hermeneutics is experienced to reach out to those yet unknown territories created by language itself. This dimension of language invites challenges to hermeneutics.

Time is the perception of change, change as innovation and deviation. Moreover, it is the perception of an individual. All the times there is only a *now moment,* within which it revolves around a flux, the following diagrams well represent the notions of time:

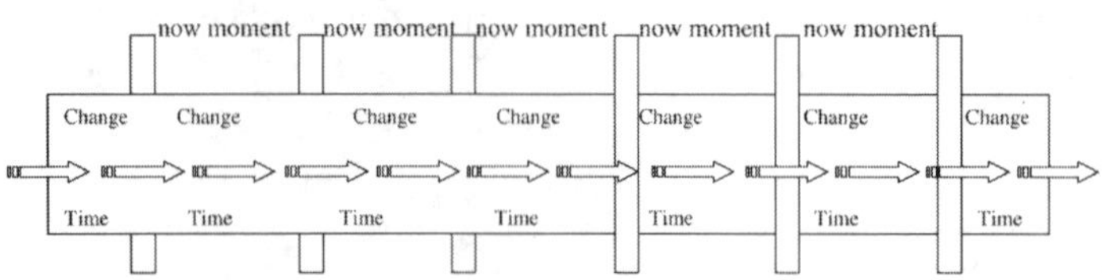

Past, present and future – are taken only as a matter of consciousness and there is no free will. There is just an illusion as all times are equally real in our black universe; this is in contrast with the conventional view of time where only the present is real, highly privileged and significant. *Present* was all that was real, as the clock tickled the moment passed and another moment came into existence, a process called flow of time as if the moon was located at one fixed orbit around the earth. But at the end of the 20th century this old notion of time was shattered. The theory of time at the end of the 20th century becomes more complex phenomena of the present moment or all time like the present and the other notions such as past and future seem to vanish. Thus, time becomes more fundamental. There is an affinity of this relation theory of time:

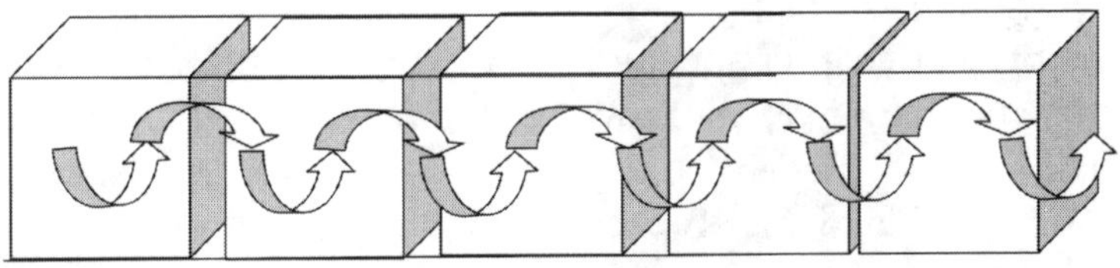

Seemingly the concept of time may not be an important topic but a "pervasive and hydra-headed problem," in Woods' language. (2) In Aristotle's physics it is a problem of holomorphic compound, a matter of *motion* as something *before* and *after*. This is true to a great extent that it belongs to such a vast range of problems that it looks impossible to comprehend and cover every aspect of the problem i. e. time and space, time and speed (time in physics, mathematics and astro-physics), time and narrative (time in language and discourse), time in cinema and films, cosmological time, universal time, global time, time in world clocks, human time, passing time, time that is *is*, time that *was*, time that *will*, fictional and historical time(lived and configured time), local time, time of sunset and sunrise, life time, UTC, GMT/ ST, Coordinated Universal Time, Green watch mean time, Standard time. A majority of scholars in modern time believe that time started from the big-bang in the Cosmos. Just like Augustine, a similar frustration is expressed by C. D. Broad when he writes that – "I am well aware how easy it is to talk nonsense about time." (138) Thus, the concept of time becomes quite a comprehensive and exhaustive phenomenon as writes David Wood in his Introduction to "Interpreting Narratives" of his book *On Paul*

Ricoeur: Narrative and Interpretation (1991), 2003) about the same problem of time:

> For time is the destroyer not just of all that we are proud of, even pride itself, it threatens the realisation of many a philosophical ideal.[2] Time is the possibility of corruption at the deepest level. And yet without organised temporal extension, there would be nothing to be corrupted. Time makes as well as breaks. Time gives and it takes away. The pervasiveness of time is an intuition that can strike us on occasion at the everyday ontic level. The Heraclitean vision that all is in flux is not uncommon, even if the force of this intuition wanes like everything else. But the pervasiveness of time in philosophy does not arise simply at the level of intuition – that all things, and all experiences are in time. It is near to the surface of most of the central problems of philosophy, and has a major impact on how we think of identity, of truth, of meaning, ofreason, of freedom, of language, of existence, of the self. The list is endless. (1-2)

The present chapter specifically aims to focus on the mechanism of time and narrative, narrative and time vice-versa with special reference to Paul Ricoeur's three volumes of *Time and Narrative.* In the words of David M. Kaplan "with the publication of *Time and Narrative*, Ricoeur's work shifts away from questions of textual interpretation to questions of human action, in particular human temporal and historic experience." (47) David Car observers that – "the study of narrative has become a meeting ground and battle ground of the disciplines, and has fast become a discipline in its own right." (160) Human beings in the present world as a matter of fact have started experiencing *less permanence* and *much temporality* – only because of the shift from linguistic turn to the phenomenon of time to find out the pervasive truth. Scholars in modern times generally consider that narratives entirely deal with the themes and nature of time by the temporal logic of story-telling, either of time or *about* time. In both the cases it seems that time is not primarily at stake or risk but rather it is the truth which *is.* David Wood tells that "Ricoeur's *Time and Narrative* is one of the most impressive attempts ever made to address and resolve the practical nature of time." (1) Getting close to the present problem that this study aims at, it seems necessary to refer to the "Introduction: About Time," of *About Time: Narrative, Fiction and the Philosophy of Time* where Mark Currie discusses the current problem objectively as:

> Imagine reading a novel with a bookmark. Suppose the novel is read from the beginning to the end, in the right order and for the first time. The bookmark will move over time from the beginning to the end of the novel and as it does, it will represent the reader's present

> in the narrative. Everything to the left of it is in the past, already known, and everything to the right of it is in the future, and not yet known. The last of the narrative is fixed in a way that the future of the narrative is not. Anything could happen. At first glance, this reflects the way that timeworks in life. We inhabit the present, which is sandwiched between affixed past and an open future. But there are some obvious differences. The present for a reader in a fictional narrative is not really the presentat all but the past. It is somebody else's present related to us in the past tense. Though it seems like the present, because it is new to us, it is tenses as the past, in what the French call the preterite, a tense otherwise known as the past perfect or the past historic. We are told the present, but we experience the past tense in the present. But because it is the past tense, we know that there is a future present, in relation to which the present of the narrative is past. (5)

3.2 Metaphor, Time and Narrative Configuration: A Productive Circularity

Metaphor has traditionally been associated with the concept of trope or with one of the figures mostly within poetic language and narrative. On the other hand, Ricoeur says that it also belongs to the theory of literary genres. For Ricoeur, both create the meaning effect with the similar phenomenon of semantic innovation in language which in both cases is brought on one level of discourse. This, in Ricoeur's words is "the level of acts of language equal to or greater than the sentence." ("Preface," IX (*TAN* Vol. I)

Ricoeur objectifies that with metaphor the innovation (the natural extension) is found in the formulation of new semantic pertinences which depends upon our perceptive ability, while the production of a new pertinence of the object of metaphor undergoes a displacement from ordinary language to a metaphorical utterance. Similarly, the semantic innovation in narratives is found in the invention of "another work of synthesis – a plot." Here within a new plot "goals, cause, and chance" and so many other things are brought together, within a "temporal unity" with all their magnitude in action at a moment's notice. This "synthesis of the heterogeneous" brings metaphor very much close to narrative in terms of creative production of language itself. The new thing that Ricoeur calls the "yet unsaid, the unwritten" or something which did not exist before it "springs up in language." This notion reaches back to the "productive imagination" and "the schematism that is signifying matrix" which has already been discussed in detail in the earlier chapter. At this point, Ricoeur through this intelligibility aims at a higher level of met language. In result, either with plot or metaphor "to explain more is to understand better. At first it is "grasping the dynamism in virtue of which a metaphorical utterance, a new semantic pertinence, emerges from the ruins of the semantic pertinence as it appears in a literal reading of the sentence." Thus, understanding in the second case as a result is "grasping the operation that unifies into one whole and complete action," this understanding is "constituted by the circumstances, ends and means, initiatives and interactions, the reversal of fortune, and all the unintended consequences issuing from human action." (x)

Ricoeur observes that seemingly keeping narrative parallel to metaphor, the mimetic function of narrative has the same problem as that of metaphorical reference. Ricoeur associate three different and distinct senses to mimesis – first is "a reference back to the familiar pre-understanding we have of the order of the action," second is "an entry into the realm of poetic composition," and the last one is "a new configuration by means of this poetic refiguring of the pre-understanding order of action" alone mentioned before. Ricoeur confirms that this is the last aspect of mimesis and its third sense which truly matches the referential nature of metaphor. On the other hand, Ricoeur says that the metaphorical description "reigns in the field of sensory, emotional, aesthetic and axiological values," this is something which "makes the world a habitable world." Comparatively it is only to draw our attention that the mimetic function of plot works in the preference of the field of action and also of its "temporal values," would be the last feature we would dwell on in detail in this Chapter. According to Ricoeur, the frontier between the two functions is the capacity of poetic composition to re-figure the temporal experience in narratives and second the referential function of the plot. The function between these two is unstable, at first "the plots that configure and transfigure the practical field encompass not just acting but also suffering." Therefore, characters in narratives are as agents of actions and victims of the temperament. Ricoeur opens up here for "the mimetic value of poetic discourse and the re-descriptive power of narrative function." This is something that the modern world is waiting for; it opens a new dimension of understanding. The chapter opens up a "vast poetic sphere" including the understanding of the metaphorical utterance and the understanding of the narrative discourse. (IX-XI)

Ricoeur starts pointing at two different aspects of time – first is the effect on narratives that Ricoeur questions that whether it is "structural identity of historiography," "philosophy of history," "fictional narrative" or this is only a case of "offering the deep kinship between the truth claims of these two narrative modes." Ricoeur observe that there is one presupposition which commands over both the narratives either it is structural identity or of its truth claim of all narrative works – "it is the temporal character of human experience" as the world which is opened by a narrative is always in Ricoeur's words "a temporal world." Hence a narrative becomes meaningful "to the extent it portrays the features of temporal experience" which is circular in nature and also a similar case with every hermeneutic assertion. Ricoeur attempts to demonstrate that this circle of narrative and temporality of experience should not be taken as something "vicious", he offers it to be a "healthy circle" generally known as the hermeneutic circle that Ricoeur tells and shows us like this:

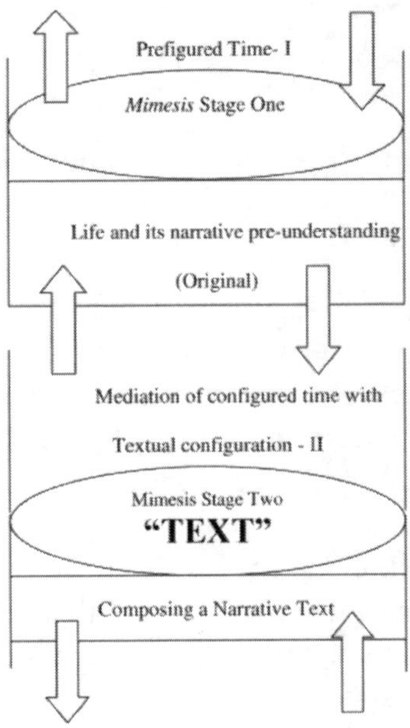

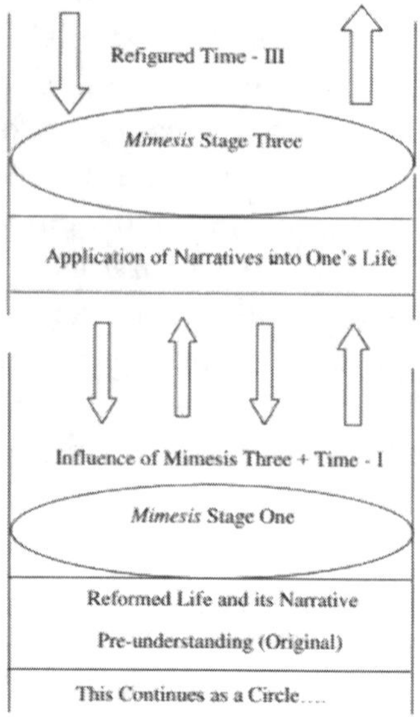

The same can also be understood as: *M* = *Mimesis*—

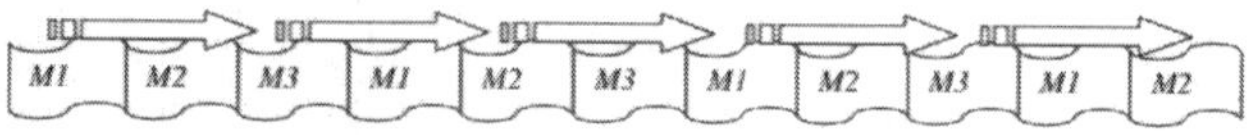

(Prefiguring, Configuring, Refiguring, Prefiguring, Configuring, Refiguring, Prefiguring, Configuring, Refiguring, Prefiguring, Configuring....)

Thus, Ricoeur observes that in Hermeneutics this is an undeniable circular – it is necessary to believe to understand, and necessary to understand to believe. It happens approximately with every hermeneutic assertion. For this Ricoeur refers to Augustine and Aristotle to understand the reciprocity between narrativity and temporality. The first one constitutes the problem "from the side of the paradoxes of time" and the later "from the side of the intelligible organisation of a narrative." Accepting this that both of them belong to two "profoundly cultural universe separated by several centuries" according to Augustine, writes Ricoeur that "the representation of time in which discordance never ceases to bite the desire for what concordance that forms the very essence of the animus," while on the other hand, in Aristoteliancorpus, it concerns about "dominance of concordance over discordance in the configuration of the plot." Ricoeur critically analyses this current model for understanding time and plot. Ricoeur establishes a relationship between concordance and discordance – taking up both Augustine's *Confession* and Aristotle's *Poetics.* Ricoeur inferences here as "the perplexity created by the paradox of time predominates toward the work in which, on the contrary, confidence reigns in the power of the poet and the poem to make order triumph over disorder." (3-4)

3.3 The Threefold Mimesis of Action

In connection with time and narrative, this is to dwell on the concept of Ricoeur's *threefold mimesis, which* is the main concern of the present study. Here first of all Ricoeur tries to unfold a relationship between "the activity of narrating a story" and "the temporal character of human experience." For this, there is a correlation between both of them, the "time becomes human to the extent that it is articulated through a narrative mode, and narrative attains its full meaning when it becomes a condition of temporal experience." It seems here that it is as if Ricoeur is trying to observe the cultural *abyss* within a structural setup. He seems to be getting back to that of some similar aspects when Ricoeur presents his thesis rejecting the traditional understanding of mimesis and plot where mimesis could open up the world of plot. He writes that the "very meaning of configuring operation constitutive of emplotment is a result of its internal mediatory position" between the two operations i. e. *M 1* and *M3 Which* themselves are constitutive of *M 2* and its two distinct sides. (52)

Ricoeur points out the "semiotics of the text" specifically the "the science of the text" which in his view can be established only upon the abstraction of *M 2* which "may concern the internal laws of literature without any regard of the two sides of the text." In connection with this textual duality Ricoeur writes that:

> It is the task of hermeneutics, in return, to reconstruct the set of operations by which a work lifts itself above the opaque depths of living, acting, and suffering, to be given by an author to readers who receive it and thereby change their acting. For a semiotic theory, the only operative concept is that of the literary text. Hermeneutics, however, is concerned with reconstructing the entire arc of operations by which practical experience provides itself with works, authors, and readers. It does not confine itself to setting mimesis2 between mimesis and mimesis[3]. It wants to characterisemimesis[2] by its mediating function. What is at stake, therefore, is the concrete process by which the textual configuration mediates between the prefiguration of the practical field and its refiguration through the reception of the work. It Will appear as a corollary, at the end of this

> analysis, that the reader is that operator par excellence who takes up through doing something – the act of reading – the unity of the traversal from mimesis 1 to mimesis 3 by way of mimesis 2. (53)

This is the time to move to the relation of time and narrative as has already been shown in the diagram of the different stages of mimesis and time. In this connection, Ricoeur constitutes a meditation where one precedes and the other succeeds (the stages). He highlights the textual configuration of the temporal experience of the constructed time, that is T1 (Prefigured time) and T3 (Refigured time) through T2 (the mediation of configured time). On this horizon of current inquiry Ricoeur seems to be super conscious about his self-made objection on the notion of the *Vicious Circle* as if it is going to be a vast tautology or if there is really something substantial! Ricoeur therefore promises something more than only a "dead tautology."

Mimesis 1: Leaving the "innovative force of poetic composition," Ricoeur argues that "the composition of plot is grounded in a pre-understanding of the world of action" along with its – (i) Meaningful Structure, (ii) its Symbolic Resources, and (iii) its temporal Character. For the first, Ricoeur sheds light on three divisions, he says "if it is true that plot is an imitation of an action" then in this case primarily a bit of competence would be required – (a) "the capacity for identifying action in general by means of its structural features." This is something Ricoeur calls semantics of action – a competence which naturally becomes a grammatical unit, (b) Ricoeur speculates that "if imitating is elaborating an articulated significance of some action" then in this case another necessary "supplementary competence is required," Ricoeur calls it "an aptitude" which becomes functional for identifying "the symbolic mediation of action." The symbols, according to Ricoeur, are the containers of the temporal elements within them. These symbols become extremely useful to narrate "the very capacity of action." For further clarification Ricoeur refers to Heidegger's corpus of understanding of the same problem. In Ricoeur's view there are some "structural networks" which distinguish "the domain of action" from "the physical movement." Ricoeur uses structural networks to define action as the term "action" is mostly taken in a very narrow sense.

Action, according to Ricoeur, implies some goals, "some foreseen or predicted result." It refers to some motives as a physical event that leads to another – "actions also have agents"; the agents are held responsible for the consequences of their actions. Their motives are, in Ricoeur's view, "complementary operation." The agents are those who *act and suffer.* They sometimes have "favorable and unfavorable occasions for their actions." Thus "to act" is always "to act 'with' other." This interaction is either in "cooperation," "competition," or "struggle," the actions may change accordingly in "fortune" either in happiness or in misfortune. This we can understand in question form e. g. "What, Why, Who, How, with Whom, Or, against Whom?" in connection with an acting domain. For Ricoeur there is a force which governs the relationship between the theory of narrative and theory of action. The relationship between narrative and practical understanding is followed by *presupposition* and *transformation.* Every narrative, explains Ricoeur, "presupposes a familiarity with terms such as agent, goal, means, circumstance, help, hostility, cooperation, conflict, success, failure etc." for both narrators and listeners. Every smallest narrative sentence becomes equal to that of an action. With this analogy, Ricoeur talks of an *action sentence,* in this way narrative is not limited only with the "familiarity with the conceptual network of action" but it adds a "discursive" feature which does not belong to the network that he calls the "network of semantics of action." These features are named as "synthetic features" which become instrumental to make any discourse "worthy of being called narrative." Ricoeur compares and applies Ferdinand de Saussure's structural understanding of language with narrative discourse, specially the paradigmatic and syntagmatic relation, synchronic and diachronic relation within the narrative discourse. Ricoeur thinks that narratives apart from the familiarity with the conceptual networks, it also requires familiarity with "the rules of composition that govern the diachronic order of a story" Ricoeur takes the plot of a narrative as the ordinary events in an interconnecting of action sentences; a constructive structure of the story becomes a "literary equivalent of syntagmatic order. There is a twofold correlation between these two understandings of actions as mentioned below:

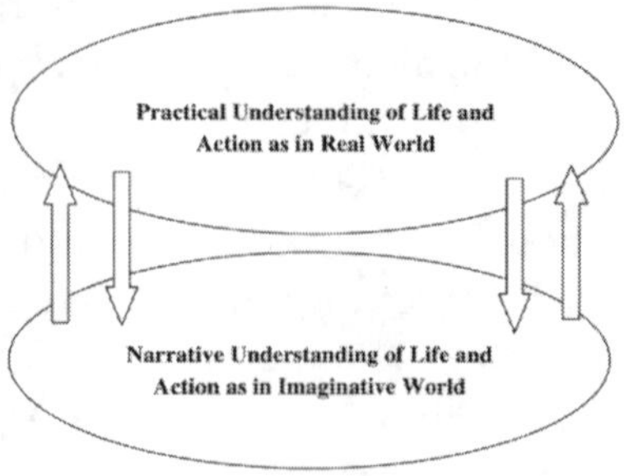

Both the worlds incorporate with each other accordingly

3.4 Symbol in the Narrative Anchorage

The twofold correlative of narrative and practical understanding undergoes from "paradigmatic order of action to the syntagmatic order of narrative." Ricoeur establishes a vivid transformation from the previous presuppositions by concluding this problem as if one has to understand a story, he has to understand "both the language of 'doing thing' and the cultural tradition from which proceeds the typology of plots" Discussing about the second anchorage, the narrative composition, Ricoeur says that it is the practical understanding that depends on the "symbolic resources of the practical field." This is what governs the "aspect of doing something," "knowing how to do something." For him, everything results from the poetic transposition of symbols. Human actions when narrated, says Ricoeur, "are always already articulated by signs, rules and norms." Human actions, in narratives are "always already symbolically articulated." Dwelling on the works of two eminent authors, an anthropologist and the other a sociologist, Clifford Geertz's *The Interpretation of Culture* (year) and Cassirer's *Philosophy of Symbolic Forms* where symbol, in Geertz's understanding is taken as a middle sense that is "hallowing between its being identified with a simple notation and its being identified with double-meaning expressions following the model of metaphor." At this juncture Ricoeur reminds us of Leibniz's dispute "between intuitive knowledge based on direct insight and symbolic knowledge by way of abbreviated signs." For 'too poor' and 'too rich' Ricoeur turns to Cassirer's *Philosophy of Symbolic Forms* (year) where he takes on symbols as "cultural processes that articulate experience." The practical aspect of autonomic symbolic whole depends more on speaking rather on writing, while in writing, there is a transfer from literal functioning to the textual world that is written here in writing symbol becomes "detached from the practical level" as an implicit or immanent one, as explicit and implicit symbolic whole. Thus, according to Ricoeur, the anthropologists and socialists' understanding of symbol "immediately accentuates the public character of any meaningful articulation." Taking Geertz's views, Ricoeur develops his ideas, especially that of "culture is public because meaning is." (12) on these lines, Ricoeur writes that "symbolism is not in the mind, not a psychological operation destined to guide action, but a meaning incorporated into action and decipherable from it by other actors in the social interplay." (57)

Turning to the aspect of symbol – Ricoeur writes that "symbolic mediation signals the structured character of symbolic system," he also mentions the process of interacting symbol and "patterns of interworking meanings." In this way symbol before being a proper text, its mediation in his view has a "texture." This symbol within a cultural and conventional framework is something that "we can interpret its gesture as meaning this or that" according to time, context, place and person. This symbolism as a whole lay "an initial readability on action". Ricoeur at this initial stage warns not to be confused with the texture of symbols with that of the text. In the meanwhile, there is also an idea of some rules. Ricoeur strengthens this view with the expression used by Peter Winch for meaningful action as "rule-governed behavior," something like 'programs' for a particular behavior, "they give form, order and direction to life." Ricoeur compares these rules with that of genetic and cultural codes which open other windows to look at the cultural codes by this comparison, in this connection writes Ricoeur that "cultural codes arise in zones not subject to genetic regulation and only prolong their efficacy at the price of a complete rearrangement of the encoding system." Ricoeur equates manners, customs, rituals etc. with what Hegel called "ethical substance." (57-58)

Ricoeur thus moves with symbolic mediation from "the idea of an imminent meaning to that of a rule, taken in the sense of a rule for description, then to that of a norm," (58) and equivalence of the rule taken by the idea that features of pre understanding of action is related to the "temporal elements." This is the base on which the narrative time grafts its configuration. The understanding of action is not limited to the awareness of the "conceptual network of action and with its symbolic mediations," it longs to recognise in action the temporal structures that call for narration. At this point narrative and time both stay quite implicit. Ricoeur promises to encounter explicitly to the former "vicious circle" at the end of his present argument he limits himself only "to examine the temporal features that remain implicit in symbolic meditations of actions and that we may take as the inductors of narratives." (55-60)

3.5 Ricoeur, Heidegger and Einstein on Time and Time Division

In the present research it is found that Ricoeur and Einstein comparatively seem to be quite relevant to understand reality in relation to time as is the view that time depends on the observer. Dealing with the temporal notion of time as past present and future, Ricoeur dwells on a new notion of three-fold time structures following Augustine's discordant-concordant structure of time where only the present is paramount e. g.:

P R E S E N T		
of past things	of present things	of future things

On the set of the reflective notion of time, this structure of time evolves some paradoxical features and one of the most "primitive temporal structure of actions which defines more specifically as:

Present 1	"*Now* I intend to do that because I *just* realised that…"
Present 2	"*Now* I am doing it, because *now* I can do it."
Present 3	"*Henceforth*, that is, from now on, I commit myself to doing that *tomorrow*."

In this regard, it should be noted that Ricoeur gets very close to Einstein's division of time for his current analysis where both of them consider the three-fold division of time as mere illusion. Apart from Augustine's notion of time – the temporal element is in relation to the "phenomenology of action." Ricoeur advances this notion by relying on Heidegger's existential understanding of time and being (Dasein). Ricoeur in his present endeavor hopes it to be quite decisive. The "place" where the 'being' is constituted he calls it Dasein, "the structure of being-in-the-world" which seems to be more fundamental comparatively than "any relation of subject to the object." (61)

Ricoeur centers his analysis of time to this Heideggerian existential understanding of time in which we normally live and act. He borrows the idea of the "structure of within – time-ness that this might be the best characterisation of temporality of action." Thus, time in this regard is something completely "desubstantialised." The conventional division of time as past, present and future has vanished. Time in Ricoeur's view, appears to be "the exploded unity of three temporal extases" therefore it seems to be, "simple succession of abstract 'nows'". Ricoeur seems to be more interested in the current understanding of time as now rather than the conventional three-fold structure. Ricoeur clarifies the existential notion of the understanding of time as:

> In this way, within-time-ness or being "within" time deploys features irreducible to the representation of linear time. Being "within" time is already something other than measuring the intervals between limit-instants. Being "within" time is above all to reckon with time and, as a consequence of this, to calculate. It is because we do reckon with time and do make calculations that we must have recourse to measuring, not vice versa. It must be possible, therefore, to give an existential description of this "reckoning with" before the measuring it calls for. Here expressions such as "have the time to," "take the time to," "to lose time," etc. are very revealing." (62)

Thus, to reach to a conclusion, according to Ricoeur, the narrative configurations at one hand is "most elaborated forms of temporality corresponding to them to share the same foundation of within-time-ness." Ricoeur's thinks this would add to the richness of mimesis stage one, before any initiation or representation of any action this become necessary to first understand that "what human action is" from multiple directions i. e. (i) semantic significance, (ii) symbolic system, (iii) the temporality of action over this pre-understanding for both addresser and addressee, "emplotment" and "textual mimetic" are developed. Therefore, the "literature would be incomprehensible if it did not give a configuration to what was already a figure in human action." (64)

Ricoeur tells us that Mimesis 1 in relation to the narrative "opens the kingdom of the *as-is if*." He does not use the expression for this as "the kingdom of fiction" as prevalent in literary criticism; he avoids it even to be taken as synonyms of narrative configuration and as "an antonym to historical narrative's claim to constitute a 'true' narrative." In this connection Ricoeur ignores both the structural aspects of fictional and historical narratives. It is here to be noted that to what extent his "kingdom of as if" is enlarged? Is it infinite or is there some limit to it at some point?

3.6 The Death of Plot and Supremacy of Character and temporality

Fiction in relation to emplotment, the functioning of imaginary faculty and some of the things called 'real' with all their manifestations will be dealt with at the end of this chapter. Getting disengaged with all this, Ricoeur focuses on the temporal structure of emplotment, which according to him, has hardly any place in Aristotle's *Poetics.* Mimesis too has an intermediary position in narratives only because "it has a mediating function." Furthermore, in this intermediary mediating connection Ricoeur writes:

> This mediating function derives from the dynamic character of the configuring operation that has led us to prefer the term emplotment to that of plot and ordering to that of system. In fact, all the concepts relative to this level designate operations. The dynamism lies in the fact that a plot already exercises, within its own textual field, an integrating and, in this sense, a mediating function, which allows it to bring about, beyond this field, a mediation of a larger amplitude between the pre understanding and, if I may dare to put it this way, the post understanding of the order of action and its temporal features. (65)

Plot: Ricoeur observes that it also mediates in three different ways: (i) it mediates "between the individual events or incidents and a story taken as a whole" which has a reciprocal relation expressed as *from* and *into* along with *thought* of the story which is "an enumeration of event in serial order" organised as an "intelligible whole." In this way, emplotment brings together factors as heterogeneous as agents, goals, means, interactions, circumstances, unexpected results," (ii) plot permits a rather greater extension after adding "pitiable and fearful incident, sudden reversal, recognition, and violent effects within the complex plot." Ricoeur tells us that Aristotle equals plot with concordance –discordance configuring character. He claims that this is the real mediating function of the plot.

Ricoeur makes it clear by saying that "narrative makes appear within a syntagmatic order all the components capable of figuring in the paradigmatic tableau established by the semantics of action." Ricoeur concludes that this process moving from paradigmatic to syntagmatic constitutes the transition from mimesis 1 to mimesis 2 which in his words is a "configuring activity," (iii) plot mediates in its temporal characteristics a means of generation as a "synthesis of the heterogeneous." But it remains a fact that Aristotle did not mention this temporal characteristic, rather it seems that these are directly inherent in the "constitutive dynamism of the narrative configuration." Thus, the feature which joins together M3 and M2 rests on the analysis of the "configurational act."

Talking about the two distinct features – the "schematisation" and the "character of traditionality," Ricoeur says that the character of traditionality and the characteristics of configurational act both have a specific and functional relation with *time*. Here in relation with configurational act, Ricoeur recalls the notion of "grasping together" by comparing the productive configurational act with that of the work of the productive imagination. The productive imagination "as a transcendental" functions rather as a "psychologising faculty." The productive imagination, as discussed before, is not only rule-governed but also it "constitutes the generative matrix of rules."' In this way, Ricoeur introduces to us the "schematism of the narrative function" which according to him gets "constituted within a history that has all the characteristic of tradition," therefore, cultures become heir to several narrative traditions including all – namely Wes, Hebrew, Christian, Celtic, Germanic, Icelandic and Slavic. Ricoeur seems to be displeased if it is applied with Western narratives. He mentions such works as *Iliad* and *Oedipus Rex*, also used as an example by Aristotle. For Ricoeur, "a universal emerges" from narrative. These paradigms are from the configuration of the productive imagination. These paradigms, influenced by earlier innovations, evolve rules "for a subsequent experimentation within the narrative field." Thus, the rules which evolve within the narrative experimentations change "under the pressure of new inventions, but they change slowly and even resist change, in virtue of the very process of sedimentation," Ricoeur, for the concept of sedimentation further adds that:

> … for the other pole of tradition, innovation, its status is correlative to that of sedimentation. There is always a place for innovation inasmuch as what is produced, in the *poiesis* of the poem, is always, in the last analysis, a singular work, this work. This is why the paradigms only constitute the grammar that governs the composition of new works – new before becoming typical. In the same way as the grammar of a language governs the production of well-formed sentences, whose number and content are unforeseeable, a work of art – a poem, play, novel – is an original production, a new existence in the linguistic *[langagier]* kingdom. Yet the reverse is no less true. Innovation Remains a form of behavior governed by rules. The labor

> of imagination is not born from nothing. It is bound in one way or another to the tradition's paradigms. But the range of solutions is vast. It is deployed between the two poles of servile application and calculated deviation, passing through every degree of "rule-governed deformation." The folktale, the myth, and in general the traditional narrative stands closest to the first pole. But to the extent we distance ourselves from traditional narrative, deviation becomes the rule. Thus, the contemporary novel, in large part, may be defined as an antinovel, to the extent that contestation wins out over the taste for simply varying the application of the paradigms. (69-70)

Moreover, the deviation may come into play in every type of narrative and genre etc., every individual work is thus constitutive of this deviation. One stands from another work because of the configuration of deviation into play. This change becomes so productive that it creates a new genre. The first example for this change is Novel in relation to other genres i. e. drama, romance, history or chronicles.

Mimesis 3 deals with the refigured time, the application of narrative into one's life – that somehow seems to be pictorial. M3, according to Ricoeur, consists of the following sections – (i) the circle of mimesis, (ii) configuration, refiguration and reading, (iii) narrative and reference and, (iv)narrated time. As metaphor and language have been mediated together in relation to time, here the same investigation of the mediation which is between time and narrative will be in focus as a second major question and problem of present endeavor. Ricoeur reminds us of his previous observation as "narrative has its full meaning when it is restored to the time of action and of suffering in mimesis 3." This is what corresponds to the concept of philosophical hermeneutics – 'Application,' something which is in Aristotle's *Rhetoric* as "the theory of persuasion" which is simply gripped "by the hearer's capacity for receiving the message." This is the effect of the cathartic structure – pity and fear, the frightening at the point and the reversal of fortune in tragedy. Ricoeur says that Aristotle did signify that when the matter reaches the audience, hearer, and reader – it gets accepted and fulfilled as well. Ricoeur dares to go one step ahead of Aristotle by dealing with the world of the text and the world of the reader as "the world configured by poem and the world wherein real action occurs and unfolds its specific temporality." (71)

3.7 The Circle of Mimesis and the Secrecy of the Text

Ricoeur ponders over linking three stages of mimesis and the mediation between time and narrative. Does it really make a progression in linking all this? Keeping in mind the possible vicious circularity, Ricoeur seriously reflects on it, which according to him travels from M1 to M3 in relation to "the semantic structure of action, it's the semantic structure of action, its resources for symbolisation, or its temporal character." Ricoeur seems to accept that this vicious circle may revolve only around the vicious circle of mimesis. He admits that "the analysis is circular" but not vicious. This vicious cycle develops from seduction in various forms of circularity i. e. (a) when one emphasises the violence of interpretation, (b)the abundance of the same. Abundance stands for a large amount of something or the relative degree of playfulness an ample quantity, affluence, profusion. In the first case "narrative gives form to what is unformed". Form, in this way, may be "suspected of treachery." There is one thing called *fiction* something in the form "as if" and – one when one stops befooling oneself at a time when one becomes "aware of the violence and the lie", the one is then "at the point of succumbing to the fascination of the absolutely unformed." This results in "radical intellectual honesty" for the act of violent interpretation. Maybe as "God is dead" metaphorically in all its violent expression. This "temporal dissonance" in narrative is related and "attached to the relationship between narrative and time." (72)

Ricoeur calls the forming of the "unformed" as one of the features of modernity. Ricoeur tells what all happens with a thinker or with any literary critic when he yields to "a nostalgia for order or, worse, to the horror of chaos" with all strife and labor they do may move then to "a genuine recognition of the paradoxes of time beyond the loss of meaning characteristics of particular culture." Thus the "mistrust" and the "suspension of the interpretative violence" according to Ricoeur, "no less legitimate" in this paradigm. This in any discourse will be "an ironic distance" which overthrows the "intention." The alleged violence can be legitimately suspected which is potentially charged with vicious characteristics.

Moving to the second objection – abundance and redundancy, he observes that there is a redundancy in the analysis of M1 in relation to the temporal features of action he strongly believes that that "the objection of a vicious circle through redundancy would offer a more propitious occasion to indicate the strategic importance of the situations." The word "propitious" stands for something likely to have or to produce good results that may appear favorably disposed.

Ricoeur strongly holds the notion that "action is in quest of narrative" and there is a "pre narrative quality of experience," there are stories in the demand to be told as well. These stories "offer anchorage points for narratives." The as yet untold stories, writes Ricoeur, "imposes itself upon us with a surprising force," therefore, this is to be noted that "telling, following, understanding stories is simply the "continuation" of these untold stories even in our real and temporal lives that we lead. Man tells stories because he "loves being narrated," there is a necessity to save the history of the victories and defeats. "The whole history of suffering" writes Ricoeur, "cries out for vengeance and calls for narrative." (73-5)

Frank Kermode observes that according to Ricoeur, some narratives aim at "obscurity and dissimulation" rather than on illuminating in nature. In the language of the evangelist Mark there is something which is not expected to be understood by those outside the privileged class and those who expel inside the substance. There are many other narratives that do not let interpreters enter into it. In fact, they are switched to be naturally barred from the text." Ricoeur writes that "these secret places are places in the text," they are in an exhaustible situation to have the unending hermeneutic potential in them. There is always some textual secrecy. This is between the narrative itself and the "as yet untold stories of our lives that constitute the prehistory, the background, the living imbrication from which the told story emerges," Ricoeur asserts that there is a possible and potential "hidden affinity." This is between the two places – the secret place from where the story emerges and the secret where it gets returned. With this Ricoeur dismisses the fear of "lifeless tautology" of the vicious circle successfully with appropriate logical justification and also declares that this in another way would be a "healthy circle."

Configuration, Refiguration and Reality: Ricoeur says that "the hermeneutic circle of narrative and time never stops being reborn from the circle that the stages of mimesis form." Here he talks about the configuration resulting from M1 and M3 by the act of reading. The act of reading according to him is similar "to the plot's capacity to model experience" because reading goes across the same line as plot fulfills the configurational act in grasping together "the details of action into the unity of the plot." Ricoeur brings back his two earlier discussed terms in this relation as a witness to reflect on the process of configuration – "the schematisation" and "the traditionality". He adds that both are from their heart "categories of the interaction between the operations [operative] of writing and reading," in the process of reading the "received paradigms" help evolve the reader's expectations, realise "the formed rule, genre and the type exemplified by the narrated story." The act of reading, whatever results and evolves to, provides a guideline to the "encounter between a text and its readers" which "govern the story's capacity to be followed." Thus, it becomes clear that the act of reading "accompanies the narrative's configuration and actualises its capacity to be followed" and therefore "[to] follow a story is to actualise by reading." Ricoeur observes that emplotment is considered similar to the act of judgmental productive imagination. It is only a joint work of the text and the act of reading similarly as Aristotle thinks that "sensation is the common work of sensing and what is sensed." The mechanism between the addresser and addressee in the narrative discourse, moreover, adds Ricoeur that the act of reading:

> … accompanies the interplay of the innovation and sedimentation of paradigms that schematics emplotment. In The act of reading, the receiver plays with the narrative constraints, brings about gaps, takes part in the combat between the novel and the antinovel, and enjoys the pleasure that Roland Barthes calls the pleasure of the text.
>
> (75-77)

Ricoeur mentions Roman Ingarden's *The Literary Work of Art* (1973) and Wolf Gang Iser's *The Act of Reading* (1978) and admits without any hesitation that "it is the reader who completes the work" and the "written work is a sketch for reading." The written work bares "holes," "lacunas" and "zones of indetermination." For example, Ricoeur writes that this is quite visible in Joyce's work *Ulysses* which openly challenges "the reader's capacity to configure what the author seems to take malign delight in defiguring. In such an extreme case, it is the reader, almost abandoned by the work, who carries the burden of emplotment." (77)

Reading operates between M1 and M2 and joins both of them. This is the last and the final indicator of the configuration of the world of action within the structure of the plot. The act of reading and its affair proceeds to the theory of reading and the theory of reception which includes the works of Robert Jauss, Iser and

Ingarden. There is an effect that is produced by the text on both the level – collective and individual. This effect, writes Ricoeur, is "an intrinsic component" or the actual meaning of the text which is a "set of instructions that the individual reader or the reading public executes in a passive or a creative way." Ricoeur stops here by referring and suggesting for any further inquiry *The Act of Reading* and *Towards an Aesthetic of Reception.* (1982)

3.8 Narrative and Reference

Ricoeur talks about narrative and reference in an old manner as it was in *The Rule of Metaphor.* Ricoeur thinks that to complete the theory of reading and writing in relation to M1 and the aesthetics of reception, the understanding of reference in narratives should also be discussed properly, this is how he reflects on the narrative reference:

> What is communicated, in the final analysis, is, beyond the sense of a work, the world it projects and that constitutes its horizon. In this sense, the listeners or readers receive it according to their own receptive capacity, which itself is defined by a situation that is both limited and open to the world's horizon. Thus, the term "horizon" and its correlative, "world," appeared twice in the definition of mimesis3 suggested earlier: the intersection of the world of the text and that of the listener or reader. This definition, close to H. G. Gadamer's notion of a "fusion of horizons," rests upon three presuppositions which underlie, respectively, acts of discourse in general, literary works among these acts of discourse, and narratives among these literary works. The order that ties together these three presuppositions is thus one of increasing specification. (77)

Ricoeur takes reference as the unit of discourse; there is an "intended discourse" with which one may get confused with that of "signified." Following Benveniste's view where language is more than a sign, in fact it is the sentence and beyond which "says something *about* something." The intent in discourse is "contemporaneous with its event character and its dialogical functioning." When someone speaks or addresses himself as "an interlocutor" only one aspect of the event is covered. The event has another aspect that is the speaker's ambition to bring a new *experience* to language and share it with someone else." The experience itself has its own world of horizons. For Ricoeur, reference and horizons are similar to that of the figure and ground – both become correlative.

Shifting to the ontological point of view willingly, Ricoeur reflects quite powerfully as "[language]is for itself the order of the same. The world is its other. The attestation of this otherness arises from language's reflexivity with regard to itself, whereby it knows itself as being *in* being in order to bear *on* being." (78) Therefore, whenever a reader reads, he is not only involved with the sense of the work but also engaged with the reference which in Ricoeur's words is the "experience it brings to language" and the world of its horizons along with the temporality that it unfolds "in the face of this experience." Thus, both discourse and literary works bring up the same experience to language, and thereafter, to the world they unfold, Ricoeur is reflecting in the following paragraph on the same problem as:

> I will say that, for me, the world is the whole set of references opened by every sort of descriptive or poetic text I have read, interpreted, and loved. To understand these texts is to interpolate among the predicates of our situation all those meanings that, from a simple environment *(Umwelt)*, make a world *(Welt)*. Indeed, we owe a large part of the enlarging of our horizon of existence to poetic works. Far from producing only weakened images of reality – shadows, as in the Platonic Treatment of the *eikon* in painting or writing *(Phaedrus* 274e-77e) – literary works depict reality by *augmenting* it with meanings that themselves depend upon the virtues of abbreviation, saturation, and culmination, so strikingly illustrated by emplotment. (80)

3.9 The Poetics of Narrativity and the Aporetics of Temporality

The function of refiguration, which originally belongs to poetic work, is a "part of a hermeneutics that aims less at restoring the author's intention behind the text than at making explicit the movement by which the text unfolds, as it were, a world in front of itself." (81) At this point Ricoeur reminds us of *The Rule of Metaphor*, that poetry with the help of *these* describes the world, in the same manner "making a narrative *[le faire narratif le*-signifies the world in its temporal dimension, to the extent that narrating, telling, reciting is to remake action following the poem's invitation." (81) In narrative the world is comprehended "from the angle of human praxis rather than from that of cosmic pathos" as is found in poetry, especially lyric poetry. Whatever is re-signified by narratives is "what was already personified at the level of human activity." Ricoeur brings this reference of practical approach of action and the cosmic pathos quite close, he further adds that:

> Human action can be over-signified, because it is already pre-signified by all the modes of its symbolic articulation. This is the sense in which the problem of reference is simpler in the case of the narrative mode than in that of the lyrical mode of poetry. Just as, in the *Rule of Metaphor,* it was by extrapolation from the tragic muthos that I

> elaborate the theory of poetic reference that joins muthos and redescription, it is the metaphorisation of action and suffering that is easiest to decipher. (89)

Writing about the narrated time, Ricoeur says that there is a reciprocal borrowing and interweaving of reference between history and narrative function. He also brings the human time in focus which is refigured by history and literary fiction commonly. Stressing on the fixed time or the narrated time, Ricoeur gives birth to a third dimension, calling it a "third partner." The narrated time cannot be discussed without meditating on this third dimension, that is, the phenomenology of time. Ricoeur reveals that this discussion may be a "long and difficult three-way conversation between history, literary criticism, and phenomenological philosophy." Ricoeur says that all three ignore each other and adds that the "dialectic of time and narrative is the ultimate stake of this confrontation." (83) Thus, in this way Ricoeur sets forth the discussion from Augustine to Husserl and Heidegger, he adds that:

> ...the poetics of narrativity responds and corresponds to the aporetics of temporality. The rapprochement between Aristotle's *Poetics* and Augustine's *Confessions* provided only a partial and, in a way, a circumstantial verification of this thesis. If the aporetic character of every pure phenomenology of time may be augmented in at least a plausible way, the hermeneutic circle of narrativity and temporality will be enlarged well beyond the circle of mimesis, to which the discussion in this first part had to be limited, so long as historiography and the philosophy of history along with literary criticism have not had their say about historical time and the games fiction plays with time. It is only at the end of what I have called the three-way conversation, in which the phenomenology of time joins its voice to those of these other disciplines, that the hermeneutic circle can then be compared with the circle of a poetics of narrativity (itself culminating in the problem of interweaving reference referred to above) and an aporetics of temporality. (84)

The paradoxical structure of the aporetic nature of temporality leads to this that "the most radical temporality bears the stamp of death – the being-towards-death." He further adds that the relation of time in depth refers to "an eternity.... Eternity by time thus lies in the stability of a soul." This conclusion seems to be rooted in Augustine's *Confession.* Turning to Heidegger's understanding of time, Ricoeur talks about the levels of temporality which in his words orients its meditation "not toward divine eternity but toward finitude seated by being-towards-death." (86-87)

The second part of the *Time and Narrative* volume deals with "History and Narrative" where he discusses that history is a very ambiguous discipline i. e. half literary, half scientific." Ricoeur establishes his argument contrary to this attitude, writing that "history the most removed from the narrative form continues to be bound to our narrative understanding by a line of derivation that we can reconstruct step by step and degree by degree with an appropriate method." (91) Ricoeur puts up those two "historical explanations" and the "narrative understanding" modes of understanding, telling us that the "refiguring of time by narrative is, I hold, the joint work of historical and fictional narrative." (94) The entire third part of *Time and Narrative* consists on "The Configuration of Time in Fictional Narrative" dealing with the metamorphosis of plot, semiotic constraints on narrating, games of time and the fictive experience of time.

In conclusion, the second part of Ricoeur's analysis in *Time and narrative* focuses on the relation between the writing of history and the operation of emplotment, something that Aristotle categorises within the imitation of an action. The first volume largely deals with the metamorphosis of historical narrative; we intend to slacken this portion from our current quest of understanding because of some strict limitation of the thesis. Nevertheless, Ricoeur has made some very remarkable observations e. g. that of Aristotle's muthos and the configuration of time. Ricoeur brings back the concept of emplotment with a valid expansion of the term what he has taught us about "quasi-plot," "quasi-character" and "quasi-event" in narratives within the hemisphere of mimesis two.

3.10 Time, Symbol, Metamorphosis of Plot and Reading Novel

Part III of volume II of *Time and Narrative* dealing with the configuration of time in fictional narratives focuses on the metamorphosis of plot, semantic constraints of narrativity and fictional experience of time. Ricoeur observes that the equation of narrative configuration with fiction can only be justified partially. Ricoeur disagrees with this while presenting his thesis "as the configuration act is, as I myself have mentioned, an operation of the productive imagination." (*TN* Vol. II 03) He also thinks that historical narratives and fictional narratives both come out in existence from configuration operation of mimesis 2. Ricoeur lingers awhile on the mimetic relation between action and narration by "broadening, radicalising, enriching, and opening up to the outside the notion of emplotment." (4) Ricoeur observes that Aristotle's muthos has extra capacity to be transformed without losing its formal identity and significance. For deepening and enlarging the notion of emplotment, Ricoeur associates the narratives as they are transmitted in culture and the "quarrel over priority that divides narrative understanding and semiotic rationality."For enriching the notion of emplotment with the notion of time Ricoeur anticipates the "great three-way debate between lived experiences, historical time and fictional time" with the narrative "utterance" and "narrative statement"for opening up the notion of emplotment along with the notion of time corresponding to it is the world of the work that the text of fiction projects in this connection Ricoeur writes that:

> In this way, epics, dramas, and novels project, in the mode of fiction, ways of inhabiting the world that lie waiting to be taken up by reading, which in turn is capable of providing a space for a confrontation between the world of the text and the world of the reader. The problems of refiguration, belonging to the level of mimesis3, begin, strictly speaking, only in and through this confrontation. This is why the notion of the world of the text seems to me still to be part of the problem of narrative configuration, although it paves the way for the transition from mimesis2 to mimesis[3]. (5)

In the "Metamorphosis of Plot" Ricoeur brings certain new aspects in account discussing the tragic muthos such as the modern novel and the notion of emplotment in the last three centuries in relation with "prodigious workshop for experiments in the domains of composition and the expression of time" (8) Ricoeur first puts a question about the "erroneous conception of plot" because it was transposed only "two of the already constituted genres,epic and drama, then because classical art, especially in France" which in fact, observes Ricoeur, was "the misunderstanding of the former principals of emplotment." Whereas Aristotle himself had subordinated the concept of Character to Plot, although, in modern novels, it is witnessed that the notion of Character has overtaken the notion of Plot clearly by becoming equal to and proceeding to surpass it completely. This can be well understood by the Modern and Postmodernnarratives. It is Henry James who says that Character is the determination of Plot and Plot is the revelation of Character, it is an interplay of Character and Circumstances which gives birth to Plot.

Ricoeur mentions three noteworthy expansions with the genre of the novel under the rubrics of Character.First: it does not deal any longer with "great deeds or misdeeds of legendary or famous characters but the adventures of ordinary men and women." The 18th century English novel testifies to this change about ordinary people and "differentiated social fabric." The second expansion of character, writes Ricoeur, "at the expense of the plot" Bildungsroman came into existence. In the 20th century another new complexity appears in the name of Stream of Consciousness novel, Ricoeur observes that:

> Yet nothing in these successive expansions of character at the expense of the plot escapes the formal principle of configuration and therefore the concept of emplotment. I will even dare to say that nothing in them takes us beyond the Aristotelian definition of muthos as the imitation of an action. As the breadth of the plot increases, so does that of action. By "action" we have to understand more than the behavior of the protagonists that produces visible changes in their situation or their fortune, what might be called their external appearance? Action, in this enlarged sense, also includes the moral transformation of characters, their growth and education, and their initiation into the complexity of moral and emotional existence. It also includes, in a still more subtle sense, purely internal changes affecting the temporal course of sensations and emotions, moving ultimately to the least organised, least conscious level introspection can reach. (10)

According to Ricoeur, the imitation of action can be extended beyond the "action novel," therefore, "to include novels oriented toward character or toward an idea, in the name of the encompassing nature of plot in relation to the more narrowly defined categories of incident, character, or thought." (10) There is something else that governs the whole – as we can see in Kafka's "K" and Becket. In this way these changes in the present history of genres novel tempts us to think "to give up the term "plot" as designating the correlate of narrative understanding." (10) Thus, there one may easily sense the defeat of plot in the narrative composition. Ricoeur writes that, although, "these problems were not abolished," but "displaced." He writes about this displacement as:

> To see this, it suffices to reflect upon the variety of novelistic procedures used to satisfy this requirement to depict life in its everyday truth in the early days of the English novel. For example, Defoe, the author of *Robinson Crusoe,* make recourse to a pseudo-autobiographical form, through imitation of the innumerable diaries, memoires, and genuine autobiographies published during the same period by people shaped by the Calvinist discipline of daily self-

> examination. Following him, Richardson, in *Pamela* and *Clarissa,* believed he could depict private experience – for example, the conflicts between romantic love and the institution of marriage – with even greater fidelity by using as artificial a device as the exchange of letters, despite its evident disadvantages: little selective power, the encroachment of insignificant matters and garrulity, much marching in place and repetition.10 But, to Richardson, the advantages won out without any need for discussion. By having his heroine immediately write things down, he could convey the impression of great closeness between writing and feeling. Moreover, use of the present tense contributed to this impression of immediacy, thanks to the almost simultaneous transcription of what was felt and its circumstances. At the same time, the unsolvable difficulties of the pseudo-autobiography, dependent as it was on the resources of an unbelievable memory, were eliminated. Finally, this method allows the reader to participate in the psychological situation presupposed by the very use of an exchange of letters, the subtle mixture of retreats and outpourings that occupy the mind of anyone who decides to confide in writing her or his intimate feelings. On the side of the reader, we find in response to this, the no less subtle mixture arising from the indiscretion of peeking through the keyhole, so to speak, and the impunity that goes with solitary reading. (11)

Ricoeur observes that this is surprising that the pseudo-autobiography and "epistolary formula" did not cause any problem to their users, "the epistolary genre presupposes, in fact, that it is possible to transfer through writing, with no loss of persuasive power, the force of representation attached to the living voice or theatrical action." (12) Ricoeur stresses that it was necessary to overcome the empire of convention.

Being deeply influenced by Northrop Frye, Ricoeur adds that a literary symbol is a hypothetical verbal structure. There is something towards "the out" and "inside." Towards the inside, "symbol provides a hermeneutic key for interpretation." When a symbol is set in any fictional context, it passes through some phases in the language of Henri De Lubac:

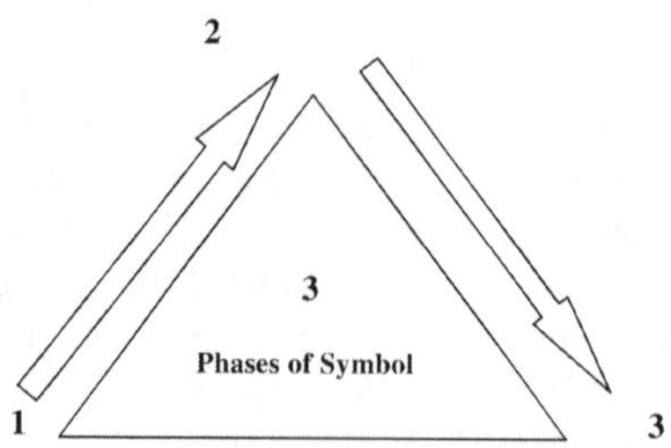

1. Phase one: (literal phase of symbol)
2. Phase two: (symbol as archetype [equivalent of the schematism, from sedimentation of tradition])
3. Phase three: (symbol as monad [the analogical sense of medieval biblical exegesis – in Frye's language, monad is an imaginative experience's capacity to attain totality in terms of some center]) (18).

Ricoeur writes about the end of the art of narrative and also mentions the death of the story teller – he asserts that we are witnessing "certain deaths," the death of the art of telling stories along with narrating in all its forms.(28) This last point made by Ricoeur may face a tough debate as the world has more ways of storytelling in an advanced way the world could ever have imagined, today there are more storytellers than ever before with a remarkable advancement from telling to showing the same – both – at a time.

In the game of time, Ricoeur mentions the paradigmatic and syntagmatic structure of tenses. He observes that languages have different tense structures which play important role to capture the temporality of time, comparatively, which in some ways can also be seen what Wordsworth calls "spots of time." Within the system of tenses, language contains "a ready-made means of modulating temporally all the action verbs throughout the narrative chain." (62) Ricoeur compares the system of tenses and the lived temporal experiences e. g. the use of prolepsis and analepsis in narratives and their pragmatism pinned therein which for certain may play very important role in the games with time – as they take a particular note of action to logical conclusion in narrative understanding. (83)

Ricoeur also takes the point of view and the narrative voice within the game of time wherein narrative "utterance becomes the discourse of the narrator while the statement becomes the discourse of a character." Ricoeur in this connection sheds light on the narrative mode e. g. direct narration of thoughts and feelings i. e. "self-narration" and "psycho-narration." For direct narration, he adds two more techniques e. g. "quoted monologue" that is by quoting the internal monologue of fictional others or where the character quotes himself/herself i. e. "self-quoted monologue." There also comes a third technique used by Flaubert and Jane Austen, the famous style known as "style indirect libre" that is the narrated monologue or in German stylistics "erlebte Rede" which is used for the magic of internal transparency and a lot of the "I" perspective of narrative technique.

Discussing novel, Ricoeur reaches to Bakhtin and Dostoevsky for his conclusion, since it is to restrict on the targeted topic here, we would not dwell into it in detail. Nevertheless, this is obvious that Ricoeur seems to be very impressed by Bakhtin's understanding of novel. Ricoeur mentions, in general, that voice is an important problem of communication for both addressors and addressees equally. He writes that "the narrative voice is the silent speech that presents the world of the text to the reader." (99) This is in the fictive experience, writes Ricoeur that "the confrontation between the world of the text and the life-world of the reader will make the problematic of narrative configuration tip over into that of the refiguration of time by narrative." (100) For Ricoeur, a work too, opens like a window onto a world, and time is "the temporal aspect of this virtual experience of being-in-the-world proposed by the text" which is either "related to," "directed to," or "is about" something. In this regard, Ricoeur does a practical analysis of three distinct works to prove his thesis. The first one is *Mrs. Dalloway* written by Virginia Woolf; second *Der Zauberberg* written byThomas Man and the third *A la recherché du temps perdu* written by Marcel Proust. He chooses these works because they are either "tales of time" or "tales about time." According to Ricoeur, very few narratives are tales about time whereas all fictional narratives are tales of time. Ricoeur discusses the above works as tales about time; he observes that these tales explore "the hierarchical levels that form the depth of temporal experience." According to Ricoeur, the functional narrative detects temporalities that are more or less extended, offering in each instance, a different figure of recollection of eternity in or out of time. (101)

This is to note here that only a framework of analysis of the above said texts would be taken into account here so that it would help frame the proposed framework for our current quest of ours in the reading of the following chapters and novels. Therein first of all Ricoeur focuses on configuration of works at first level and the worldview or the temporal experience at second level that the configuration projects "outside itself." Ricoeur discusses the narrative voice which addresses the readers – offers the reader "armful of temporal experiences to share." The stream of consciousness in his view is a kind of narrative configuration in which the narrative voice wants to communicate with the reader. The narrative technique progresses through some numerous events i. e. the list of coming, going of the events and the meetings including the narrated time. Ricoeur tells that in literary criticism more attention is given on character than on the exploration of the narrated time, in this connection he writes:

> ...the time lived by the characters in the narrative, there is no doubt that this plunge into the past along with the incessant weighing of souls that the characters practice on one another, contribute along with the actions described from the outside to reconstruct from within the characters in their present state. By giving a temporal depth to the narrative, the entanglement of the narrated present with the remembered past confers a psychological depth on the characters without, however, giving them a stable identity, so discordant are the glimpses the characters have of one another and of themselves. The reader is left holding the scattered pieces to a great game of character identification, but the solution to it escapes the reader as much as it does the characters in the narrative. The attempt to identify the characters certainly corresponds to the promptings of the Active narrator, when this voice leaves the characters to their interminable quest. (104)

Thus, the temporal configurations serve to share temporal experiences with the reader that is a tale about time running into the narrative through the character's configuration. Ricoeur brings in the clock time with the notion of monumental history where the time from inside is the same but not from outside where we divide time into hours and minutes. Thus, it is only fiction that can bring to language the "divorce between worldviews and their irreconcilable perspectives on time." At the end of the analysis of *Mrs. Dalloway,* Ricoeur concludes that although the character may have the individual worldviews and experience of time but there may well also be a single experience of time as "as the proximity between the "caves" visited constitutes a sort of underground network that *is* the experience of time in *Mrs. Dalloway.*" This experience of time in Ricoeur's view is "suggested to the reader by the reverberation..., of one solitary experience in another solitary experience." There is a network that is taken as a whole – the experience of time as a whole.

Turning to *The Magic Mountain*, Ricoeur starts discussing about "effacing of chronological time" throughout the basic storyline including the narrative technique as it confirms characterisation through which Ricoeur makes a distinction between "the time of narration" and "the narrated time." In this analysis, he distinguishes between chronological time and internal time as the current novel incorporates with three dimensions i. e. time, sickness and culture, more clearly it is about the experience of time, the deadly sickness and the debate over culture – especially the destiny of European culture. The novel's technique is observed in Bildungsroman dealing with the epic of death and tragedy of culture. The novel is full of the adjectives of time which help the series of events get narrated through them. The novel turns to let the reader experience the eternity unfolding its paradoxes whereunsetting situations become more unsettling. The function towards sickness carries us to an eternity of death whereas the hero "makes a precarious victory over the eternity of death that borders on stoic ataraxy." (130)

Dwelling on the analysis of the last work *Remembrance of Things Past,* Ricoeur takes the narrator, the hero "as a fictive entity supporting the tale about time that constitutes Remembrance" where he says that the remembrance is not about time but truth through the exposition of memory. Thus, Ricoeur hears here two narrative voices, i. e. that of the hero and the narrator. Ricoeur makes a three-way division of time as – the lost time, the time regained and the time from time regained to time lost. Ricoeur discusses metaphor as the stylistic figure as he writes that the:

> …metaphorical relation, brought to light by the elucidation of happy moments, becomes the matrix for all the relations in which two distinct objects are, despite their differences, raised to their essence and liberated from the contingencies of time. [….]. Metaphor reigns where cinematographic vision, which is purely serial, fails to relate sensations and memories. [….]. Style, here, does not designate anything ornamental but the singular entity resulting from the union, in a unique work of art, of the questions from which it proceeds and the solutions it gives. Time regained, in this first sense, is time lost eternalised by metaphor.

In this way Ricoeur proceeds to the conclusion saying that "time envelops us" in narratives. Summing up the second volume of *Time and Narrative,* Ricoeur mentions the three-fold mimesis and the rule-governed compositions of tale with the mimetic relation, his broadening the concept of plot, the distinction between utterance and statement, and the great pain in taking up the game of time, Bakhtin's notion of novelisation and the comparison of epic and novel. Ricoeur tells us that that novel is born by the destruction of "epic distance" which is under pressure of the ridicule of the "Carnivalesque," therefore, "it is the epic distance that provides the definitive basis for opposing "low" literature to all the rest of the "high" literature." (153-55)

Ricoeur supports the opinion that the modern novel belongs to its time and there is a distance between fiction and the nature of the novel which is more complex than ever before. Ricoeur associates it with emplotment which enriches the very fabric of the text. It enriches the notion of action.

Ricoeur now moves to the historical and fictional configuration of time. He observes that historiography and literary criticism together would evolve a "grand narratology" by giving equal status to historical and fictional narratives; he adds that "both narrative modes are preceded by the use of narrative in daily life." The knowledge about the world comes through "hearsay" (including all the information and events). The act or the art of narrating requires a symbolic meditation of action that is related to the pre-mediatory state which Ricoeur already has discussed under the discussion of mimesis M1. Ricoeur also adds that both the modes follow the law and rule of emplotment equally, it is discovered at the end that historical and fictional narratives share the same configuring operation that historical explanation was confronted with, he opens up as:

> It was a plea for the precedence of narrative understanding over narratological rationality. The universal character of the formal principle of narrative configuration was thereby confirmed, to the extent that what this understanding confronts is the emplotment, taken in its most extreme formality, namely, the temporal synthesis of the heterogeneous. (158)

In this way, to a proper understanding of time, Ricoeur suggests that in the next volume he is going to discuss how historical and fictional intentions "interweave" by bringing up the world of the text and the awaiting emplotment of the life-world of the reader.

3.11 The World of the Text and the World of the Reader: A Hermeneutic Challenge

The third volume of *Time and Narrative* or the fourth part of the book completely deals with the narrated time. This last part contains two sections (1) "The Aporetics of Temporality" and (2)" The Poetics of Narrative: History, Fiction, Time." In the first part Ricoeur discusses the dispute between Augustine and Aristotle over the time of the soul and the time of the world. It also includes the confronting views of Husserl and Kant on intuitive and invisible time, summing up the first section of the last volume, Ricoeur also analyses Heidegger dwelling on temporality, historicality, within-time-ness and the ordinary concepts of time. The second section of the last part of *Time and Narrative* entirely deals with the lived and universal time – the historical time, fiction and its imaginative variations on time, reality of past, the world of the reader and the text, interweaving of history and fiction. He ends with the discussion of the hermeneutics of historical consciousness.

This is to state it here that the only section that is needed in the present quest is the "The World of the Text and the World of the Reader" for the present interest of the book in detail. Here, Ricoeur takes up the reality of past – history and the unreality of the past – fiction together. The pastness of the past is not observable as he reminds us again that "the literary text transcends itself in the direction of a world," which belongs to both the worlds – the internal and the external as adds Ricoeur here:

> … the world of the text marked the opening of the text to its "outside," to its "other," in that the world of the text constitutes an absolutely original intentional object in relation to its "internal" structure. It must be admitted, however, that apart from reading, the world of the text remains transcendence and immanence. Its ontological status remains in suspension – an excess in relation to structure, an anticipation in relation to reading. It is only in reading that the dynamism of configuration completes its course. And it is beyond reading, in effective action, instructed by the works handed down, that the configuration of the text is transformed into refiguration. In this way, we link up once again with the formulation whereby I define mimesis 3 in volume 1. Mimesis 3 I said, marks the intersection between the world of the text and the world of the listener or the reader, the intersection, therefore, between the world configured by the poem and the world within which effective action is unfolded and itself unfolds its specific temporality. The significance of the work of fiction stems from this intersection. (Ricoeur 158-59, Vol. III)

Ricoeur says that the theory of reading that according to him, in a way, falls in the field of Rhetoric similarly as persuasion in the art of Rhetoric. This is something which "sets up the act of reading as the supreme authority" which initially belongs to rhetoric but eventually "slips over into a phenomenology or hermeneutics." (166) Here Ricoeur includes Husserl, Ingarden, Iser and Jauss in his discussion through which arises a new dimension and enriching poetics of reader i. e. the "aesthetic" rather "rhetoric." Through aesthetic he takes its full range of meaning which Aristotle associated with his "aesthesis" including all multiple ways that affect the reader. The nature of being affected combines the experience of the reception of the text by the "act" of reading.

Amidst all of this, Ricoeur introduces three dialectics in the act of reading. The first one is that reading tends to become" response to the strategy of deception" as well projected in Joyce's *Ulysses.* Ricoeur writes that this strategy "consists in frustrating the expectation of an immediately intelligible configuration and placing on the reader's shoulder the burden of configuring the work." (168) The reader expects a configuration that "reading is a search for coherence." It designates the "lacuna of text with respect to image-building concretisation." Reading becomes "picnic where the author brings the words and the readers the meaning." Thus, the first dialectic gives rise to the second act of reading that reveals "not only a lack of determinacy but also an excess of meaning." Reading reveals "the unwritten side of the text." The third dialectic evolves on the horizon of the search of coherence, if it is successful the familiar becomes familiar the reader comes to believe in it and also loses himself within it. In this ease, Ricoeur writes that "[concretising] then becomes an illusion in the sense of believing that one actually sees something." (169) But unlikely if the search for coherence fails then "what is foreign remains foreign." The reader goes on some other train which may possibly leave him to some uneven horizons, for this Ricoeur adds:

> The "right" reading is, therefore, the one that admits a certain degree of illusion – another name for the "willing suspension of disbelief" called for by Coleridge – and at the same time accepts the negation resulting from the work's surplus of meaning, it's poly semanticism, which negates all the reader's attempts to adhere to the text and to its instructions. This process of "defamiliarising" on the side of the reader corresponds to that of depragmatising on the side of the text and its implied author. The "right" distance from the work is the one from which the illusion is, by turns, irresistible and untenable. As for a balance between these two impulses, it is never achieved. (169)

In conclusion, Ricoeur sums up saying that the power of refiguration belongs to the works of fiction and reading adds a new impetus to action and also becomes an interruption, "[these] two perspectives on reading result directly from its functions of confrontation and connection between the imaginary world of the text and the actual world of readers." (179) In the act of reading, the reader subordinates his expectations evolved from the text, for him they become "unreal to a degree comparable to the unreality of the fictive world towards which they emigrate," thus reading takes a place of unreal and reflective pauses. The configuration between the world of the text and the world of the reader at the same time becomes "a stasis and an impetus." Ricoeur is all praise to the contribution of Wolfgang Iser and Jauss at the end of his long and exhausting research, by talking of the ideal reading as:

> The ideal type of reading, figured by the fusion but not confusion of the horizons of expectation of the text and those of the reader, unites these two moments of refiguration in the fragile unity of stasis and impetus. This fragile union can be expressed in the following paradox: the more readers become unreal in their reading, the more profound and far-reaching will be the work's influence on social reality. (179)

Ricoeur concludes by writing that in fiction there are imaginary variations which lead to the "problem of the duality of the phenomenological and cosmological interpretations of time" and the "extreme concentration on temporality leads to a variety of limited experiences worthy of being placed under the sign of eternity." Moreover, he adds that "fiction multiplies our experiences of eternity," and "each work of fiction unfolds its own world," in every instance of the act of unfolding, "it is in a different possible world that time allows itself to be surpassed by eternity." It is the function of fiction which serves as "a laboratory for an unlimited number of thought experiments." Ricoeur also suggests that in other domains e. g. religion, ethics and politics a choice, accordingly, should be there but "the imaginary does not tolerate censorship." (271)

In this way, it seems very clear that "the lived temporal experiences" are "aporetic" or discordant and "the aporetics of time and the poetics of narrative correspond to each other" and – life is in a constant quest of narrative. Therefore, there comes a need for hermeneutic labor and the problem of interpretation of action too.

CHAPTER 4

'Exigesis,' Hermeneutics and the Textuality of Text

4.1 'Exigesis,' Hermeneutics and the Textuality of Text

4.1.1 Exegesis, Existence and Hermeneutics

This is to re-enter Ricoeur's Hermeneutic cosmos, the cosmos of his hermeneutics. In the beginning, when it was just an evolutionary stage of his scholarship, Ricoeur concentrated on the existential and the phenomenological aspects of hermeneutics through the structural and psychological hermeneutics to the final stage of his theory in his essays e. g. "Hermeneutics and Existence," (1974) "Structure and Hermeneutics," (1974) "Structure, Word, Event," (1974) "Phenomenology and Hermeneutics," (1981) "Consciousness and the Unconscious," (1974) "Psychoanalysis and the Movement of Contemporary Culture," (1974) "A Philosophical Interpretation of Freud," (1974) "The Hermeneutical Function of Distanciation," (1981) "What is a Text: Explanation and Understanding," (1981) "Metaphor and the Central Problem of Understanding," (1981) "The Model of the Text: Meaningful Action Considered as Text," (1981) "Appropriation" (1981) and "The Task of Hermeneutics" (1981).

Now coming back to Ricoeur's core ideas of the theory of interpretation and philosophy of hermeneutics, let us begin with Ricoeur's essay – "Existence and Hermeneutics," where he introduces his initial ideas of "the hermeneutic problem which was first raised within the limits of exegesis, that is, within the framework of a discipline which proposes to understand a text – to understand from its beginning with its intention, on the basis of what it attempts to say. If exegesis raised a hermeneutic problem, that is, a problem of interpretation, it is because the very reading of a text always takes within a community, a tradition, or a living current of thought, all of which display presuppositions and exigencies-regardless of how closely a reading may be tied to the quid, to "that in view of which" the text was written.

The term exegesis implies the entire theory of sign and signification only. Ricoeur mentions that there are instances that a text is capable of having multiple meanings e. g. a historical meaning and a spiritual meaning and there is a "notion of signification" that is extremely complex; and that is more than "the so-called univocal signs." Thus, the work of interpretation "reveals a profound intention, that of overcoming distance and cultural differences and matching the reader to a text." Then looking at its meaning in present comprehension, tells Ricoeur, "a man is able to have himself." In this way, according to Ricoeur, hermeneutics does not stand only for the interpretation of oracles and marvels – rather possess a general problem of comprehension!

Ricoeur mentions the concept of "general hermeneutic" as a second development after "exegesis," which was the classical philology and "historical sciences" at the crossroads of the eighteenth and nineteenth century. Ricoeur states that it is with Schleiermacher who is the father of modern hermeneutics, and Wilhelm Dilthey wherewith the hermeneutic problem becomes a philosophical problem: Dilthey's problem, in the age of positivistic philosophy was to give to the Geisteswissensch after validity comparable to that of the natural sciences. Posed in these terms, the problem was epistemological; it was a question of elaborating a critique of historical knowledge of nature and of subordinating to this critique the diverse procedures of classical hermeneutics: the laws of internal textual connection, of context, of geographic, ethnic and social environments, etc. But the resolution of the problem exceeded the resources of mere epistemology. An interpretation, like Dilthey's, bound to information fixed by writing is a province of the much vaster domain of understanding, extending from one psychic life to another psychic life. ("Existence and Hermeneutics," 5)

Ricoeur puts a question by saying that if hermeneutics is seen from the perspective of psychology, then "to understand a finite being, is to be transported into another life" as Dilthey says –a man is "a man totality–in- himself." Ricoeur now opens up another new chapter when he says:

> Historical understanding thus involves all the paradoxes of historicity: how can a historical being understand history historically? These paradoxes, in turn, lead back to a much more fundamental

> question: in expressing itself, how can life objectify itself, and, in objectifying itself, how does it bring to light meanings capable of being taken up and understood by another historical being, who overcomes his own historical situation? A major problem [….] of our investigation is thus raised: the problem of the relationship between force and meaning, between life as the bearer of meaning and the mind as capable of linking into a coherent series. If life is not originally meaning, understanding is forever impossible, but in order for this understanding to be fixed, is it not necessary to ease back to life itself the logic of immanent development which Hegel called concept? Do we not then surreptitiously provide ourselves with all the resources of a philosophy of the spirit just when we are formulating a philosophy of life? (5-6)

According to Ricoeur, the above-mentioned problem in the paragraph is solved by a phenomenological method. He describes two ways to ground hermeneutics in phenomenology, calling them short and long routes: the short one is the "ontology of understanding," the understanding of finite being, that is not a mode of knowledge" but as a "mode of being." To enter this mode, Ricoeur says that we do not get in little by little or degrees, or by "methodological requirement of exegesis, history, or psychology." It is only, according to Ricoeur, by means of "a sudden reversal of question or it's a moment laddered with the experience of essence or meaning. Ricoeur argues that instead of asking "on what condition can a knowing subject understand a text or history?" One may ask such as "what kind of being is it whose being consists of understanding?" This is what is generally called the understanding of Dasein. Thus, the hermeneutic problem becomes the subject, being of the language and the being that is neither out nor inside of all these. Professor Ricoeur makes a choice to take the long route, the linguistic or semantic consideration. Ricoeur, keeping the view of ontological understanding, moves from it to pose certain problems such as:

> My problem will be exactly this: what happens to an epistemology of interpretation, born of a reflection on exegesis, on the method of history, on psychoanalysis, on the phenomenology of religion, etc. when it is touched, animated, and, as we might say, inspired by the ontology of understanding? (7)

Ricoeur observes the paradigm shift that "[we] see the degree of radicality to which the problem of understanding and that of truth are carried." Going back to the concept of historicity in hermeneutics, Ricoeur declares that the "question of historicity is no longer the question of historical knowledge conceived as a method. Now, it designates the manner in which the existent "is with" existents." Here, Ricoeur rejects the concepts of the old notion of understanding that is "no longer the response of human sciences to the naturalistic explanation; it involves a manner of being akin to being, prior to the encounter with particular beings." Ricoeur writes more specifically about the transcended concept of history and being as:

> At the same time, life's ability to freely stand at a distance in respect to itself, to transcend itself, becomes the structure of an infinite being. If the historian can measure himself against the thing itself, if he can compare himself to the known, it is because both he and his object are historical. Making this historical character explicit is thus prior to any methodology. What was a limit to science – namely, the historicity of being – becomes a constituting element of being. What was a paradoxnomely, the relation of the interpreter to his object – becomes an ontological trait. Such is the revolution brought about by the ontology of understanding. Understanding becomes an aspect of Dasein's "project" and of its openness to being. The question of truth is no longer the question of method; it is the question of the manifestation of being for a being whose existence consists in understanding being. (9-10)

Ricoeur radically criticizes the ontology of understanding as it poses "the extraordinarily seductive power"; this is the reason that he explores another path in a different manner. For the justification of this diversion, Ricoeur puts some questions such as "How, we ask, can a canon be given to exegesis, to the clear comprehension of texts? How can historical science be founded in the face of the natural sciences? How can the conflict of rival interpretations be arbitrated? These problems are not properly considered in a fundamental hermeneutics and this by design: thus, hermeneutics is intended not to resolve them but to dissolve them. (10)

On Heidegger: according to Ricoeur, Heidegger did not specify and consider 'this' or 'that' being clearly. His only aim was to realise and look forward to gazing at subordinate historical knowledge with the ontology of understanding "derived form of a primordial form." Ricoeur claims that Heidegger does not show how historical understanding is derived from that mode. Ricoeur asks that – "Is it not better, then, to begin with the derived forms of understanding and to show in them the signs of their derivation?" (10). According to Ricoeur, the understanding of Dasein or understanding of being takes place within one's being itself:

> The difficulty in passing from understanding as a mode of knowledge to understanding as a mode of being consists in the following: the understanding which is the result of the Analytic of Dasein is precisely the understanding through which and in which this being understands it as being. Is it not once again within language itself that we must seek the indication that understanding is a mode of being? (10-11)

Thus, according to Ricoeur, understanding operates on the level of language; this is the point Ricoeur is confidently moving from the ontology of understanding to the epistemology of interpretation that is only by the analysis of language. Ricoeur explains why and how he tries to reach the question of existence by semantic analysis:

> A purely semantic elucidation remains suspended until one shows that the understanding of multifocal or symbolic expression is a moment of self-understanding; the semantic approach thus entails a *reflective* approach. But the subject that interprets himself while interpreting signs is no longer the *cogito:* rather, he is a being who discovers, by the exegesis of his own life, that he is placed in being before he places and possesses himself. In this way, hermeneutics would discover a manner of existing which would remain from start to finish a *being-interpreted.* Reflection alone, by suppressing itself as reflection, can reach the ontological roots of understanding. Yet this is what always happens in language and it occurs through the movement of reflection. (11)

4.1.2 Symbol and Symbolic Expression

In this connection, Ricoeur comes close to his soul discussion of semantic level, and his well-defined arena, the "symbolism of evil," that is a "multi-vocal expression," generally called "symbolic." A symbol to Ricoeur is "any structure of signification in which a direct, primary, literal meaning designates, in addition, another meaning which is indirect, secondary, and figurative and which can be apprehended only through the first." Ricoeur announces that this is the field of hermeneutics and the "circumscription of expressions with a double meaning."

Having defined a symbol, Ricoeur turns to another very important word – turned-term-that is "interpretation," which also, in a way, recovers distinct and distant meaning. Ricoeur gives this term the same extension as does with symbol. According to him, it is the "work of thought which consists in deciphering the hidden meaning in the apparent meaning, in unfolding the levels of meaning implied in the literal meaning." In this way "symbol" and "interpretation" naturally become correlative. Thus, there is "interpretation," whenever there is a "symbolic." It is an interpretation that brings into light the extended multiple meanings and manifests in the plurality of meaning.

This delimitation of the field of semantics – the symbolic interpretation, says Ricoeur, has "a certain number of tasks." For symbolic expression, the task of linguistic analysis is of twofold: first, "the matter of beginning an enumeration of symbolic forms which will be as full and as complete as possible." This is the only way to access the investigation, thus Ricoeur elaborates the first nature of the symbolic:

> This enumeration should include the cosmic symbols brought to light by a phenomenology of religion (…); the dream symbolism revealed by psychoanalysis with all its equivalents in folklore, legends, proverbs, and myths; the verbal creations of the poet, following the guideline of sensory, visual, acoustic, or other images or following the symbolism space and time. In spite of their being grounded in different ways– in the physiognomical qualities of the cosmos, in sexual symbolism, in sensory imagery – all their symbolisms find their expression in the element of language. There is no symbolism before man speaks, even if the power of the symbol is grounded much deeper. It is in language that the cosmos, desire, and the imaginary reach expression, speech, is always necessary if the world is to be recovered and made hierophany. Likewise, dreams remain closed to us until they have been carried to the level of language through narration. (13)

Turning towards the "symbolic expression" and its operations of interpretation Ricoeur focuses on the problems given by symbolic expression in the methodology of interpretation, alluding to the phenomenology of religion, and psychoanalysis. Ricoeur makes a distinction between Freudian hermeneutics and philosophical hermeneutics. For him, Freud only "confines the rules of decipherment to what could be called a semantic of desire." It can only find and reach to what it searches for – the economic "meaning of representations and affects operating in dreams, neuroses, art, morality and religion". Thus, Ricoeur claims that Freud cannot trace anything other than the "disguised expressions of representations and affects belonging to the most archaic of man's desires," which gives only a single level of semantics. Philosophical hermeneutics "begins by an expanding investigation into symbolic forms and by a comprehensive analysis of symbolic structures." It happens by the confrontation and varying hermeneutic styles and by the critical analysis of symbols of interpretation. The critical function of this hermeneutics is purely semantic.

Coming to the level of reflection and the expression of double or multiple meanings, Ricoeur claims that "a semantic of expression with multiple meanings is not enough to qualify hermeneutics as a philosophy." This linguist analysis treats those multiple "signification as a whole closed in on itself," the language as an absolute. "This hypothesis of language," according to Ricoeur, "repudiates the basic intention of a sign, which is to hold "for," thus transcending itself and suppressing itself, in what it intends." (16) In this way, language itself, being as a "signifying milieu" should be referred to as "existence." Re-visiting Heidegger, Ricoeur says that "what animates the movement of surpassing the linguistic level is the desire for an ontology." Furthermore, Ricoeur adds that "it is the demand this ontology makes for an analysis which would remain a prisoner of language." Thus, according to Ricoeur semantics and ontology which in the beginning of this discussion seemed quite difficult? This intermediate step in the direction of existence is "Reflection." This is the link between the understanding of signs and self-understanding, because, this is, "in the self that we have the opportunity to discover an existence." By the effort to relate symbolic language to self-understanding, Ricoeur says that he fulfills "the deepest wish of hermeneutics," according to Ricoeur:

> The purpose of all interpretation is to conquer a remoteness, a distance between the past cultural epoch to which the text belongs and the interpretes himself. By overcoming this distance, by making himself contemporary with the text, the exegete can appropriate its meaning to himself: foreign, he makes it familiar, that is, he makes it his own. It is thus the growth of his understanding of himself that he pursues through his understanding of the other. Every hermeneutics is thus, explicitly, or implicitly, self-understanding by means of understanding others. (16-17)

4.1.3 The Problematic of the Cogito

Ricoeur makes another extension to hermeneutics saying that hermeneutics should not be the only graft on the phenomenological level, but "also at the level of the problematic of the "*cogito*," that is purely Cartesian dictum. Talking about "*cogito*" as an object of his thought, Ricoeur seems curious that how it is enriched and deepens by this recourse to hermeneutics," before thinking that "how the cogito is exploded," he first tries to reflect upon "what the self of the self-understanding signifies, whether we appropriate the sense of an analytic interpretation or that of textual exegesis." Ricoeur mentions two reasons why it is that "we do not know beforehand, but only after word," and why does the self through which the interpretation is guided, able to recover the self-itself, only as a result of the interpretation for this, Ricoeur says:

> The celebrated Cartesian *cogito*, which grasps itself directly in the experience of doubt, is a truth as vain as it is invincible. Do not deny that it is a truth; it is a truth which posits itself, and as such it can be neither verified nor deduced. It posits at once a being and an act, an existence and an operation of thought: I am, I think; to exist, for me, is to think; I exist *insofar as* I think. But this truth is a vein truth; it is like a first step which cannot be followed by any other, so long as the *ego* of the *ego cogito* has not been recaptured in the mirror of its objects, of its works, and, finally, of its acts. Reflection is blind intuition if it is not mediated by what Dilthey called the expressions in which life objectifies itself. (17)

After the minute operation of Descartes' *cogito* and relating it to Freud's ego as to exist to me is to think at first, and necessary as if "I" has to exist and "thinking," that is an act of linguistic competence, cognitive or pragmatic in nature. Thus, to exist is necessary, and for existing is "thinking" vis-a-viz in reverse. Then, what is that thinking which becomes the base of existence as – *cogito*? Where and how does this thinking come? Should we trust our existence which is primarily based on our thinking, which comes passing through our "false or fake-consciousness?" Can we trust our existence? Or, what is that we reflect, either in ontology or epistemology? Referring to Jean Nabert, Ricoeur specifies that "reflection is nothing other than the appropriation of our act of existing by means of a critique applied to the works and the acts which are the signs of this act of existing." The cogito, in Ricoeur's view, is "an empty place" which has all the time been occupied by a false cogito! According to Ricoeur, the so-called immediate consciousness that is actually a "false consciousness" has to unmask its tricks, which has already been done by Marx, Nietzsche, and Freud. In this way, "it becomes necessary to join a critique of false consciousness to any rediscovery of the subject of the *cogito* in the documents of its life." That is why, to Ricoeur, the philosophy of reflection should just be the opposite of a philosophy of consciousness. Because, the "I" of cogito is not able to recapture itself only within the expression of life that objectifies it; and the "textual exegesis of consciousness," in Ricoeur's view, "collides with the initial "misinterpretation" of false consciousness." Thus, suggests Ricoeur, that it is, for all the times necessary "to rise by means of a corrective critique from misunderstanding to understanding." (17-18)

Coming from the problematic of ontology to the dialectic of language and reflection we now join the problem of existence. Commenting on Heidegger's ontology of understanding that is for knowing and considering it as a mode of being, Ricoeur states, about this notion of being and knowing that "separate ontology is beyond our grasp: it is only within the movement of interpretation that we preserve the being we interpret." The ontology of understanding, by Ricoeur, is also included in the methodology of interpretation. As in his view, "it is only in a conflict of rival hermeneutics that we perceive something of the being to be interpreted, while on the other hand, comparatively, "a unified ontology is as inaccessible to our method as a separate ontology." Thus, each hermeneutics discovers the aspect of existence. Now, talking of philosophical reflection on psychoanalysis, Ricoeur explores that:

> "What can we expect from the latter in the way of a fundamental ontology? Two things: first, a true dismissal of the classical problem of the subject as consciousness; then, a restoration of the problematic of existence as desire." (19)

It is indeed through a critique of consciousness that psychoanalysis points to ontology. The interpretation it proposes to us of dreams, fantasies, myths and symbols always contests to some extent the pretension of consciousness in setting itself up as the origin of meaning. The struggle against narcissism and the Freudian equivalent of the false *cogito* leads to the discovery that Language is deeply rooted in desire, in the instinctual impulses of life. The philosopher who surrenders himself to this strict schooling is led to practice a true access of subjectivity allowing himself to be dispossessed of the origin of meaning. (20)

In this connection, the abandonment is linked again to reflection, which becomes a "loss of the most archaic subject: the self," as is the loss with psychoanalysis, which is expected to be found again symbolically. Ricoeur says that the philosophy of reflection "must integrate this discovery with its own task," he further adds:

> The self [*le moi*] must be lost in order to find the "I" [*leje*].... The most archaic signification is organised in a "place" of meaning that is separate from the place where immediate consciousness reigns. The realism of the unconscious, the topographic and economic treatment of representations, fantasies, symptoms, and symbols, appear finally

> as a condition of a hermeneutics free from the prejudices of the ego. (20)

4.1.4 Psychoanalysis and Hermeneutics

Thus, Ricoeur comes close to the conclusion pondering over "how is the order of significations included within the order of life?" In his view, this progression that is from meaning to desire is the mark of "a possible transcendence of reflection in the direction of existence." After the understanding of ourselves, says Ricoeur, "we appropriate ourselves" and, thus in this way, "the meaning of our desire to be or of our effort to exist." Therefore, in this way existence becomes-to effort and-to desire. The existence that psychoanalysis brings into prominence is that of the archeology of man's deepest desire – where, to exist is to desire first. This is the hermeneutics of psychoanalysis, while on the other is the hermeneutics of spirit, the hermeneutics of gods coming, which suggests another manner of shifting the origin of sense that is a hermeneutics of representing the prophecy of consciousness. Ricoeur makes a minute and meticulous observation, by comparing these two different kinds of modes of hermeneutics with psychoanalysis and hermeneutics of phenomenology:

> This is what animates Hegel's *Phenomenology of the Spirit.* I mention it here because its mode of interpretation is diametrically opposed to Freud's Psychoanalysis offered us a regression toward the archaic; the phenomenology of the spirit offers us a movement in which each figure finds its meaning, not in what precedes but in what follows. Consciousness is thus drowning outside itself, in front of itself, toward a meaning in motion, where each stage is suppressed and retained in the following stage. (21-22)

Ricoeur asserts that this is the reason that philosophy is identified as a hermeneutics in which hidden meanings are traced and deciphered that are in and outside the text. And, thus, it becomes the task of hermeneutics to project and bring the meaning into prominence – that existence first arrives at its expression, its meaning and at its reflection. In this way existence naturally becomes a self, a human and an adult only through the appropriation of the, meaning, which first of all "resides outside," in works, institutions and cultured monuments," wherein, in Ricoeur's view, "the life of all spirit is objectified" each hermeneutics, in a way or the other, "affirms the dependence of the self upon existence." Psychoanalysis, thus, projects its dependence on the archeology of the subject, the hermeneutics of phenomenology of the spirit on the teleology of figures, and the phenomenology of religion on the sacred and divine signs, or on eschatology-all are the examples of the "ontological implications of interpretation." In spite of the precariousness of ontological understanding, it is not merely a language game in Ricoeur's view. On the other hand, he says in linguistic philosophy, "all interpretations are equally valid with the limits of the theory which finds the given rules of reading." According to Ricoeur these language games remain equally valid "until it is shown that each interpretation is grounded in a particular existential function." In the ending, Ricoeur seems to be helpless in his argument for the solution of the problem – that how can these three, the dialectic of archaeology, the problematic of teleology and the problem of eschatology be brought together in a unitary mode or circle? Ricoeur mentions that Heidegger also faces the same problem of making these three dimensions unitary. Though he tries resolving the problem in the second half of his *Being and Time*, as a being, coherent of all these figures, which we are, wherein rival interpretations are implanted – is only within the dialectic of interpretation. Thus, in this connection, "hermeneutics is," according to Ricoeur only "a hermeneutics instructed by symbolic figure can show that these different modalities of existence belong to a single problematic," for it is,' adds Ricoeur, "through the richest symbols that the unity of these multiple interpretations are assured." These rich symbols have all the vectors of both kinds; the regressive and progressive. For Ricoeur, "true symbols contain all hermeneutics." The symbols, which are potential for "the emergence of new meanings," and also for those, "which are directed toward the resurgence of archaic fantasies." (20-23)

Unsurpassable, existence as it relates to a hermeneutic philosophy "always remains an interpreted existence." It is only interpretation through which different modes of the self – in the philosophy of language are discovered, as "its dependence on desire glimpsed in an archeology of the subject, it's on the spirit glimpsed in its teleology," moreover, "its dependence on the glimpsed in its eschatology." Thus, ontology is, in this way, a "promised land" for philosophy that begins with language and with reflection. The reflection which "suppresses itself as reflection," just like the prophet Moses' (PBUH) community, would die after having a glimpse of the Speaking and the Reflecting Subject in life. (24) One of the grafts of hermeneutics according to

Ihde, of Ricoeur, is the question of faith. The hermeneutics of belief is in latent religious sense as comments Don Ihde:

> With the question of faith in the background, the dialectic of hermeneutics which emerges is one which counter plays those interpretations of meanings which demythise with existential *cum* religious significations with those which seek a "recovery' of "forgotten" significations. (XVII)

"Hermeneutics of faith," that is motivated by the "willingness to listen" and respect the object as a revelation of the sacred, and, in the "hermeneutics of suspicion" comparatively, is in contrast. There is skepticism from willingness to listen, and a rejection of the respect of the object. After a suspicious hermeneutics, the simple faith cannot be recovered. For its survival, it should be informed and a critical faith, which should also be an object of criticism e. g. demythologisation. "Demythologisation," writes Ihde, "is a process of interpretation which accepts the loss of all pretensions to direct "rationality" in symbolic discourse, but at the same time this loss is seen as the way towards a freeing, a recovery, of the symbolic – existential dimension." The symbol word opens the ways which explore the possibilities of men to the understanding of the sacred. Thus, Freud without his unconscious mind, and Hegel without his "Absolute Idea" do not appear the same. Here, the respective justifying metaphysics is now removed through hermeneutics.

4.2.. The Textuality of Text

4.2.1. Text and Discourse

This is to shift the focus now from metaphor and Hermeneutics of metaphor to text and textuality. With reference to the essays discussed earlier. This quest will again reflect on the world of discourse, event, distanciation, text and self-understanding in a bit of detail. The central focus will rest on distanciation, text and self-understanding. It will dowel the focus on our problem between writing and text as the text is not simply identified within writing. To be more specific, this is to state that we will examine and analyse the essay "The Hermeneutic Function of Distanciation" first and later at the end of this chapter the last essay will be "What is a text? Explanation and Understanding" to complete the present debate that we have here; herein will talk on certain issues i. e. the realisation of language as discourse, discourse as work, world of the text, and lastly, the self-understanding: a subjective turn which seems to be predominant problem in Ricoeur. For him, as text is not simply identified only because "it is not writing as such which gives rise to the hermeneutical problem, but the dialectic of speaking and writing." The dialectic that Ricoeur mentions is basically "constructed upon a dialectic of distanciation" which according to him is "more primitive" than the opposition which is in between speaking and writing. This opposition is associated with the oral tradition of discourse. Ricoeur seems to be in search of the most primitive "roots of all subsequent dialectics"; he suggests searching for these primitive dialectics and ends this dispute with the realisation of language as discourse which is a "structured work." He thinks that the objectification of language in the "work of discourse constituted the proximate condition of the inscription of discourse in writing." (131)

Thus, in the world of the text Ricoeur finds the "gravity of the Hermeneutical question," and says that there is a way of displacing the problem of the text towards that of the world which it opens up. The confrontation with this new open world emerges as the problem of self-understanding. The world of discourse bases the "primitive types of distanciation." This seems a challenge to understand what Ricoeur is trying to say. Is he trying to translate Northrop Frye, or other myth critics? Ricoeur calls it the deflection of events. For him it is "something which happens when someone speaks." This notion of discourse as an event is actually when we consider the passage moving from linguistics of language to the linguistics of discourse or message." (132)

There are two stages of discourses: one is when it does not appear in the virtual time, though it is there but not spoken. Second, when it gets a proper identity and appears in real time. At first a language had no subject, nevertheless it gets a subject in the second category as: "who speaks?" and this discourse refers back to its speaker, then the event is now seen associated with the person as well. This becomes openly self-referential. Therefore, discourse is always about something "it refers to a world which it claims to describe, express or represent." When the virtual element of discourse is transformed from speech to writing it becomes a "purely external and material factor." Discourse is presented by its fixation in the web of writing, "it shelters the events of discourse from destruction," the fixation in writing thus becomes important. Paul Ricoeur in this connection gets externally close to Roland Barthes when he says that writing makes the text "autonomous with respect to the intention of the author." Here, in another way, the text no longer, according to Ricoeur, coincides with whatever at the time of writing the author meant. That is why the "psychological" and "textual" seem to be separated into two different directions. Thus appears a duality here: one is that the "text may escape from the finite intentional horizon of its author" and second on the contrary adds Ricoeur attributing to writing as "the world of the text may explode the world of the author." The psychological aspect of the discourse gets sociological conditions in the contraction of the text. The literary work transcends its psycho-linguistic conditions with the text. Therefore, it opens up with endless and "unlimited series of reading," which is associated with so many different socio-cultural conditions. According to Ricoeur, "the text must be able, from sociological as well as psychological point of view to 'contextualise' itself in such a way that it can be 'recontextualise' in a new situation so that it could get accomplished, precisely, by the act of reading. (134-39)

Thus, it is writing which displaces the discourse and, in the result, it does not remain in relation to the speaking-hearing domain. It gets fated with the dialogical condition of reading. The written and fixed discourse extends the audience; anyone can read it by getting into the dialogical process. The impression of discourse gets changed. Ricoeur observes that the "passage from speaking to writing affects discourse in several other ways." By confronting the theory of Romantic hermeneutics including Dilthey, he recalls that Romantic hermeneutics laid emphasis on the expression of genius; therefore, it was a prime task of hermeneutics. The notion of the world of the text extends to the nation of 'reference' which he now calls "denotation of discourse." The reference for him is the truth value which claims to access or reach reality. Ricoeur following Frege also distinguishes clearly between 'sense' and 'reference'. For this, the sense, he writes, is "the ideal object which the preposition intends," it is "purely immanent in discourse." The 'reference' is the "truth value of the proposition", something which claims to be close to the reality it refers to. It separates discourse from language and later it stands in no relation with reality. At this point it is only discourse which "intends things" and further it "applies itself to reality." Through this process, it exposes the world. Here arises another problem at the time when the discourse becomes a text: what all happens when something gets the textual identity? Because in oral discourse "the problem is ultimately resolved by the ostensive function of discourse." Because in the oral discourse the "here" and "now" are determined by the specific situation of the discourse. Whereas on the other hand, with 'writing' things appear quite different. Here writers and readers both have no such situation, for Ricoeur "the abolition of the ostensive character of reference" constitutes the identity of literature. This 'literature' has intrinsic quality and capacity to abolish all references associated here to a given, particular and specific reality. On the cost of abolition certain types of literary genes are associated and linked with writing. Ricoeur thinks that literature may play a role in destroying the world. He claims it to be true with fictional literature and literature that is also categorised as poetic for him. This happens, writes Ricoeur, when and "where language seems to glorify the function of ordinary discourse," although he believes that "there is no discourse so fictional that it does not connect up with reality." (140-41) Ricoeur's thesis on the current problem of reference in writing is this when he writes that:

> The abolition of a first order reference, an abolition affected by fiction and poetry, is the condition of possibility for the freeing of second order reference, which reaches the world not only at the level of manipulable objects, but at the level that Husserl designated by the expression *Le-benswelt* [life-world] and Heidegger by the expression 'being-in-the-world.' (141)

Thus, the notion of the secondary referential dimension appears to be the "most fundamental hermeneutical problem." This is the result of fixation. If hermeneutics are not able to bring out and project the psychological insertion concealed inside the text and do not dismantle its structure. What else remains untouched here, and what else would be left uninterpreted? Ricoeur answers it as "to interpret is to explicate the type of being-in-the – world unfolded in front of the text" (141). In this description, Ricoeur gets very close to Heidegger's concept of "being-in-the-world," given in *Being and Time*. For this, Ricoeur writes that "the moment of understanding' corresponds directly to being in a situation, "exactly at the same moment we also have the "projection of our own most possibilities" in the situation where we are as human in real time. Ricoeur applies this notion of possibilities with the text, which, according to him, "must be interpreted in a text." This is a "proposed world" where, Ricoeur thinks; he can inhabit and also project one of his own most possibilities. This is the way of understanding a text in Ricoeur's corpus of subjective wholeness.

This world of the text is not, according to Ricoeur, the language of everyday language, "it constitutes a new sort of distanciation." This is something he calls "a distanciation of the real from itself." For fiction and for poetry Ricoeur writes, both "intend being, not under the modality of being-given, but under the modality of power to be," where tells Ricoeur that "fiction is the privileged path for the rediscription of reality" on one hand, and on the other hand "the poetic language is *par excellence*." (141-3)

4.2.2 Appropriation and Distanciation

While discussing the metaphorical language, Ricoeur relates it with Aristotle's concepts of *mimesis* of reality as "tragedy imitates reality only because it recreates it by means of a mythos, a 'fable' which reaches the profound essence of reality." Ricoeur teaches us that this is the "third sort of distanciation which the hermeneutic experience must incorporate." In the fifth section of the essay "The hermeneutical function of distanciation," that is the self-understanding in confrontation with this opens a fourth dimension of text which appears as a medium to understand ourselves. The fourth dimension of the text, says Ricoeur, constitutes "the subjectivity of the reader," which in his view "extends the fundamental characteristics of all discourse written or spoken. The second one: the written discourse – is in the dialogic framework; in its reception with the written text the instant subjectivity is absent. The same as in oral discourse is not found here with the written discourse. The gap or the gulf has to be filled with the work itself. The work itself opens up its reader and "creates its own subjectivity vis-à-vis." (143)

With this understanding of text arises a new problem of 'appropriation' that is well known in traditional hermeneutics. The concept of 'appropriation' is dialectically associated with the notion of distanciative characteristic of writing. This distanciation is not abolished by appropriation as each of them is counterparts for each one. "Appropriation" for Ricoeur is the "understanding at and through distance," it is also linked dialectically with "the objectification characteristic of work. Appropriation corresponds to the 'sense' rather than the author. Therefore, according to Ricoeur, we understand ourselves "only by the long detour of signs of humanity deposited in cultural work." (143) Ricoeur asks, "what would we know... that we call the self?" If it would not have been recorded in language and expressed through literature? According to Ricoeur, in this way the "most contrary to subjectivity and structural analysis discloses the texture of the text... is the very medium within which we can understand ourselves." Ricoeur agrees that appropriation is the same thing that Gadamer calls – 'the matter of the text.' This is what Ricoeur himself calls 'the world of work.' For him this 'world' is not believing if it is true, Ricoeur admits that the concept of 'appropriation' seems to be "directed against 'Verfremdung'" and therefore, needs an internal critique. In connection with "[the] metamorphosis of ego" writes Ricoeur, "implies a moment of distanciation in the relation of self to itself." Thus, for Ricoeur, 'understating' becomes 'appropriation' and 'misappropriation,' he suggests that the illusion of the subject should be put to be examined under the Marxist and Freudian concepts incorporated with the castle of 'self-understanding'. Here hermeneutics become most important and one should not stand against criticising the illusion of subjectivity or whenever the same gets developed and shaped as ideology. Ricoeur tells us that "the critique of ideology is a necessary detour which self-understanding must take," if the ideology is supposed to be formed on "the matter of the text" rather on "the prejudices of the reader." Thus, for the very heart of self-understanding, explanation taken at the "level of text, it structures its sense and its reference," therefore, distanciation is a must for understanding and its analysis as well. (132-144)

4.2.3 Ricoeur's Understanding of Text

Moving toward the understanding of the textuality of text, we will dwell on the essay – "What is a Text? Explanation and Understanding" which seems to be the Ricoeurian manifesto of his textual hermeneutics. It is divided into four sections: 'What is a text?' 'Explanation or Understanding,' and 'Towards a New Concept of Interpretation.' Ricoeur mentions two distinct accounts of similar attitudes with a fine difference, specifically W. Dilthey's views on 'explanation' and 'interpretation.' Before Ricoeur, it was Dilthey who summed two concepts up as one for natural sciences and the second for human sciences. This is Ricoeur who examines the fate of these two oppositions and the internal conflicts. Ricoeur stands against Diltheyean notion of the understanding of the word 'explanation.'

Before discussing the essay, which starts with the understanding of text, we will have a look at the same that what other writers have written and said about text in short. The word 'text' is derived from Latin – 'texture' or 'textum' meaning "to weave." 'Text' in the community of critics, especially structuralists and poststructuralists do not consider a 'work' or a literary 'product' rather an impersonal text. This is Roland Barthes in 1968 who talked about text loudly and significantly in his epoch-making essay "The Death of the Author." (1968) According to the structuralists and poststructuralist critics, the linguistic system and literary conventions constitute a literary text. Roland Barthes in his *S/Z* (1970) proposes a distinction between a text which is 'legible' or 'readable' and a text which is 'scriptable' or writable meaning 'illisible' that is 'unreadable.' Barthes in his work "The Pleasure of the Text" (1973) assigns the readable text, the response of mere "plaisir" – that is 'quasi-erotic' pleasure and the unreadable text to the response of "jouissance" – the 'orgasmic ecstasy.' There appears another work of Stanley Fish in (1967) "Surprised by Sin: The Reader in Paradise Lost," and the famous one, a reader-oriented account of the understanding of the text, a more influential one – "Is There a Text in This class?" (1980).

Not discussing much of what writers before Ricoeur have said and written, we will start from Ricoeur himself, this is because of the limitations that present study has. For Ricoeur, 'text' is "any discourse fixed by writing," the fixation is essentially a constituent of text. "Any discourse" may be virtual in the pre-linguistic abstract stage (langue) or may be linguistic or written text (parole). In an event of discourse, "writing as an institution is subsequent to linear script, all the articulations that have already appeared orally." If the text is a discourse fixed, it is "a discourse that could be said," but because it is not said but written. Here in this way of understanding in the process of "fixation" by writing takes the very place of speech that could have emerged." (146) Then this "writing" tells Ricoeur "calls for reading," And this act of reading invites the concept of interpretation. Reading is not an instance of dialogue with the author. The relation of the reader to the book is different to that of a dialogue, as a "dialogue is an exchange of questions and answers." Whereas between the reader and writer there is not like that but a book involves two acts, act of writing and act of reading. The following image will explain the reader-writer diachotomy:

Ricoeur thinks as…

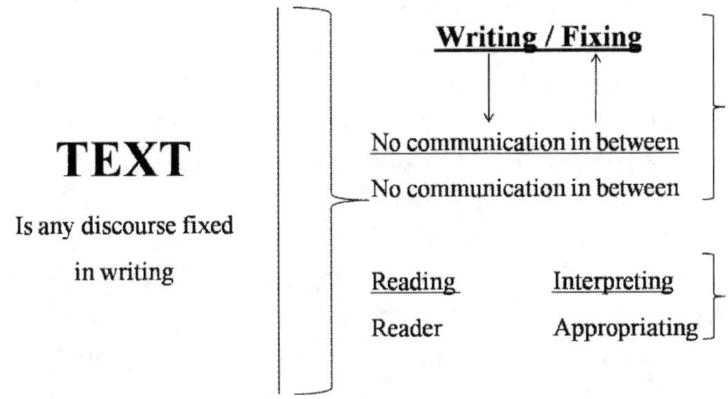

Ricoeur shows us that the "reader is absent from the writing process." Thus, in this way the text experiences "a double eclipse of the reader and the writer." Similar as Barthes in 1968 announced the *death of the author*, Ricoeur writes that, "to read a book is to consider its author as already dead and the book as posthumous." (147) It is as the writer is no longer able to respond. The only thing that is left is the act of reading his work. Ricoeur makes a difference between dialogue and reading as:

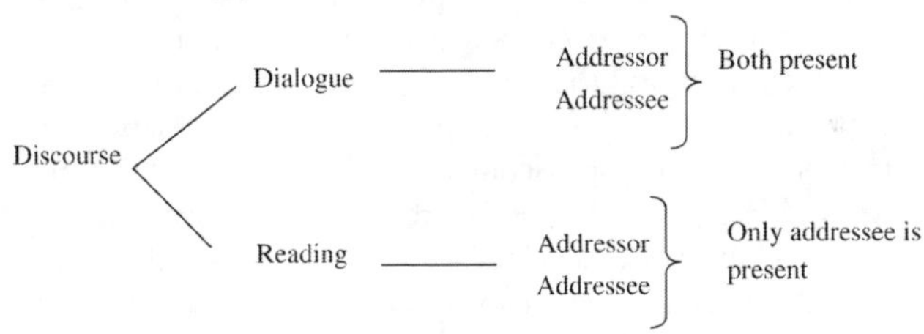

For writing, Ricoeur observes that it is a "realisation comparable and parallel to speech, a realisation that takes place of it and, as it were, intercepts it." Thus, within this writing process comes a direct inscription of discourse and the intention within it, "the emancipation of writing, which places the latter at the site of speech, is the birth of the text." Ricoeur thinks that when the statement is directly pronounced, it just passes away in general but it is written that "preserves discourse and makes it an archive available for individuals and collective memory." This is the point where our common sense would put an objection, a valid objection against the prejudice with speech, as it lacks something preserving discourse and being unavailable, speeches, it is a fact now, are preserved, or can preserve discourse in the same way as the written text. In fact, now speeches as a text are more preserving and safe than any written document. Ricoeur becomes ignorant of this fact. Modern technology has brought back those primitive days in the sense that speeches can be saved in the same way as people might have thought at the invention of printing. Now written and spoken are equally safe and preserved. Now the discourse can be preserved and archived for future generations that man would have ever imagined. Now texts in speeches are more easily accessible than texts written – a new attitude towards the modern discourse. Nevertheless, Ricoeur observes that the "emancipation of the text from the oral situation entails a veritable upheaval in the relation between language and the world as well as in the relation between language and various subjectivities concerned (that of the author and that of the reader)." Ricoeur goes further saying that there is a same upheaval when the referential function of language undergoes at the time when the text takes the place of speech. The subject of the discourse, which is referential, says something about something, it is as addressor to addressed. This referential function which gets us back to the inherent world, it sends us to the universe closed in the text: Ricoeur explains about speach in the following way:

> When the text takes the place of speech, something important occurs. In speech, the interlocutors are present not only to one another but also to the situation, the surroundings and the circumstantial milieu of discourse. It is in relation to this circumstantial milieu that discourse is fully meaningful; the return to reality is ultimately a return to reality, which can be indicated "around" the speakers, "around," if we may say so, the instance of discourse itself. Language is moreover, well equipped to secure this anchorage. Demonstratives, adverbs of time and place, personal pronouns, verbal tenses, and in general all the "deictic" and "ostensive" indicators serve to anchor discourse in the circumstantial reality that surrounds the instance of discourse. Thus, in living speech, the *ideal* sense of what is said turns towards the *real* reference, toward that "about which" we speak. At the limit this real reference tends to merge with an ostensive designation where speech rejoins the gesture of pointing. Sense fades into reference and the latter into the act of showing. (148)

Ricoeur turns to the text again saying that the ideology of the "absolute text" should not be suppressed but interpreted by saying it is distant from that ideology. This gives Ricoeur a secular image in terms of reading and interpreting a text. He writes that the text is never without a reference "the task of reading, qua interpretation, will be precisely to fulfill the reference," but if reading appears different from the real reference, the suspense will put away all reading and interpretation; it will go in the air out and outside without a world proper.

The text has a relation with so many other texts; the circumstantial references etc. engender the "quasi world of texts on *literature*." When in the civilisation of writing, writers have to talk about the world that does not exist i. e. The Greek, Byzantine or Vedic world is called "imaginary" in the sense that it is represented by writing in lieu of the world present by speech, but this imaginary world is itself a creation of literature." (149)

4.2.4 Explanation, Interpretation and Understanding

There is a complex relation of the author with the text. This relation enables us to see that the author is instituted by text. The author stands in the space that is the meaning of the text as "the text is the very place where the author appears," the text becomes a morning where King Hamlet appears to say something! The author appears as a first reader of the text. Then in the meanwhile arises the need for explanation and interpretation when the dead author is resurrected as the reader. The readers thus may have two distinct attitudes:

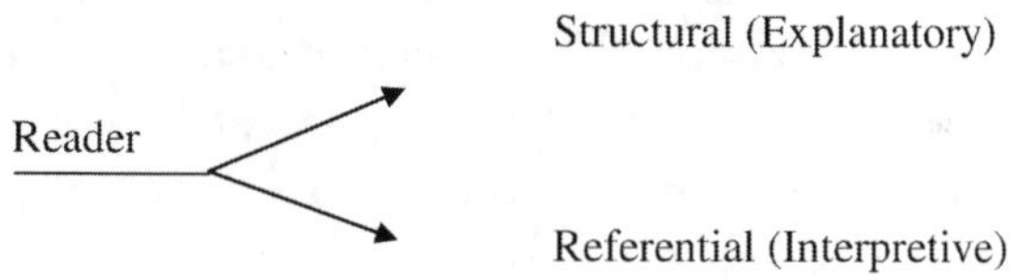

Ricoeur abandons Dilthey's term 'Understanding' and replaces it with the term 'interpretation.' This relates to Dilthey's division of 'explanation' for human sciences. But Ricoeur confronts her and says that 'Explanation' is related to linguistic analysis, to language sequences, to the written and spoken monuments as well. Ricoeur declares that 'interpretation' comes in between explanation and understanding. But nevertheless, this is not the main problem here with Dilthey for Ricoeur. He writes that "[mind] is the region of psychological individualities into which each mental life is capable of transposing itself. Understanding is such transference into another mental life." (150) The act of interpreting is the "art of understanding" and therefore "hermeneutics fulfills the aims of understanding." In Ricoeur's opinion understanding "seeks to coincide with the inner life of the author, to liken itself to him (sich gleichsetzen), to reproduce (nachbilden) the creative process that engendered the work," including both the interior or exterior forms of the work in Schleiermacher's language, this altitude somehow gets the dialogic values.

Hermeneutic, therefore, in Ricoeur's words "proceeds from the objectification of the creative energies of life in work that come in-between the author and us." This, according to him, is a "mental life itself, its creative dynamism, that calls for mediation by "meanings," "values," or "goals." The "eclipse of surrounding world" discussed above as the "quasi-world of text" belongs to two different possibilities: first, it is up to the reader to let the text remain in suspense, considering it as a wordless and some authorless orphan and explain only its structural and textual internal or external relation with depth semantic of the text before him. Second: the reader may lift and carry up the suspense and fulfill it. Restoring the text to communicate the real reference, reproducing the real sense through the referential function by interpreting the exterior structures of the text, the world that it belongs to along with the *subject* as well. Both these two distinct attitudes belong to the act of reading. "By means of this special project, the reader decides to situate himself in the place of the text." But if it is considered that there is no outside world, if the referential function is ignored then in the closure of this point. According to Ricoeur, this projection is not only possible, but also legitimate. The constitution of the text, for him is "the body of the text as literature justifies the interception of the double transcendence of discourse, towards the world and towards someone." At this point of understanding arises the need for an explanatory attitude to Ricoeur in his own way. He rejects Dilthey's concept of understanding the explanatory attitude once more that is formed from the field of knowledge. Thus, for Ricoeur it belongs to the linguistic domain rather than the natural sciences, as parole belongs to speech and *langue* to the abstract systems, rules and regulations of language in the game of language use. For him, "*language-speech* distinction is the fundamental distinction which gives linguistics a homogenous subject," on the other hand this is a fact that "speech belongs to physiology, psychology and sociology." Each unit of spoken words or written which are put/set together are different from other units. They may be either phonological units or lexical. For him, "the interplay of opposition and their combination with an inventory of discrete units is what defines the notion of structure in linguistics." Therefore, this structure model requires and, in his words, furnishes an explanatory attitude.

Apart from this linguistic structure model, Ricoeur also digs into Mythical and Narrative structure. Ricoeur reveals that there is a larger structure than that of the linguistic one, longer than the units of language in general; these are the units of higher order than the sentence apart from the units lower than a sentence, the smaller units of language. Quoting from Levis Strauss' *Structural Anthropology* (1958) Ricoeur writes that "like every linguistic entity myth is made up of constitutive units... namely the phoneme, the morphemes and the sentences.... Each form differs from that which precedes it by a higher degree of complexity.... Large constitutive units…." He is, perhaps, talking about *mythemes*, the signifying function, and the structure of myths where there is a "bundle of relations" on the higher level. This is to say that "only in the form of a combination of such bundles do the constituent units acquire a signifying function." (P. 234[P.211]) For the justification and concretely examining this larger structure, Ricoeur refers to Levis Straus' division of Oedipus Myth into four columns i. e. (i) All sentences that speak of overrated blood relations i. e. Oedipus' Marriage to Jocasta – his own mother, (ii) the same relationship modified by inverse signs: that is the blood relation and killing of his own father Laius by his own self, (iii) the monster and his destruction, (iv) the fourth column groups all parts specially all those names whose meaning-reflected as – lame, clumsy, swollen and fool. Within this large structure it is seen that the fourth one is connected and correlated with the third part and the first one is to the second. The relation shown here is quite visible as a larger structure – that is larger than the sentence. Here the power of myth is reactivated in a particular situation.

Ricoeur also dwells on the narrative structure of folklore, a domain exposed by the Russian Formalists, the school of Propp and the French specialist in structural analysis. There too, the units which are above the sentence have the same composition as is with the units below or over the sentence, therefore, "the sense of the narrative consists in the very arrangement of the elements." It is the interconnectedness of the series of actions. The actions are related to the "actants". The actants are the "predicates of action," in other words "the actant is the one by whom, to whom, with whom... the action is done." In this way the structural analysis "brings out a hierarchy of actants correlative to the hierarchy of actions." The narrative gets assembled as a whole, and is ready for "narrative communication," and when it is, it becomes a discourse being presented before an audience.

In the structural analysis it must be sought by the two interlocutors in the text as the narrator, according to Ricoeur, is designed by the signs of narrativity in the text. The signs belong to the constitutive structure of narrative, beyond the three levels: *action, act* and *narrative* are the *world of narrative users*. Getting back to the two different attitudes: The Explanation – (closed-only within the text.) and the Interpreting – (open-referential-outside the text).

4.2.5 Interpretation-Appropriation: Subjects and Texts

Ricoeur clearly writes that lifting the suspense and fulfilling the text in present speech in the second attitude "is the real aim of reading text" as the true nature of the suspense derives us to the real textual meaning. "The text," writes Ricoeur, "as writing, awaits and calls for a reading." This seems to be a fact, that if in any ways "reading is possible; it is indeed because the text is not closed in on itself but opens out onto other things." To read, therefore, is "to conjoin a new discourse to the discourse of the text." In the text there is an original capacity, an open character for the reversal of the text. This is the act of interpretation which concretises this reversal.

Therefore, the act of interpretation retains appropriation in Schleiermacher's language. Meditating on the concept of interpretation-appropriation, Ricoeur writes that "the interpretation of a text culminates in the self-interpretation of a subject who thence forth understands himself better, understands himself differently, or simply begins understanding himself." The self-understanding belongs to reflective philosophy- therefore, for Ricoeur hermeneutics and reflective philosophy, both are reciprocal. There in this connection appear two perspectives understanding, (i) "self-understanding passes through the detour of understanding the cultural signs in which self-documents and forms itself," (ii) "[understanding] the text is not an end in itself; it mediates the relation to himself of a subject who, in the short circuit of immediate reflection, does not find the meaning of his own life." Ricoeur observes that in any way "reflection is nothing without the mediation of signs and work." (157-58)

Thus, in the second attitude of reading the *self* is "contemporaneous with the constitution of meaning." In the meanwhile, 'appropriation' underlines two more additional features. The first is the "structure against cultural distance," a struggle "against secular estrangement," "against the estrangement from meaning itself, that is, from the system of values upon which the text is based." In this process the act of interpreting makes something (text) "one's own what was initially alien." The second additional feature of interpretation," as the act of reading appears to be a realisation or an "enactment of the semantic possibilities of the text." Here the act of realisation is paramount as it fulfills the discourse of the text in a similar instance to that of speech. Here it is not uttered as in speech; here it is an event, an instance of discourse. Thus, while *reading* "the sentence of the text signifies *here* and *now* moments," similar happens in speech, in this way, to interpret is to interpret the here and now intention of the text. Therefore, the entire hermeneutics relies on the mediation of interpretation-appropriation, the labor that is with the text in the act of reactivating what was all about the text. Ricoeur ends his debate by adding that "reading is the concrete act in which the destiny of the text is fulfilled." (163-64) With this we observe that Ricoeur stands quite close to Barthes as he also proposes to fulfill the gaps in the text that is expected to be filled by the reader.

CHAPTER 5

From Sacred Scripture to the "Secular Scripture" (Literature): A Framework for Literary Hermeneutics

"You're young. You know people but little!"

Pavel stopping before him said seriously:

"Let's not talk of being old or being young. Let us rather see whose thoughts are truer."

"That is, according to you, we've been fooled about God also. So! I, too, think that our religion is false and injurious to us."

Here the mother intervened. When her son spoke about God and about everything that she connected with her faith in him, which was dear and sacred to her, she sought to meet his eyes, she wanted to ask her son not to chafe her heart with the sharp, bitter words of his unbelief. And she felt that Rybin, an older man, would also be displeased and offended. But when Rybin calmly put his question to Pavel, she could no longer contain herself, and said firmly: "When you speak of God, I wish you were more careful. You can do whatever you like. You have your compensation in your work." Catching her breath, she continued with still greater vehemence: "But I, an old woman, I will have nothing to lean upon in my distress if you take my God away from me."

Her eyes filled with tears. She was washing the dishes, and her fingers trembled.

"You did not understand us, mother!" Pavel said softly and kindly.

"Beg your pardon, mother!" Rybin added in a slow, thick voice. He looked at Pavel and smiled. "I forgot that you're too old to cut out your warts."

"I did not speak," continued Pavel, "about that good and gracious God in whom you believe, but about the God with whom the priests threaten us with a stick, about the God in whose name they want to force all of us to the evil will of the few." [….] "They have mutilated even our God for us, they have turned everything in their hands against us. Mark you, mother, God created man in his own image and after his own likeness. Therefore, he is like a man if man is like him. But we have become, not like God, but like wild beasts! In the churches they set up a scarecrow before us. We have got to change our God, mother; we must cleanse him! They have dressed him up in falsehood and calumny; they have distorted his face in order to destroy our souls!" (Maxim Gorky, *Mother* 147-49)

5.1 The Problem with Writing

It will be very difficult to deny that any "fixation" in human discourse will not be complex enough to interpret. How far will it be correct to believe that king Thebes was right in condemning the art of writing and the act of fixing? Keeping the modern-day consequences in mind, this might lead to a long debate. Is it true that there will come no Hermes again? Will the Theologians, clergy-men including the general readers knock the doors of prophet-hood to be reopened again? Or, has everyone today acquired the art of Hermes? Are we not living in a time where the textual territories have been occupied and colonised by "some groups" or "communities" who have their grip over all the intellectual think–tanks? Do they not use the so-called theorists which very much sound as literary terrorists – as a strong weapon and instrument befitting their policies, plans, goals, aims, ideologies? Do they not evolve an attitude of looking at the world of the texts? Are we not living in the age of constant gatekeeping?

Fixing, according to Theuth would make men wiser and more capable of containing knowledge than ever before but the prophetic king Thebes comes up with a "No!" in his reply, an open reply that seems to be correct as the modern-day students and scholars look to have more information and less knowledge. The king rightly cried that in this way "[souls] will become more forgetful once they have put their confidence in external marks instead of relying on themselves from within." (Ricoeur 39, *Interpretation Theory: Discourse and the Surplus of Meaning*) For Socrates, too, writes Ricoeur that, "writing is like painting which generates non-living beings, which in turn remains silent when asked to answer." (38-39) Presenting a short apology for this harsh critique, Ricoeur writes that discourse is "written in the souls of the one who knows, the one who is able to defend himself and keep silent or talk as required by the soul of the person addressed" (39) Although, Rousseau and Bergson "link the main evils that plague civilisation to writing." (39) According to Rousseau, adds Ricoeur in this regard that:

> … [As] long as language relied only on the voice, it reserved the presence of oneself to oneself and to others. Language was still the expression of passion. It was eloquence, not yet exegesis. With writing began separation, tyranny and inequality. Writing ignores its addressee just as it conceals its author. It separates men just as property separates owners. The tyranny of the lexicon and of grammar is equal to that of the laws of exchange, crystallised in money. Instead of the word of God, we have the rule of the learned and the domination of the priesthood. (39)

Might this not be one of the reasons that the majority of prophets from Adam to Jesus Christ including Prophet Mohammad and the mystics believed in instant statesmanship as they articulated thought and they did not leave anything written primarily? But the problem with us is that we have 'Writings!' The present chapter will be an attempt to look into the matter within the phenomena of writing and reading dialectic for communication and human survival inventing a hermeneutic framework for all sorts of fixation and affairs in and with writing.

5.2 Hermeneutics from Sacred Scripture to the "Secular Scripture"

Before the summation of Ricoeur's overall theory of hermeneutics and presenting the proposed hermeneutic-framework consisting of the overall study to reach the hypothesis the other topics and the remaining essays will also be taken into account. This may be observed on the basis of the study of metaphor and language that how hermeneutic theory and praxis continued throughout the times from Sacred-hood to the general literary arena. Precisely, it is to say that the new critics and the praxis of practical criticism brought into focus realised the gravity and power of metaphor and verbal imagery. Richards reaches to an impressive analysis of Aristotle's understanding of metaphor where Aristotle associated metaphor with genius. In English literature it was S.T. Coleridge makes metaphor central to poetics far before Richards'.

In literary history, before that, language was never taken for serious scholarship – neither it was supposed to be a medium of the expression of man's passion, and sacred messages nor was it an object of any serious discourse and research. Here one may ask a very obvious question that – if hermeneutics belongs to religion, then what gives rise to associate it with literary text? How and why hermeneutics became so common?

The question can be answered by tracing the history of biblical translation for which Wycliffe, Tyndale and Coverdale were beheaded because of their translation of Bible into common language similarly as the case with the invention of printing which later in India and the other subcontinent printed images and pictures of gods and goddesses which reached in the hands of every untouchable then now called dalits. Similar was the case with the translation of the Bible. When biblical translation took hold Protestantism came into existence – and the art and the science of hermeneutics became important – in effect it gave birth to the Reformation in Christendom. In this way the question of the interpretation became a serious problem for individuals in Christianity.

The other reasons might also have been responsible for becoming hermeneutics common e. g. the spread of the democracy and its compact, tightly composed and condensed constitutions in the modern world. Thus, the lawyers, judges, politicians, students and scholars in general and people in particular would become interested in their political rights, citizenship, native privileges and opportunities that were there for them. The laws, regulations, and judiciary drew hermeneutics from Temples, Churches and Mosques to the modern academia and to the common readers as well. In this way hermeneutics becomes instrumental to the interpretation of worldly manmade laws and judgments from the Godly laws, jurisprudence, 'fiqh,' commandments etc. Thus, Hermeneutics shifts its paradigm from being theocentric to the geocentric world and enters the literary arena. It is commonly known that earlier, to an extent in Hinduism, Christianity, Islam and the other religion the Scriptures were and some extents even now are the same as the national constitutions are in today's the so called modern civilised world. The interpretations of the laws and their meanings become crucial; hermeneutics entered where-ever the meaning of some text seemed to be important. The Constitution becomes as important as the scriptures. The question of meaning in divorced opinions provides ground to the experience of the hermeneutic gravity. Hermeneutics in this way entered the way where meaning of something was more important and very difficult to grasp even in the absence of hermeneutic arts for literature. This absence is visible in English literary history from 17th, 18th and 19th centuries to a very recent time (namingly the age of Dryden, Pope, Dr. Johnson, Coleridge, Wordsworth, and Arnold etc.) We only know that they produced good literature but no emphasis was given on interpretation or the art of the interpretation. Writers and scholars were more interested in analysis and appropriation, satirising or glorifying.

The publication of the great essay – "The Rise of Hermeneutics" (1900) by Dilthey provided a real challenge in the act of reading. Reading metaphor, poetry, and largely the narrative text required a hermeneutic labor since then. Still, there is something which should link it to hermeneutic praxis to the present before moving ahead. This is to ask why after all hermeneutics for literature again? Because literature was to amuse and please to a great extent, the creative process, the mechanical understanding of the literary production and the principles of poetry and their revival was on the grounds of morality and the sense of aesthetics. Because writing was something clear to understand which did not depend on interpretation. It seems to be reasonable that the playwrights of that age wrote prologues to the obscure, ambiguous and difficult aspects of the texts. They, in fact, used to condemn each other because of their obscurity and complexity. Writing was so simple that metaphors were not very difficult to grasp and to be understood with labor. Since it was not a convention and habit to deal with metaphors – language was just a matter of rhetoric, an instrument or a medium of literary or non-literary communication. This can be well seen that the interpretive principles were neither studied nor even they were thought of to be so.

It is observed that in the Romantic revival and at the end of the 19th century the notion of 'genius' in relation to the creation of poetic text gets associated with it. The division of Coleridge between fancy and imagination, and later primary imagination and secondary imagination along with his realisation of metaphor to poetry associated poetry and literature with genius – literature became something manufactured by and created by genius. Wordsworth creates a divine inspiration in nature; thus, the spiritual insight of the author was weaved within the literary text. Jonathan Swift comes to be known as a genius of his age and time. Thus, the importance of the expression of genius became a general phenomenon. The literary creator gets equated with the divine creator on the basis of his creation.

The increase of secularism during the last two centuries with the romantic hermeneutics laid emphasis on the expression of genius too. The community of poets falls in love with nature in the Romantic Revival. The strongest and daring comment given by Northrop Frye declares the hermeneutic play open when he describes romantic literature as "secular scripture." Thus, meaning becomes more difficult than ever before. It turns subjective rather than merely a shared value. With the rise of secular scripture rises the art and science of hermeneutics too and finds a legitimate way open to the access of literary meaning. That is why Schlarmacher, the theologian of romantic tradition devotes his energies to apply hermeneutics with literature equally as with scripture and even a common reader gets a privilege to play the role of Hermes. The problem of the interpretation of secular scripture increases to the heights. Eliot gets influenced by Gadamer and in recent times the reader-response critics by Dilthey and phenomenology. A road goes from phenomenology to hermeneutics.

5.3 Metaphor, Language and Time

A nerve stimulus, first transposed into an image – first metaphor. The image, in turn, imitated by a sound-second metaphor…when we speak of trees, color, snow, and flowers; and yet we possess nothing but metaphors for things…. […]. What then is the truth? A mobile of metaphors, metonyms, and anthropomorphism…. (Nietzsche 1, "On Truth and Lie in an Extra-Moral Sense," 1873)

With the great move and paradigm shift of the problem of interpretation in general and particular engages the reader to understand the nature of language as a serious problem. The dance of metaphor and imagery comes in the show on stage which has ended many debates, discussions, discourses, essays, articles, chapters and even books without any clear conclusion. To a great extent, Ricoeur's *The Rule of Metaphor* seems to be justifying the thirst to understand metaphor in its complete manifestation. Metaphor in the act of interpretation always emerges as a big challenge, as serious and hard intellectual labor.

It will be very difficult to distinguish whether metaphors constitute and construct narratives or narratives create metaphors. Ted Cohen in one of his forum discussions on metaphor mentions that the talent to understand narratives has to be the talent of understanding metaphors. This debate will be left untouched in this study for some future endeavors.

It has already been shown and proven in the previous chapters that the nature of language is deeply metaphoric in its structure and evolution. Here we will proceed to a partial conclusion of the. The view that language is all made of live and dead metaphors has strongly supported our and hypothesis as well. Metaphor on its own, productive and poetic both is full of power and all surprises till the time it remains alive like a promising and evolving green plant. When the greenery of the plant starts fading, it starts dying. Having given its fruits, it becomes dead as woods in the forest – dead but still equally useful. In language, when metaphors die, they join the party of 'dead society,' they get listed in the dictionary as one of the semantic meanings the roads to semantics goes from metaphors. This is to be noted here that the plant does not die in vain. It leaves uncountable seeds for other new plants to grow and evolve in multiple shapes and cases for the evolution of new metaphors. Thus continues the vehicle of metaphor and metaphorics.

Metaphor and narrative go hand in hand; the demand of human life to be narrated provides a necessity to both of them to come into existence. Human life demands it to be narrated with full vigor and spirit. Metaphors fulfill this demand and record the vast, rich and complex aspects of human life and reality. They project the narrative linear and chronically configured time and experiences in progress to eternity, to death.

Ricoeur has made a journey on the vehicle of metaphor from rhetoric, semiotics and semantics getting across the different and distinguished functioning stations of language and meaning. The division that has been made by the authors and thinkers of meaning earlier was as such: explicit and implicit, cognitive and emotive, denotative and connotative, linguistic and non-linguistic, literal and figurative, primary and secondary meaning. All in a way fail to give a fine and clear conclusion to reveal the true nature of language. Thanks to Mr. I. A. Richards took metaphor as an object of his serious attention and scholarship. Since then, metaphor appears to be a governing and central trope in language and literature. It becomes very fundamental to understand human language, action, history and the world at large as well.

Hilary Lawson supports our argument and observers that language as being metaphoric by nature, our factual discourse goes on dead metaphors which earlier were very much alive. Metaphors always hold openness; while it is alive it is infinitely rich; it is immensely potential. In Lawson's view we close off all the times within metaphors. It enables us to intervene and operate in the world and make sense of which we come across. Metaphors deal with the physics of human emotions, chemistry of the human heart and music of the human soul. Language does not describe reality, but rather it enables us to perceive the world as something. In a sense we also function as metaphors. ("Language Metaphor and Reality," a forum discussion at the Institute of Art and Reality, Published on 19 Sep 2014)

This would be a matter of great interest that why the Pope believed metaphor as an abusive speech and Nietzsche stated that one cannot escape it. It is observed that if the entire knowledge system were to be destroyed and removed from the face of the earth except language – then, can the entire loss would well not be recovered or retrieved through language, through live and dead metaphors? Language as a whole imitates time, the determination of mind to our inner states as it is believed that "[time] is nothing but the form of inner sense, that is, of the intuition of ourselves and our inner state." (*Transcendental Aesthetics*, S6b)

Is there any secrecy or any special provision in the directions that the languages move? For example, Sanskrit, Hindi, English, French and many other languages move from left to right and similarly Hebrew, Arabic, Persian and Urdu move from right to left directions. In space, the earth and all other planets including our galaxy and an infinite number of other galaxies according to modern science revolve from left to right, although, it may be defined accordingly to the point of reference. The planets in space revolve in equal measure as language; it revolves in paradigmatic and syntagmatic ways both. Thus, are we moving ahead? Or getting back? Is our past and future back or in front? Is it before us or behind us the time we live? There are other languages which go from bottom to top and top to bottom. This will remain a mystery till we understand time and the true nature of language – the time and the language through which we live. It is true that learning a new language always gives a whole new world of a new universe – a universe, approximately, of seven thousand stars, which according to an estimate are constantly in flux – always evolving. Language comes across the same change – the flux. Language which is in flux keeps on shaping us according to its color, depth and status. This development seems to be purely metaphorical. Languages, we know, do not evolve out of nothing. They evolve only because they are used and in situations, cases, conditions, events and happenings they fall short and hence there arises semantic innovation. The flux in time brings flux in language and human life in return. The 'metaphorics' of language contains information about objects and about human electrons and intentions of genes, universe, human emotions, attitudes, tendencies, ideologies, histories, signs, symbols, all myths and all non-verbal modulations of language. The planet, like language, revolves in two directions similarly as synchronic and diachronic structures of language. This time too has the same moves synchronically it brings days and nights, and diachronically it brings different seasons in nature.

Michael Erard in good humor observing on metaphor says that metaphor is the ultimate software for human brain to work and to function ("Language Metaphor and Reality" a forum discussion at the Institute of Art and Reality, Published on 19 Sep. 2014). This is true that if any language stops producing metaphors, it is destined to be dead e. g. Greek, Hebrew, Sanskrit etc. There are many languages which have recently been found dead only because of the stagnancies caused by some internal and external affairs of the places and people they belong. In recent times it can also be seen how modern languages such as English, German, French, Hindi, Urdu etc. have been expanding. They are expanding and evolving only because they are creating new metaphors and making semantic innovations. When in language new metaphors are not created, it experiences a silent pause – if this serious pause gets longer, it starts decaying. Thus, it is proven that metaphor prevents language from dying. The active role of metaphorisation and semantic innovation in Paul Ricoeur's language helps language expand and evolve to reach to eternity itself.

The discovery of metaphor grabs a serious and simultaneous attention in a 'wow' or 'waah' moment if we talk in English or Hindustani (Rekhta). Some authors believe that metaphors are of primary and secondary disposition as there are green and pale fruits, cooked meat and fresh ones that can be hardly eaten easily.

Metaphor and discourse both have approximately three references – (i) "an extra linguistic reality" (ii) "a self-reference" or "a reference to reality" and (iii) "to whom it is addressed as to its own speaker." Understanding metaphor carries a reader to reach to a larger and wider canvas of the text. The act of explanation concerns only the sense; hence it covers only one aspect of meaning – a one way to go. But the "understanding of a work taken as a whole gives the key to metaphor" on the upper hand. (Ricoeur, "Central Problem of Metaphor," 169-173)

Ricoeur distinguishes between interpretation and explanation keeping two views in mind. First: understanding of metaphor to a larger and wider understanding of a text that is going and reading something from metaphor to 'Text.' Second is the understanding of the larger and wider layers of the text to understand a metaphor – and that is from text to 'Metaphor.' There is something always new with metaphor that is the – "description of metaphor as a new meaning in a new context." (174-76) Sometimes, it is the text which provides the key to reach to the hermeneutics of metaphor. There are some features, adds Ricoeur, that they get active only if the discourse becomes a literary work. He observes that texts speak of the possible worlds and of the possible ways of orienting in the worlds. The act of interpretation becomes the act of 'apprehension' of the "proposed worlds," in this connection he further adds that "[to] understand is to follow the dynamic of the work, its movement from what it says to that about which it speaks. Beyond my situation as reader, beyond the situation of the author, I offer myself to the possible mode of being-in-the-world which the text opens up and discloses to me." (177)

In Ricoeur's view interpretation is not only appropriated – but is made one's own that was alien and foreign before. He adds that "what we appropriate for ourselves, is not an alien experience or distant intention, but the horizon of the world towards which a work directs itself." (178) Ricoeur associates a sense of metaphor to Aristotle's mythos and reference of metaphor with his concept of mimesis.

5.4 The Transposition and the Appropriation of the Text

At this point there are two concepts left and yet unclear – first is the mechanism involved in the imaginative acceleration or imagination itself, second, the partially discussed concept that is – 'appropriation,' in his essay "Appropriation," one of the key concepts which govern the methodology of interpretation in his own words. 'Appropriation' is a counterpart of his concept 'distanciation' it is a "playful transposition of the text" and relates it to the critique of the "illusion of the subject," a work on the 'distanciation' and the "relinquishment of the self." The act of appropriation goes throughout the whole process of interpretation. The dialectic of distanciation and appropriation according to Ricoeur "concerns the way in which the text is addressed to someone." He compares this dialectic with that of the concept explanation and understanding. (182-3)

Historically, in the 19th century the focus used to be on the historicity of the literary text, therefore, "[to] explain a text was essentially to consider it as the expression of certain socio-cultural needs and as a response to certain perplexities located in space and time." Later, this attitude developed an alternative tendency – namely "historicism" being influenced by Frege and Husserl as for them meaning was as "an ideal object" which is later understood as "the theory of the fixation of life expressions by writing." At the turn of the century the current practice of understanding becomes more logical than historical and this change affects the whole discourse of human sciences. This change can be seen in the domain of literary criticism, specifically in America "a turn from historicity to logicity in the explanation of cultural expressions" in the name of 'anti-historicism.' The same gets followed by what Ricoeur calls 'psychologism and 'sociologism'. (184)

5.5 The 'Play' of Heuristic Fiction, Author and the Reader in the Text

With a new dimension again mentions Ricoeur that "the text is not primarily a message addressed to a specific range of readers…, it is not a segment of an historical chain…, it is a kind of atemporal object which has, as it were, broken its moorings with all historical development." According to him the development of writing "implies the 'suspension' of the historical process," it transfers human discourse to an infinite expansion of communication. Ricoeur openly accepts and supports this anti-historicist and later develops an attitude of understanding and analysis in his account. Here meaning is a medication between the writer and the reader. This medication has an existential character; he calls it the appropriation of meaning that is again the making – making of the foreign one's own which were one's alien before. In this way "the aim of all hermeneutics is to struggle against the structural distance and historical alienation. Interpretation brings together, equalises, renders contemporary and similar." The act of interpretation "actualises the meaning of the text for the present reader." Thus, appropriation becomes "the actualisation of meaning as addressed to someone." It becomes similar to that of the dialogical process. In this way the interpretation and appropriation happen when "the reading releases something like an event in the present time." With this notion the act of appropriation becomes dialectical and the counterpart of the timeless distanciation. (185)

Being influenced by Gadamer, Ricoeur mentions "the theory of heuristic fiction" teaching us that "it is not only reality which is metamorphosed by the heuristic fiction but also the author and reader." (185-86) Ricoeur centers his theory on three grounds: (a) the heuristic fiction as play, (b) the author as playful figure, and (d) the reader as playful figure. The play is rooted in the "subjectivism of the aesthetic consciousness" coming from Kant's "judgment of state," Ricoeur in this connection further adds:

> Play is an experience which transforms those who participate in it. It seems that the subject of aesthetic experience is not the player himself, but rather what 'takes place' in play. In a similar way we speak of the play of waves, of light, of parts of a machine and even of words. We play with a project, with an idea; we can equally 'be played'. What is essential is the 'to and fro' (*Hin-und Her*) of play. Play is thereby close to dance, which is a movement that carries away the dancer. That we say that the part 'is played,' or again that something 'is in play' between … All of these expressions betray that play is something other than the activity of a subject. The to and fro of play occurs as if by itself, that is, without effort or applied intention. This 'in itself' of play is such that, even in solitary play, there must be something with which or against which one plays (with luck as one's partner in times of success!). (186)

Thus, for Ricoeur "worlds are proposed in the mode of play," it is the heuristic fiction that is at play and in this process "we hand ourselves over, we abandon ourselves to the space of meaning." Ricoeur states that within the play "metamorphosis" occurs which stands for two things – (i) the "imaginary transposition marked by reign of figures," (b) "the transposition of everything into its true being." The art abolishes the "non-metamorphosed reality" and a true mimesis becomes a true metamorphosis. The imaginary part, in Ricoeur's view, elicits recognition of the "presented being" and its essence. This is the reason that Aristotle on the basis of the 'essence' he considered poetry superior over history as it "proceeds to the essential." Thus, in this way Ricoeur presents a "significant link between fiction, figuration and recognition of the essential." (187)

For Ricoeur it is not only the presentation of the world in the text which is playful but also the author does the same as he too brings himself onto the stage and gives himself in the representation of the world, the author "is rendered fictitious." He can disguise himself but can never disappear. Here, to disguise will be to have different voices – at this instance Ricoeur asserts that "[…] is this not to play?" Ricoeur writes that the French structuralists stressed to cut this link of the author with the text. Ricoeur strongly seems to oppose and disprove this notion as "the narrator is never the author; nevertheless, the narrator is always the one who is metamorphosed in a fictional character which is the author. Even the death of the author, Ricoeur says, is a 'game' that the author plays. The reader too, is in the text as a playful figure as "the author's subjectivity submitted to imaginative variations becomes a world offered by the narrator to the subjectivity of his reader." (189)

5.6 The Critique of the Subject and Ideology

Ricoeur proposes in this regard that "the subject must be submitted to a critique," the critique of all prejudices and the notion on which metaphor gets exercised. The critique of the subject links to the "general theory of ideology" as "we are," adds Ricoeur, "propelled to act the hidden interests" and thus comes the falsification of reality and consciousness which also must be submitted to a justful hermeneutics. For Freud the critique of the subject is the critique of illusion – but instead illusion Ricoeur insists on the self or better called the self-analysis or the "self-criticism." This is what he calls "the relinquishment of the subject." For Freud "the subject is not master in his own house" and the self-criticism for him was the "narcissism of the reader." The notion of relinquishment is "a fundamental moment of appropriation." Ricoeur ends his essay teaching us that the hermeneutics of understanding, meaning and self-understanding belong to the "hermeneutics of reflective philosophy." Thus, hermeneutics emphasises more on the notion of 'I am' rather than the hermeneutics of 'I think' in the theory of the critique of the illusion of the subject. (191-93)

5.7 Identity, Self and Narrative

According to Ricoeur, identity is always narrative. The narratives constitute the identities of the individuals. Identity is nothing recalling and tracing the history to establish and to constitute it. The self is always oneself as another. All the times when we pass with it, we become a different self, the one-self: as another. Thus, Ricoeur discusses the narrative identity. In this view we all are the product of our narratives that we have or that we produce. Oneself as another, one may arise in many ways of relationship with others – the others that inhabit us. There are parts of others that we live and get influenced by, too. There is the other which reveals us – the shortest road to self goes to the other. There is always an 'Other' in us which we always are on an existential level. In other, to recognise oneself is necessary to be the other a bit that which we are also a part. Memory is something that makes us away from becoming other in the same way narrative is to become another. Everything that happens with us manages us. In this way-narrative also becomes an act and when it happens, we accordingly get changed by it, we no longer remain the same as we are before getting across any narrative. It is the subject which experiences the meaning in his horizons. The common words such as – love, hate, anger, happiness, sympathy, empathy etc. are not truly meaningful until or unless one experiences them within the self or one subject.

Ricoeur in his book *Oneself as Another* (1992) presents a continuation of his arguments made in *Time and Narrative*. In the sixth study of the book entitled "The Self and Narrative Identity" of *Oneself as Another* writes that the "genuine nature of narrative identity discloses itself, in my opinion, only the dialectic of self and sameness. In this sense, this dialectic represents the major contribution of narrative theory to the constitution of the self." (140) Ricoeur's 'identity' is the identity acquired by "the narrative function." The identity gets constituted on the level of the configuration and reconfiguration of time and narrative. The reconfiguration of narrative destroys the self which was before – another self takes birth and this newly born self is legitimately fathered by the narrative entwined or enjoined with the subject. The self every now and then acquires new knowledge, a new way of looking, reading, seeing, perceiving, being and interpreting.

The identity is a mixed form of *idem-* identity (sameness) and *ipse-* identity (selfhood) which responds to time and change, and leads us to the dialectic of narrative and the ethical self. It is a matter of relation and relation of relation which is related to the modality of the "presence in time." Ricoeur provides three grounds on which the sameness can be seen: (i) numerical identity – as opposed to plurality, (ii) qualitative identity – the sheer resemblance, and (iii) the uninterrupted continuity between the first and the last stage in individual's development. Ricoeur adds in this regard that "[the] entire problematic of personal identity will revolve around this search for a relational invariant, giving it the strong signification of permanence in time. (118) The sameness and selfhood, here seem to have an analogy with the sense and reference of metaphor. In the same context, Ricoeur further adds about the narrative identity in his third volume of *Time and Narrative* as:

> ...the notion of narrative identity brings to the initial aporia of temporality. Certainly, the constitution of narrative identity does illustrate in a useful way the interplay of history and narrative in the refiguration of a time that is itself indivisibly phenomenological time and cosmological time. But it also includes, in turn, an internal limitation that bears witness to the first inadequacy of the answer narration brings to the question posed by the aporetics of temporality.... narrative identity is not a stable and seamless identity.... narrative identity continues to make and unmake itself." (248-49)

The identity of a person as we understand finds a way either from history or from fiction. It gets constituted through the very fabric of the structure of emplotment which goes across some unified whole. This unified whole is further defined by Ricoeur as:

> As for the notion of the narrative unity of a life, it must be seen as an unstable mixture of fabulation and actual experience. It is precisely because of the elusive character of real life that we need the help of fiction to organise life retrospectively, after the fact, prepared to take as provisional and open to revision any figure of emplotment borrowed from fiction or from history. In this way, with the help of the narrative beginnings which our reading has made familiar to us, straining this feature somewhat, we stabilise the real beginnings formed by the initiatives (in the strong sense of the term) we take. And we also have the experience, however incomplete, of what is meant by ending a course of action, a slice of life. Literature helps us in a sense to fix the outline of these provisional ends. As for death, do not the narratives provided by literature serve to soften the sting of anguish in the face of the unknown, of nothingness, by giving it in imagination the shape of this or that death, exemplary in one way

> or another? Thus fiction has a role to play in the apprenticeship of dying. (*OA* 162)

5.8 Imagination and Semantic Innovation

In the previous sections some of the important aspects were proposed to be taken for further and final clarifications i. e. imagination, self and the "I am" or if better call its identity. For now, we would dwell on the problem of imagination comparatively with metaphor. This aspect was taken in *The Rule of Metaphor* in the beginning, but it was in brief. For further reflection on this aspect, we have chosen an inaugural lecture "Imagination in Discourse and Action" of Paul Ricoeur delivered at the "5th International Phenomenology Conference," 1975 in Paris. Ricoeur strives to associate the conception of imagination with the theory of metaphor and with the "poetics of violation" which moves from theory to praxis. There is a tie between imagination and semantic innovation. Imagination in Ricoeur's view "suffers from the dispute in which the term 'image' is held." (4)

The theory of imagination has references to the theory of *sense* – the *objective* or the *ideal* sense. Ricoeur mentions four dimensions of imagination: first it shows arbitrary evocation of things which are absent, although they exist elsewhere as absent and present things. Second, that it designates – portraits, paintings, drawings, diagrams, all of them take the place of the things they represent – as all have physical existence as we know around us. Third, the image of fiction brings to us which are existential things e. g. dreams, the products of sleep to the purely literary existence i. e. drama, novel or a short story. Fourth, the term image is used for the domain of illusions of the existents and non-existent things on something that the subject knows as the reality of the object. Thus, the theory of imagination is centered on the two different axes (i) the axes of presence and absence in regard with the object and (ii) the axes of the fascinated consciousness and the critical consciousness in regard with the subject. The first axis according to Ricoeur refers to "the perception of which it is merely the trace in the sense of a lesser presence." All theories of productive imagination move to this pole. In a way, on the other hand within this same axis "the image is thought of essentially in relation to absence, of the other-than the present, the various key figures of productive imagination – portrait, dream, and fiction – all refer in different ways to this fundamental otherness." (5)

The subject can make distinction between imagination and the real but sometimes, writes Ricoeur that "the image is confused with the real, taken for the real." Imagination becomes an instrument to give a critique of reality. Ricoeur compares the theory of imagination to the theory of metaphor which renders itself with the semantic innovation or rather call the theory of language use in this connection he further adds:

> …many prejudices were linked with the idea that the image is an appendix to perception, a shadow of perception. To say that our images are spoken before they are seen is to abandon what we initially – but mistakenly – take for granted, namely, that the image is first and foremost a "scene" being played out on the stage of a mental "theatre" for the benefit of an internal "spectator"; but this also means giving up a second point we also mistakenly assume, namely, that this mental entity is the stuff out of which we construct our abstract ideas, our concepts, the basic ingredient in some sort of mental alchemy. (6)

Ricoeur seems curious that if image does not come from perception but language, then what will happen? The poetic image comes out of reverberation, which "comes not from things seen but from things said" or even written. Ricoeur again indicates that metaphor takes birth on new semantic pertinences – and the new pertinence results in the imaginative pole. He further adds that "imagination is apperception, the sudden view of a new predicative pertinence." This view brings us close to the "mechanical attraction of mental atoms. Imagining is first and foremost restructuring the semantic fields" – something he has already said that is the "seeing as." Here he reaches very close to the Kantian theory of schematism as "a method for giving an image to a concept." This was the point where Ricoeur paused in his *The Rule of Metaphor*. In the "Editor's Introduction" of Ricoeur's *Lectures on Ideology and Utopia*, J. H. Taylor adds on the innovative aspect of the imagination in relation to ideology and utopia as a process of imagination:

> If ideology is imagination as picture, utopia is imagination as fiction. "In a sense all ideology repeats what exists by justifying it, and so it gives a picture… of what is. Utopia, on the other hand, has the fictional power of re-describing life" (lecture 18). Ricoeur builds on Kant to say that the comparison between picture and fiction may be characterised as one between *reproductive* and *productive* imagination. (xxviii)

5.9 Ricoeur's Freud and Earlier Philosophy

One of the important aspects of Freudian critique which was introduced and to some extent discussed as well in the previous chapter, here again would be brought to the final conclusion of it by referring Ricoeur's an earlier work *Freud and Philosophy,* one of the finest works on hermeneutics and psychology including the limitations of Freud and his scholarship. This should be noted here that many of the earlier ideas of the book have been modified in Ricoeur's later works which he brought in consideration. Nevertheless, *Freud and Philosophy* still seem to have a lot of serious concerns over here. Accordingly, we would like to dwell on this work partially as required. Here we would stress and reflect on his understanding of the theory of interpretation. In the first chapter of the book "Language Symbol and Interpretation," Ricoeur asks some fundamental questions as how can language be put to account for multiple functions of the human act of signifying? Language means something more than what we just say or write. Ricoeur writes that in language "a symbol is a double meaning linguistic expression that requires an interpretation, and is a work of understanding that aims at deciphering symbols." (6-9) On the other hand, on the problematic of symbolism, he adds that in "hermeneutics symbols have their own semantics, they stimulate hidden meaning, far from falling outside the bounds of language, they raise feeling to meaningful articulation" and the "interpretation is any voiced sound endowed with significance." (19-21)

In Ricoeur's hermeneutics, interpretation is always a tactic of suspicion; it is "a battle against masks." He also accepts that "there is no general hermeneutics" as there are literary 'Theories, in the same way there is "no universal canon for exegesis" but some rules of interpretation which are "at variance with itself." For the enumeration of hermeneutic style, Ricoeur adds that "hermeneutics is understood as manifestation and restoration of meaning addressed to me in the manner of a message, a proclamation, or as is sometimes said, a kerygma" or in other words it is "a demystification, as reduction of illusion." (27) The school of the hermeneutics of suspicion and the practice of interpretation include – (i) the interpretation of the interpretation, (ii) the recollection of meaning, (iii) reduction of the illusions, (iv) and the lies of the consciousness.

This is to remind here that it was mentioned in the introduction about the three masters of suspension upon whom Ricoeur is said to lay the foundation of his hermeneutics. Ricoeur himself admits that "[three] masters, seemingly mutually exclusive, dominate the school of suspicion: Marx, Nietzsche, and Freud…., [all] three show their common opposition to a phenomenology of the sacred, understood as a propaedeutic to the 'revelation' of meaning, then their interrelationship within a single method of demystification." These thinkers, in Ricoeur's views belong to three different and distinct practices of suspicion – and all differ to each other. Ricoeur writes that "Marx is relegated to economics and the absurd theory of the reflex consciousness; Nietzsche is drawn toward bilogism and a perspectivism incapable of expressing itself without contradiction; Freud is restricted to psychology and decked out with a simplistic panasexulism." (32-33)

The only thing that they have in common is the notion of "false consciousness" each in a different way. Ricoeur mentions the "Cartesian doubt" here and the doubt of Descartes' who commonly think that things are not as they appear. But these two did not have any doubt about consciousness. The human consciousness was spared, but these three masters include consciousness also to their critique and legitimising the nature of suspicion by giving proper justification. Here the suspicion should not be understood with skepticism, Ricoeur says that they are "a new foundation" including all institution – as a "new reign of truth" not by destructive critique but "by the invention s of an art of interpretation." Ricoeur concludes this by saying that "understanding is hermeneutics." (33) The suspicion thus, goes on three different and distinct levels – first, economic, political, or social level. Second, psychological level, and third, on the level of faith, value, truth or religion. Ricoeur believes that "Marxists are stubbornly insistent on the 'reflex' theory." Ricoeur bases his theory of deciphering on these three masters of suspicion. Freud reaches to "the problem of false consciousness via the double road of dreams and neurotic symptoms but Freud's limit is only to the economics of instincts." For Marx, Ricoeur adds that he attaches the economics of ideology and politics, whereas Nietzsche on the other hand focuses on the problem of 'value,' Ricoeur better clarifies the distinctions as:

> What Marx wants is to liberate *praxis* by the understanding of necessity; but this liberation is inseparable from a "conscious in sight" which victoriously counterattacks the mystification of false consciousness. What Nietzsche wants is the increase of man's power, the restoration of his force; but the meaning of the will to power must be recaptured by meditating on the ciphers "superman,"

> "eternal return," and "Dionysus," without which the power in question would be but worldly violence. What Freud desires is that the one who is analysed, by making his own the meaning that was foreign to him, enlarge his field of consciousness, live better, and finally be a little freer and, if possible, a little happier. One of the earliest homages paid to psychoanalysis speaks of "healing through consciousness." (34-35)

5.10 Paul Ricoeur: A Citizen of "Lebenswelt"

As it appears, Paul Ricoeur in his poetics and praxis very much seems to be quite close to those of the Geneva School of Phenomenology and Criticism with a difference that he proceeds from phenomenology to hermeneutics. Husserlian influence seems to be dominant in his analysis of human consciousness including the consciousness of the addresser and addressee if we use Jakobson's vocabulary for instance in the literary and linguistic communication that describes the lived world called – "lebenswelt." It was Husserl who had concluded that consciousness is a unified "intentional act," this is not something which is deliberately willed, but it is "to be conscious is always to be conscious of something." This is to be noted here that phenomenological analysis always starts with an "epoché" that is what we have been calling as "suspension" of all presuppositions about the previous nature of human experience and understanding.

It is in 1930, the Polish Theorist, Roman Ingarden (1893-1970) writing in both Polish and German talked of the intentional acts of the consciousness of the author of a literary work recorded and fixed in writing to a reader's response to the same. There are many 'places of determinacy' to be taken forward – this is something he calls an active reading which responds to the text through a temporal process of consciousness by filling up the potentialities of textual indeterminacies, he calls it a "co-creative" process which results in an actualised "aesthetic object" in association with the reader's consciousness. This on surface does not depict a reality which exists independently in the text rather it constitutes a "quasi-reading," that is something Ricoeur has already mentioned in his philosophy, that is something its own fictional world. In practice this approach becomes subjective. Thus, after Husserl, Ingarden, Heidegger, Gadamer, Jauss and Iser, it is Paul Ricoeur in the convention. The bard of hermeneutics, borrowing the notion of suspicion, he brings it to prominence calling it as – hermeneutics of suspicion. The real contribution of Ricoeur is this that not only he abridges between phenomenology and hermeneutics, but also strongly establishes it for general practice. Ricoeur's hermeneutics ruins the *Husserlian Idealism* and the interpretation of phenomenology. He reaches from the polysemy of the word to the polysemy of the text including the inter-subjective aspects of reading and understanding. Ricoeur also talks of historical connections in this context. He invites the exegesis of the text rather than the exegesis of the word only. In his article "Phenomenology and Hermeneutics," critiquing the Husserlian idealism Ricoeur remarks as:

> [We] are not content with the sense which is its ideal object, but we ask further about its reference, that is, about its claim to truth, so in the text, we cannot stop with the immanent structure, with the internal system of dependences born of the intersecting of "codes" that the text uses; we want to unfold the world that the text projects. I am not, in saying this, ignoring the fact that one important category of texts, what we call *literature* – namely, narrative fiction, drama, poetry – seems to abolish all reference to every reality, to the point that language glorifies itself at the expense of the referential function of ordinary discourse. But it is precisely in the measure to which the discourse of fiction "suspends" this referential function of the first degree that it frees a reference of the second degree, in which the world is no longer manifested as an ensemble of manipulable object, but as the horizon of our life and our project, in short as a Lebenswelt, as being-in-the-world. This referential dimension only attains its full development with works of fiction and poetry, which pose the fundamental hermeneutical problem. (39)

Andreea Deciu Ritivoi în *Paul Ricoeur: Tradition and Innovation in Rhetorical Theory* – observes that "Ricoeur belongs to the camp of European philosophers who have "colonised" American academia in the last few decades. In this category are also Jürgen Habermas, Michel Foucault, Jacques Derrida, Emmanuel Levinas…." (1). Even so, one may criticize Ricoeur for possessing any important philosophical and intellectual identity: maybe because of the extensive and inclusive character of his work, because of non-polemic and nonsensical style of writing. It may be because of his lack of interest and ambition toward establishing a school. Although, he often admitted very frankly that he had no master plan in his philosophy. It is a fact that Ricoeur never presented a unified and systematic presentation of his thought.

Nevertheless, Ricoeur's decisive contribution to the future course of French philosophy would be hardly possible to capture in a single phrase or a sentence. It is true that Ricoeur is extremely influential, but his position and status remained enigmatic to the modern philosophical arena. We have found that Ricoeur has never involved himself in any fierce arguments and stormy debate. Ricoeur rather seems to be following the essentially humble and intellectual approach. In Ricoeur's hermeneutics, epistemology and ontology meet with a focus on the ontological investigation into the nature of self and self-awareness, and its relation to the linguistic phenomenon of the first-person pronoun *I*. In the "Introduction" of *Fallible Man,* Walter J. Lowe observes that:

> Rich in texture, expansive in scope, and indefatigably exploratory in character, Ricoeur's is not a philosophy that lends itself to a tidy summary. Still, it may be possible, by way of introduction, to retrace something of the pathway along which his thought has moved: to indicate a few of the most basic concerns and then to show how those concerns, and the interaction between them, came to generate the particular works which he did in fact write. As a means of interpreting the institutions and works of art which constitute our culture, Ricoeur has often sought, in and through those various expressions, an underlying human act, a generative "affirmation" of effort and desire. Without pressing the point unduly, we may ask to what extent Ricoeur's own thought, and particularly his early work, may be interpreted in the light of such an originary affirmation. (vii)

5.11 The Fashionable 'non/Sense' of 'Theory' and Literary Hermeneutics

In the year 1996, it was Alan Sokal (physician), a mathematician's "affair" known for his "Transgressing the Boundaries: Toward a Transformative Hermeneutics of Quantum Gravity" (1996), a parody article which dressed down and exposed the hypocrisy of the so-called American intellectuals in humanities especially the professors in English Departments claiming to be critics of modern sciences and ethics or if better call critics of science wars. I, myself doubt that many of the contemporary literary theories and their forceful and illegitimate intrusion in English departments would have been because of the national and foreign American policies and plans. One of the recent guides to the Contemporary Literary Theory, especially the recent edition of Raman Selden by Peter Widdowson and Peter Brooker is recording the awareness of 'post' theory cry and its failure. The trend till very recent, was this that we waited for the emergence of some new, substantial and potential theories only for the sake of theories as movie buffs restlessly wait for some Bond films to be released – thus to the great extent theory replaces the literary discourse. In recent times, many thinkers have started questioning the future and fate of literary theories and the nature of contemporary criticism. It is as if it has crashed, failed and is a beginning time of 'post-theory period.' Theory is seemingly failing and slowly becoming obsolete because of its excessive and unnecessary involvement in humanities, more theories and less or lesser practices. It was Raman Selden in 1985, long ago from now had realised that:

> [Until] recently ordinary readers of literature and even professional literary critics had no reason to trouble themselves about developments in literary theory. Theory seemed a rather rarefied specialism which concerned a few individuals in literature departments who were, in effect, philosophers pretending to be literary critics.... Most critics assumed, like Dr. Johnson, that great literature was universal and expressed general truths about human life. . . [and] talked comfortably about the writer's personal experience, the social and historical background of the work, the human interest, imaginative 'genius' and poetic beauty of great literature. (1)

The very semantic innovation of 'post theory' shows that something has recently gone amiss, and the moment of theory is now over. There arises a curiosity whether, do we require a new approach to literature to a level that it does not affect the pure literary discourse – or what is called literature. It is a fact that theory made literary reading empirical; it only revolved around Jakobson's framework of linguistic communication. Is it not true that humans are more than just linguistic beings? Are there no affairs larger than this linguistic connection, communication, and comprehension? Is there no meaning beyond linguistic empire? Does it mean that a literary text is only all about linguistic meaning and nothing else?

The present resentment finds favor from Raman Selden. It is to confront Peter Widdowson and Peter Brooker for their justification and legitimising the presence of 'theory' by giving a kind of counter to the present view in the fifth edition of *A Reader's Guide to Contemporary Literary Theory* (2005) for theory in 'post theory period.' This is to be observed here that the theoretical discourse in association with literature or literary product is not put to justice. Reading under this umbrella gets imperialised rather than actualised. Saying this does not mean to end affairs with theoretical discourse. It should be noted here that theory is never applied as it is discussed. Theory does add to an understanding of a literary text better but if it is strictly followed and practiced it bounds and limits more than it facilitates. It is doubtful whether these theories may not belong to some various dying and recently ignored disciplines of modern-day scholarship. It is generally known that the bureaucrats and corporate cultures seem to be gripping, limiting and controlling the modern-day world universities. The universities as institutions are supposed to challenge the status-quo; this might be a constant threat to them, the so-called modern-day ideologues. Is there anyone talking about the death of universities and the death of criticism? Yes, a modern-day mighty genius, Terry Eagleton. He has reflected very deeply on the nature and ways in which universities are functioning at present. He rightly claims that they have just become training centers and, therefore – dying. The subjects which had potential to challenge the absurdities of the status-quo have been demotivated from the very underground.

Raman Selden in 1985 had rightly observed that the theories did not actually belong to literature but to philosophy, psychology, anthropology, linguistics or some other scholars of other disciples trying to be literary theorists. The general view is that they would survive only if they themselves were literary penmen and not by some philosophers, linguists, psychologists or anthropologists at all. Theory helps understand literature to some extent but even then, the intrusion of theory in literary discipline seemed to be uninvited. A possible threat which has already been articulated that literary discourse and literary bodies are trying to camouflage as cultural studies. This situation forces us to raise a pertinent question whether we are really headed to see the death of literary convention and witness all the expected and predicted dystopias? There is no answer as yet! There may possibly be one solution – that hermeneutics of suspicion and peace for meaningful, healthy and productive reading rather than theorising things – a return to the basics.

The fascination towards theories may be taken in addition as a temporary literary fashion in English and other Departments of Humanities as well. Metaphors and narratives as a whole should be brought to the hermeneutics of suspicion – to a justful hermeneutics. Suspicion does not mean that it leads to anarchy but on the contrary, it leads to the truths and meanings exposed as it is. It does not mean deconstruction or destruction at all. Suspicion may and may not give the same or the different results, but help to demystify and decipher something which is hidden as it is. The world of the text should be submitted to honest meditation, as a battle against the mask. It should set aside all the presuppositions. There should be a free and careful speculative reflection on the world of the text. The readers must look at the possibility which is neither an error nor a lie with a tactic of suspicion. The temporal orientation and the schema of the system must be taken carefully in the act of reading. Every possibility of the duality of meaning should be properly explored and brought to logical conclusion including the *integral discourse*, the univocal and pluri-vocal *empire of language*.

Theoria must be substituted by Humanitas as it is seen in modern sciences; the fundamentals have been set aside after quantum mechanics, physics and the development of microbiology. Following theories and approaches, in humanities may limit and may carry prejudices as well. There should be an honest hermeneutics rather than surrendering to some disguised ideological, empirical power or propaganda. If it be so, then the death of theory should be understood as the birth of peaceful hermeneutics. If there is any delay in understanding these problems, then the consequences will appear much more precarious than ever before – the dangers of the present that the world may face in future.

Ricoeur has no theory except some very basic principles, but he does talk of the ways of reading and writing process and its formal function. Hermeneutics begins from one subject to the other subject – by configuration of time, distanciation, writing, reading, explanation, interpretation, reconfiguration of time, understanding, application and appropriation in the sequential order. In a way, time is experienced in three different stages – prefiguration, configuration and reconfiguration. This leads to explanation, understanding and appropriation of the text. The island where the mystery of time is slightly revealed is only in the *understanding* of the subject only. Reading narratives, as Ricoeur already did, for instance, in his *Time and Narrative,* with a few additions, should lay emphasis on ideology, Irony, intention, metaphor, plot, place, people, pattern, action, actant, actor, action-text, atmosphere, attitude, character, chronotope, context, coherence and cohesion, texture, theme, truth, technique and time. There are also a few important terms, already established and discussed, which are borrowed herein with Ricoeur's overall hermeneutics. The horizons of Ricoeurian hermeneutics of suspicion can be easily glimpsed by the following table and figures:

***VOICE* in hermeneutics (Human and Holy)**

I # 5	I (Cogito)	Irony	Intention	Ideology	Identity
M # 4	Metaphor	Mimesis1	Mimesis2	Mimesis3	
P # 4	Plot	Place	People	Pattern	
A # 5	Action	Actor	Actant	Attitude	Atmosphere
C # 5	Character	Chronotope	Context	Coherence	Cohesion
T # 5	Text (action)	Texture	Truth	Technique	Time- 1, 2, 3
S # 1	Suspicion (Marx, Freud and Nietzsche)				

The Channel of Ricoeur's Hermeneutics of Suspicion and Literary Interpretation: A Framework

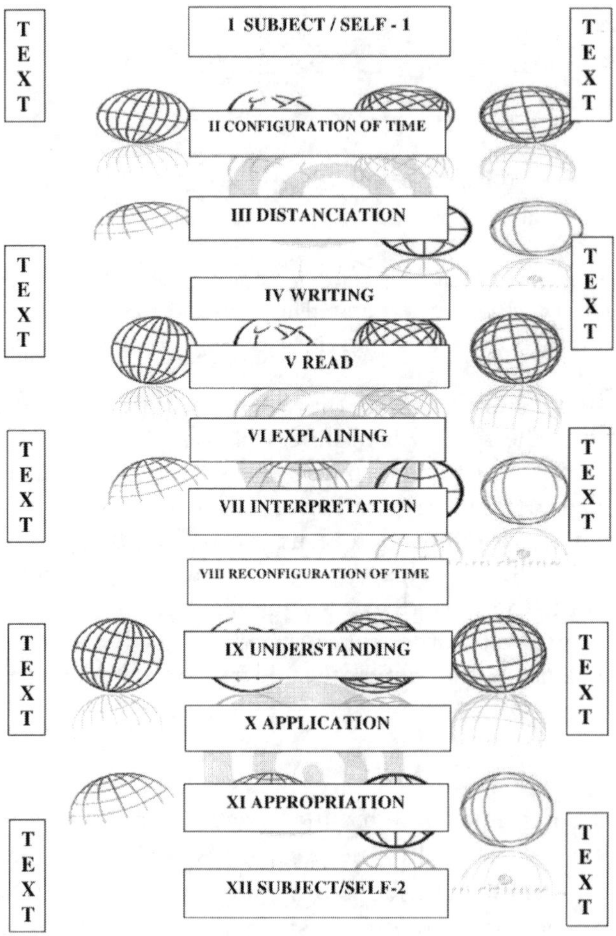

CHAPTER 6

'Fic*tory*,' '*Fa*ction,' or 'Hi*terature*'?: Rushdie's Metaphor of Midnight and *His* '[Re]Configuration' of Time – the Mystery Called Maya

ہستی کے مت فریب میں آ جائیو اسد
عالم تمام حلقہ دام خیال ہے

हस्ती के मत फ़रेब में आ जाइयो 'असद'
आलम तमाम हल्क़ा-ए-दाम-ए-ख़याल है

Be not left deceived in the existential deception, Asad!
The-whole-encircled-world is screwed up in imagination.

Mirza Asad-u-Allah Khan Ghalib

It was the best of times, it was the worst of times, it was the age of wisdom, it was the age of foolishness, it was the epoch of belief, it was the epoch of incredulity, it was the season of Light, it was the season of Darkness, it was the spring of hope, it was the winter of despair, we had everything before us, we had nothing before us, we were all going direct to Heaven, we were all going direct the other way – in short, the period was so far like the present period, that some of its noisiest authorities insisted on its being received, for good or for evil, in the superlative degree of comparison only. (*A Tale of Two Cities,* 3)

6.1 The Text and the Author

The proposed framework in the previous chapter for literary interpretation will be used in the present hermeneutic labor to testify the book on Salman Rushdie's magnum opus *Midnight's Children (1981).* The novel has a syllogistic structure and set-up. It tells a tale of three similar and dissimilar countries – India, Pakistan and

Bangladesh. The world of the text opens up with a world that is the undivided India – in person, public, family and nation. Harish Trivedi in his article "Salman the Funtoosh: Magic Bilingualism in *Midnight's Children*" writes that:

> When in 1981, that madman-from-somewhere Salman Rushdie came out of nowhere and won the Booker Whatshisname *Midnight's Children*, the whole of India went wild with joy and received him into its bosom as a darling Piece-of-the-Moon. (By the whole of India is of course meant that an infinitesimal fraction of it reads fiction in English and Rushdie believes that India is only as old as Rushdie – and therefore only half as old, for example, as Nirad C. Chaudhury.) Nothing like this had happened, everyone agreed, since Tagore won in 1913 – even though not many had heard of Booker before, and hardly anyone of Rushdie. (69)

The so-called bloody narrator of the Indian Subcontinent – Salman Rushdie is rather known or in other words "mark[et]ed" for his *The Satanic Verses* (1988). The mighty fashionable genius in technique is more known for his notorious and blasphemous gambling with history, myth, politics, religion and culture than his literary product at least in South Asia – specifically in the Indian Subcontinents. It may be a postmodern narrative technique, but Rushdie appears equally skilled in the articulation of his 'things' right from the gutter-tongue to the narrative grand poetic style, from the big city Bombay's cheap-street vernacular to the high and sophisticated literary language use. In the novel, to some extent, the narrator speaks as a recently converted, jilted and prejudiced crusader. Nevertheless, Mujeebuddin Sayed in his "*Midnight's Children* and Its Indian Con/Text" comments on Rushdie's success and the novel as:

> When *Midnight's Children* was first published it was hailed as a masterpiece that demanded comparisons with such widely different writers as Swift, Joyce and Marquez and traditions as varied as modernism, postmodernism, and the epic modes of the Mahabharata and Ramayana. If Midnight's Children achieved its success in the West partly owing to its modernist/postmodernist techniques, its ability to "tell strange stories in familiar ways," in India itself, its success owed much not only to the deliberate evocation of the post-colonial Indian imagination and … […] … despite a certain cynicism about its own method, a newer and fresher picture of India and Indianness. (149)

6.2 The Reading Plan

At this point of reference, this is to clarify that the main focus of this chapter will be to a justful hermeneutics. The hermeneutics of suspicion applied on the text of Midnight's Children following the ways of interpretation suggested and discussed in the previous chapter – *Voice IMPACTS* the acronym will be brought to be practiced. The analysis will be based on the central metaphors of the text, that is from metaphors to text, and from text to the metaphors – especially with the reconfiguration of time and the narrative technique with its central voice. The reading of the novel will also lay emphasis on *narrative identity* and its *subjects* as well taking up the function of *application* and *appropriation* with the text. The text from its very inception seems to be a product of the hermeneutic suspicion with the historical knowledge which offers, in a way, a possible alternative and subjective history of India, of Rushdie's version, of India from a distance to West.

6.3 The World of the Text

The text opens many unknown and consciously locked windows of Indian Carnivalesque – full of polyphony. The novel also opens a world of its own – quite similar to the "willing suspension of disbelief" sort, screwing it in surrealistic or super-realistic manner, a self-recreated and appropriated world. The text appropriates family and national history and fiction-cum-fantasy. Rushdie appears meticulously setting the dates of history with his events that he narrates.

The events, facts, and figures of history cover approximately – almost a century from 1910 to 1977, till the declaration of emergency imposed by Mrs. Indira Gandhi. The novel breaks and denies the authenticity and the general truth claim of history. It was Kamala Das in the same context confessing somewhere about the *experience of Emergency* that "after Indira Gandhi I feared my husband the most…!" Rushdie himself in the "Introduction" of the novel remarks that "her [Mrs. Indira Gandhi] action during the Emergency was so heinous that she could no longer be considered a person of good character, and could therefore not be defamed. In other words, we would have had, in effect, to put her on trial for her misdeeds." (xvi)

The novel appears to be half a tale *of* time and half a tale *about* time. It exposes the mental, psychological and physical torture inflicted upon people by the greedy leaders. The text takes account of the separation of the families – where more than one million people were killed; and, approximately twelve million people were lost forever in the aftermath. The events and incidents also include the largest horrific migration on the face of the earth that human history has ever recorded.

Midnight's Children articulates the socio-economic biases, refugee crises and riots. It seems that the novel is paradigmatically a postcolonial text subverting the general notion of historiography. Any reader having a small understanding of Indian politics may be able to appropriate the text very easily into historical discourse associating it with the notion of history and narrativity – constituting 'a version' of narrative identity on a large stage and scope. The story starts from Kashmir South to the big city called Bombay, from Karachi to East Deccan, from India's independence to the horrors of the *Emergency Period.* The texture of the text coincides with the historical facts and fictional events and characters i. e. India's birth to independence and Saleem Sinai's birth on August 15, 1947 throughout the novel.

If it is not an exaggeration, then the novel holds on the entire 20th century Indian history in the background of Sinai saga carrying us from Jallian Walla Bagh massacre, Quite India Movement, the Cabinet Mission, the Role of Muslim League in partition, the rejection of seven states, language issues, riots, violence caused by bullies and military, the Indo-China war, the theft of the Prophet's hair from Hazratbal mosque, Kashmir, Kashmir massacre and all bloodshed, the war with Pakistan, to the liberation of Bangladesh etc. into three different sub-books of the novel.

6.4 The [Re] Configuration Time: A Mystery Called Maya

Paul Ricoeur in his *Freud and Philosophy* writes that "the structure of the narrative that tells of events that happened "once upon a time," our experience receives a temporal orientation, an élan extended between a beginning and an end; our present becomes changed with a memory and a hope." (39) In the same way Rushdie problematizes historical discourse through his imagination and a post-colonial reflection on the marginalised India by making history an artifact or using it as a raw material for his cause. Thus, the *stroke of midnight* gives a promise to a *brave new world, an independent* world (India). In the novel, this is the point of reference as far as the configuration of time is concerned, specified with the historically recorded time in a different and strange manner in which the long cycle of life continues as Sinai starts – "I was born in the city of Bombay…. once upon a time [….] … on the stroke of midnight. Clock-hand joined palms in respectful greetings as I came." (3) This is the way the clock-ridden twin time starts in the novel, it is as if it was an organised memory and recapitulation of the lived time fixed in writing, the novel begins with such expressions: "He seemed happy enough," "his beard was thick and red," "his hear, however, was darker," "there it was," "when young Adam was barely past puberty the dilapidated boatman said, '[that's] a nose to start a family on, my princeling. There'd be no mistaking whose brood they were. Mughal Emperors would have their right hand for noses like that one. There are dynasties waiting inside it," "he had a pile," "[he] was a living antithesis," "[memory] of my blue bedroom wall," "it was magic talk," "once it was set down," "he had had breath and good heart," – this is the way Rushdie sets [hi*story*] in motion. (1-40)

The reflection on time in the novel is like that of a prophet's revelation. The experience of time in the novel seems to be the revelation of humans as if the person is burning, bursting, fainting or dizzying. The narrative voice bares the same pain of the revelation on the spots of time; the narrator of the novel in the section "Hit-the-spittoon" starts reflecting on the same as – "I have begun to crack all over like an old jug-that my poor body, singular, unlovely, buffeted by too much history, subjected to drainage above and drainage below, mutilated by doors, brained by spittoons, has started coming apart at the seams. In short, I am literally disintegrating, slowly for the moment, although there are signs of acceleration." (43) Discussing the horror of 1947 Rushdie opens a window telling us that "[there] followed an illusionist January, a time so still on its surface that 1947 seemed not to have begun at all." (82) Within the experience of the time of 1947 with a minor character of Musa in the novel configures in an ambiguous way the time period of Moses who "once when he returned to destroy the world by accident" somewhere from the mountain Sinai, the "Tur-e-Sina." Within the subsection of the novel "Many Headed monsters," Sinai reflects on the same subject, the same allusion and the same configuration of time as:

> Unless, of course, there's no such thing as chance; in which case Musa-for all his age and servility-was nothing less than a time-bomb, ticking softly away until his appointed time; in which case, we should either-optimistically-get up and cheer, because if everything is planned in advance, then we all have a meaning, and are spared the terror of knowing ourselves to be random, without a why; or ebe, of course, we might-as pessimists-give up right here and now,

> understanding the futility of thought decision action, since nothing we think makes any difference anyway; things will be as they will. Where, then, is optimism? In fate or in chaos? Was my father being optimistic when my mother told him her news (after everyone in the neighborhood had heard it), and he replied with, 'I told you so; it was only a matter of time? My mother's pregnancy, it seems, was fated; my birth, however, owed a good deal to accident.
>
> 'It was only a matter of time,' my father said, with every appearance of pleasure; but time has been an unsteady affair, in my experience, not a thing to be relied upon. It could even be partitioned: the clocks in Pakistan would run half an hour ahead of their Indian counterparts.... (102)

After using the Hindustani myths such as Prince Ram, Hanuman Ji – the monkey Hindu god along with the many headed monster, called Ravana – Saleem Sinai, one of the most highly learned and well-read characters in the history of English literature captures the experiences of time using all his Faustus-style-knowledge. He himself starts suspecting his own memory and perception. Saleem brings his conscience or *cogito* to the court of self-critique in terms of narration, perception, conception and understanding things and time, he remarks on the same problem as:

> What, I ask, would be a fair description of the seer's match? And memory-my new, all-knowing memory, which encompasses most of the lives of mother, father, grandfather, grandmother and everyone else-answers: soft; squashy as corn flour pudding. Again, reluctantly, I ask: What was the condition of his lips? And the inevitable response: full; over fleshed; poetic. A third time I interrogated this memory of mine: what of MS Hair? The reply: thinning; dark; lank; worming over his ears. And now my unreasonable suspicions ask the ultimate question... did Amina, pure-as-pure, actually... because of her weakness for men who resembled Nadir Khan, could she have... in her odd frame of mind, and moved by the seer's illness, ... (116)

The forceful abduction of properties and the time of despair for those who were in business, the time of paradigm shift, shifting power at the time of India-Pakistan partition, the game of rich for rich, the Christian characters' anxiety, the Mary Pereira's lover Joseph and his Marxist assertion for socio-economic shift or change. His short assertion reveals a long background story untold in history as he cries that partition will benefit the rich only and not the poor at all. The scene where in the narrator sketches it out is this – the truth that Joseph was anxious about:

> On June 4th, my ill-matched parents left for Bombay by Frontier Mail. (There were hangings, voices hanging on for dear life, fists

> crying out, 'Maharaj! Open, for one tick only! Ohe, from the milk of your kindness, great sir, do us a favour!' And there was also-hidden beneath dowry in a green tin trunk-a forbidden, lapis-lazuli-encrusted, delicately-wrought silver spittoon.) On the same day, Earl Mountbatten of Burma held a press conference at which he announced the Partition of India, and hung his countdown calendar on the wall: seventy days to go to the transfer of power… sixty-nine… sixty-eight… tick, tock. (120)

This is the starting point from where Rushdie starts making his readers become conscious of clock-ridden time, the suspense of the experiencing partition time. Before coming forward Rushdie goes backward in time to tell how and when Britishers started dreaming for India and the time when finally they got settled here starting from 1633 they developed and fancied the idea of a British Bombay which was Methwold's vision, 1660-Charles II of England, the Catharine of the Portuguese House of Braganza till September 21st 1668 when the company finally captured and gripped over Bombay bay – the British Bombay, it "was a notion of such force that it set time in motion" and thus the historical time in this way "churned ahead" till the time where in August 1947 ending their India forceful illegitimate settling. (122)

Through the departure of the English William Methwold, Rushdie combines three different experiences of time together – the ancient, the medieval and the modern one as "… [There] are thirty days to go to the transfer of power," "Mr. Methwold is a little eccentric, that's all-can we not humor him? With our ancient civilisation, can we not be as civilised as he?'… and he drains his glass at one go," "Amina pictured herself as a convicted murderer in Mughal times, when death by crushing beneath a boulder had been a common punishment… and in the years to come, whenever she looked back at that time which was the end of the time," "time in which the tick tock of countdown calendars was rushing everyone towards August 15th, she would say: 'I don't know about any of that. To me, it was like time had come to a complete stop," "days and nights I've waited and still you won't get to being born!" "[salt] water washes the confessional floor.,. and now," "[tomorrow] I'll have a bath and shave," "[tomorrow], at last, there will be an end to stories," "Mountbatten's countdown calendar can be ignored no longer," and finally at the end – he adds that the "old Musa is still ticking like a time-bomb; but he can't be heard, because another sound is swelling now, deafening, insistent; the sound of seconds passing, of an approaching, inevitable midnight" (130-141). After this hard work of putting three different experiences of time together in the novel Rushdie starts pondering over the mysterious nature of time seriously in the subsection of the novel "Tick, tock," the narrator adds:

> Padma can hear it: there's nothing like a countdown for building suspense. I watched my dung-flower at work today, stirring vats like a whirlwind, as if that would make the time go faster. (And perhaps it did; time, in my experience, has been as variable and inconstant as Bombay's electric power supply. Just telephone the speaking clock if you don't believe me-tied to electricity, it's usually a few hours wrong. Unless we're the ones who are wrong... no people whose word for 'yesterday' is the same as their word for' tomorrow' can be said to have a firm grip on the time.) (142)

Rushdie as usual, plays or better gambles even with the clock time – and by doing that he succeeds to create suspense through his narrative technique. Saleem tells that "I am still over a day away from being born... but now the remorseless tick tock reasserts itself: twenty-nine hours to go, twenty-eight, twenty-seven...," "[but] now the countdown will not be denied... eighteen hours; seventeen; sixteen... and already, at Dr. Narlikar's Nursing Home," describing the "rituals of blood" and the "collective fiction in which anything was possible, a fable rivaled only by the two other mighty fantasies: money and God," "[twelve] hours to go," "eight hours to go," "six hours to go. The cocktail hour," "a cocktail containing equal proportions of panic, excitement and triumph... 'Arre Ahmed!' Amina Sinai yelled, 'Janum, the baby! It's coming-bang on time!'," "[suddenly] everything is saffron and green," "[it] is twenty-nine minutes to midnight," "twenty-seven minutes to midnight," "[twenty] minutes pass, with aaahs from Amina Sinai, coming harder and faster by the minute, and weak tiring aaahs from Vanita in the next room," "Jawaharlal Nehru begins:'... Long years ago we made a tryst with destiny; and now the time comes when we shall redeem our pledge-not wholly or in full measure, but very substantially...' It is two minutes to twelve," "[it] is two minutes to twelve," "[Wee] Willie Winkie rocks, rocks, his eyes as empty as a blind man's... will she live? won't she? ... and now, at last, it is midnight..." (146-56). And thus, in the expression "[are] Ahmed!' Amina Sinai yelled, 'Janum, the baby! It's coming-bang on time!" indicates the beginning of the world, the beginning of the time, the beginning of the independence, the beginning of a brave new world. The bang also reminds us the big bang theory of the beginning of the scientifically defined notion of time. But comparatively this midnight is a different one; it has got a different beginning, Saleem in this context adds:

> The monster in the streets has begun to roar, while in Delhi a wiry man is saying,'… At the stroke of the midnight hour, while the world sleeps, India awakens to life and freedom…' And beneath the roar of the monster there are two more yells, cries, bellows, the howls of children arriving in the world, their unavailing protests mingling with the din of independence which hangs saffron-and-green in the night sky-'A moment comes, which comes but rarely in history, when we step out from the old to the new; when an age ends; and when the soul of a nation long suppressed finds utterance…' while in a room with saffron-and-green carpet…. (156)

In the novel a time comes when Ahmad Sinai's assets are freezed and the "so called secular state gets some dam clever ideas," aftermaths Nirankar adds "[these] are bad times, Sinai bhai-freeze a Muslim's assets, they say, and you make him run to Pakistan, leaving all his wealth behind him. Catch the lizard's tail and he'll snap it off!" On another instance Ismail Ibrahim says 'It's my fault,' [….] 'I should have warned you, Sinai bhai. I have heard about these freezings-only well-off Muslims are selected." After the controversial abduction of properties another dark moment of time is recorded in the novel, and that is of the horror spread by doubtful rumors. The sub section of one of the books starts as "other omens: comets were seen exploding above the Back Bay; it was reported that flowers had been seen bleeding real blood; and in February the snakes escaped from the Skaapsteker Institute. The rumour spread that a mad Bengali snake-charmer, a Tubriwallah, was travelling the country, charming reptiles from captivity…." (185-88)

It is noted in the novel that Rushdie after a regular pause in his *fictory* keeps on reflecting on different aspects of time such as time – the mystery called maya in Indian vernacular. Considering this notion, the narrator opens up in the novel from Indo-Anglian angle as:

> Think of this: history, in my version, entered a new phase on August 15th, 1947-but in another version, that inescapable date is no more than one fleeting instant in the Age of Darkness, Kali-Yuga, in which the cow of morality has been reduced to standing, teeter-ingly, on a single leg! Kali-Yuga-the losing throw in our national dice-game; the worst of everything; the age when property gives a man rank, when wealth is equated with virtue, when passion becomes the sole bond between men and women, when falsehood brings success (is it any wonder, in such a time, that I too have been confused about good and evil?)…. Began on Friday, February 18th, 3102 b.c.; and will last a mere 432,000 years! Already feeling somewhat dwarfed, I should add

> nevertheless that the Age of Darkness is only the fourth phase of the present Maha-Yuga cycle which is, in total, ten times as long; and when you consider that it takes a thousand Maha-Yugas to make just one Day of Brahma, you'll see what I mean about proportion. (269)

For time, for glory, for goddess, for love, Rushdie revives the Indian mythical notion of the understanding of time. Starting from Indian Lotus goddess who possesses Dung to the sacred rivers Ganga, Yamuna and Sarasvatito glorify Padma, "his Padma: beguiling and comforting mortal men while they pass through the dream-web of Maya.... Padma, the Lotus calyx, which grew out of Vishnu's navel, and from which Brahma himself was born; Padma the Source, the mother of Time!" (270) After this deep reflection on time, Saleem Sinai on his tenth birthday calls on in his unique audio-visual conference with the help of his gifted nose – at this time this gathering seems to be a happy gathering, Saleem interacts each one of them name by name, discussing every body's unique gift that the all the children have. He also reveals that there were 1001 children born at the stroke of midnight. This was the time of "...Kali-Yuga; the children of the hour of darkness were born, I'm afraid, in the midst of the age of darkness; [...] ... [certainly] it was a hallucinatory time in the days leading up to my tenth birthday." (177-9)

As was confessed in the beginning that the novel, in a way, was an organised and coherent record of memories of Rushdie's 'his*tory,'* Saleem (Salman Rushdie) himself reveals about the memory's truth that "memory has its own special kind. It selects, eliminates, alters, exaggerates, minimizes, glorifies, and vilifies also; but in the end it creates its own reality, its heterogeneous but usually coherent version of events; and no sane human being ever trusts someone else's version more than his own."' (292) In memorising or in recapitulating time Rushdie seems to be so obsessed with the expression "once upon a time," "night," and "midnight" that it starts looking like extreme repetition in the novel. In most of the cases "midnight" appears to be a metaphor for Rushdie's representation of his Indian picture at large. Night represents darkness, danger; despair division, horror, terror, and freedom as well. Therefore, in the novel, anything that is important mostly happens at night or rather at midnight. For midnight, Saleem adds that "[midnight] has many children; the offspring of Independence were not all human. Violence, corruption, poverty, generals, chaos, greed and pepper pots... I had to go into exile to learn that the children of midnight were more varied than I-even I-had dreamed." (405)

In some other instances where Saleem deeply reflects on the nature of time that is always slippery on its own, he says that "[what-chews-on-bones] refuses to pause… It's only a matter of time. This is what keeps me going: …when the telegram arrived… once upon a time. No, that won't do, there's no getting away from the date…." In the same subsection of the novel "Drainage and the desert" he further adds that "And the time? The time matters, too. Well, then: in the afternoon. No, it's important to be more… At the stroke of three o'clock, which, even in the north, is the hottest time of day…" Thus, the novel slowly, slowly but gradually moves to some ending points as does time, time that leads humans towards certain ends, this is what observes Rushdie in "[how] Saleem achieved purity" on the same subject here [what] is waiting to be told: the return of tick tock. But now time is counting down to an end, not a birth; there is, too, a weariness to be mentioned, a general fatigue so profound that the end, when it comes, will be the only solution, because human beings, like nations and fictional characters, can simply run out of steam, and then there's nothing for it but to finish with them." (454)

The tick-tock technique of Rushdie is to make the readers conscious of time. He observes that if one desires to understand the modern history and time he must understand the modern bombing pattern – it seems here that he may be conscious of India, Pakistan, China wars, or in broad, the bombing pattern of USA, Russia and other dominating nations have done in modern history, he adds in the novel "[in] order to understand the recent history of our times, it is only necessary to examine the bombing-pattern of that war with an analytical, unprejudiced eye." (469) This may also be noted to strengthen the point that most of the time measuring watches in modern time tell us one significant time of bombing on Hiroshima or Nagasaki, that is 10: 10 am. It reminds us of the horrors of World Wars. In the third part of the novel that is about "Buddha" opens up with 1965 and aftermath horrors, here the narrator seems to be responding to Buddha's shrine metaphorically as:

> How the Buddha regained his name: Once, long ago, on another Independence Day, the world had been saffron and green. This morning, the colours were green, red and gold. And in the cities, cries of 'Jai Bangla!' And voices of women singing 'Our Golden Bengal', maddening their hearts with delight… in the centre of the city, on the podium of his defeat, General Tiger Niazi awaited General

> Manekshaw. (Biographical details: Sam was a Parsee. He came from Bombay. Bombayites were in for happy times that day.) And amid green and red and gold, the buddha in his shapeless anonymous garment was jostled by crowds; and then India came. India, with Sam at her head. (527)

The "memories of invisibility" continues and Parvati meets Saleem in real time and space opening up with time in present excitement, she says in joy and excitement as "'O God, too much excitement!' she cries. 'Arre baap, Saleem, you remember-the Children, yaar, O this is too good! …. So many years I only saw you inside here,' she taps her forehead, 'and now you're here with a face like a fish. Hey, Saleem!" The entire novel is full of the expressions such as "at night," "tonight," "afternoon" etc. and at the end Rushdie adds great Buddha, the person in his *chutney* and thus reflects Saleem "and Time was assassinated in consequence; and there were houris in a temple, and we only just escaped in time." (567) In the meanwhile, Rushdie takes on Indira trial of emergency and another birth of Saleem type/ version whom he names Adam Sinai, he adds on the birth of another unique and gifted child:

> He was born in Old Delhi… once upon a time. No, that won't do, there's no getting away from the date: Aadam Sinai arrived at a night-shadowed slum on June 25th, 1975. And the time? The time matters, too. As I said: at night. No, it's important to be more… On the stroke of midnight, as a matter of fact. Clock-hands joined palms. Oh, spell it out, spell it out: at the precise instant of India's arrival at Emergency, he emerged. There were gasps; and, across the country, silences and fears. And owing to the occult tyrannies of that benighted hour, he was mysteriously handcuffed to history, his destinies indissolubly chained to those of his country. Un-prophesied, uncelebrated, he came; no prime ministers wrote him letters; but, just the same, as my time of connection neared its end, his began. He, of course, was left entirely without a say in the matter; after all, he couldn't even wipe his own nose at the time.

He was the child of a father who was not his father; but also, the child of a time which damaged reality so badly that nobody ever managed to put it together again. (586)

6.5 The Metaphor of Midnight: An Interpretation

Focusing on the *metaphor of midnight,* it is observed that the night is more than a night or a period. Rushdie notes it as an "[endless] night, days, weeks, months without the sun, or rather (because it's important to be precise) beneath a sun as cold as a stream-rinsed plate, a sun washing us in lunatic midnight light; I'm talking about the winter of 1975-6. In the winter, darkness; and also, tuberculosis." (590) The technique of storytelling in the novel seems to be full of fabulative inventiveness. The events and the facts of history of different nations, theology, philosophy, literature, and politics including all artificial and self-made metaphors seem to be instrumental to reach out to the richness and vastness of senses, references, reflections and experiences of time, the time which has recently passed on! The time which has been experienced and which was full of pain, despair and hope, a time which evolved with saffron and green colors by making the states red.

In its fashion and structure, the text can be called a saga novel with postmodern tone and technique full of bilingual expressions, portmanteau, compound words and constant conscious repetitions of words and expressions. The text also has allusions from multiple traditions in the novel. The technique called magic realism serves the pleasure of fancy with superlative imaginative heights. The plot does not appear paramount but story, characters and time, the time that Ricoeur calls concordance and discordance. The story moves in linear, nonlinear, chronemic and non-chronemic order, space and time in its setting. Rushdie brings estrangement and foregrounds his ideas and fancy hyperbolic descriptions in his own unique style and diction. Time and characters take over the plot of the novel, and the text interestingly remains a novel as a genre. AND this is what proves Ricoeur's thesis and his hard work right that narratives entirely deal with time, they are either of time or about time. Luckily *Midnight's Children* appears to be both – half *of* the time; and half *about* the time – this is something which has been named *fictory* as Ricoeur had said in *Time and Narrative* that the true configuration of time should be half historical and half fictional.

In the novel, it is observed that there are three invisible and active characters, one that of an eccentric historian and second that of the magician's time – both equally play with the game of time – both equally interest the readers. The third one is the logician in the novel who never appears or acts but governs the entire narrative discourse of *Midnight*. In present assessment and interpretation, the novel may not be equal, but it surely reminds us of another great text, War *and Peace* (1869) by Leo Tolstoy. *Midnight's Children, like* Nietzsche's "mobile army of metaphors" narrates the truth and also takes into account everything else that remains unsaid in history or otherwise.

The metaphor of midnight symbolises the modern or recent history of India and the Indian sub-continent in a serious discourse of narrative fiction using history as its raw material. The text opens the true spot of time in a fictional manner. The midnight metaphor reconfigures time and thus it rather helps to configure the same. Midnight is the night that has recently passed, the recent past. Sinai recalls time through his memories, the metaphor also tells a story of terrible time in an ambivalent way, as a plea for terrible and broken self, beings, countries, colors, and languages. The text reveals to be a post-colonial self-reflexive Indian Saga and a national and family genealogy as well. The text as a whole seems to be a revelation on a single subject advocating multiple human *Voices,* a subjective assertion to the official historiography. In the novel, Rushdie has tried to pour every drop of his blood to put forward his subjective vision, truth and reality in his self-made fresh metaphors. The subjective version of Sinai, as has been discussed, denies some of the facts provided by the so called official Indian history – and in return the novel [co]ordinates, re-writes it with a revisionist attitude in fiction. Here Rushdie and Ricoeur are found on the same line of the understanding in which they believe that the truth and reality is something that the individual subject perceives in both the ways – the fictional and historical one. Ricoeur and other eminent authors long back had discussed that true configuration of time must be quasi-fictive and quasi-historical or in a new coinage within the *Fictory.*

The novel brings the haunting others, or the marginal in front. It also sheds light on the socio-political frustration, the rise of the middle class, and the anxiety of poor and rich conflicts and divide, decaying empirical power of British Empire, power politics, and an indirect socio-political and religio-cultural encounter. The entire text seems to be a "quest/ion" on historical narratives and historical truth.

The novel narrates a painful tale, conflict, clash, terror, hope and peace. The text gives the pleasure of purgation. The fantasy and the illusions of the novel narrate the possibility or probability of the unrecorded history; the history which institutions do not record. The novel is a bare critique of the same. Rushdie motivates a great deal to take history as a text and to reconstruct (appropriate) it accordingly in a humanistic manner to reach to the events recorded and the unrecorded.

The novel as a whole also questions the notions of human identity that we have by suggesting a peaceful direction "the narrative identity" which has remarkably been exemplified in two different characters of the novel: Saleem and Shiva both have the narrative identities although they belong to their other identities differently. But what they are, they are because of what they have lived, the so-called other blood identities they cannot wear with them and whatever they have been, they can never wear it off...! Thus, it is practically proved here that identity is always narrative. The sole aim of Rushdie's novelistic crusade in the novel is to show that history discusses only the surface of reality but fiction the inner conflicts. The novel smells against Islam, the religion and has a negative tone and texture towards Hinduism. This is something which seems the weakest point in the novel. Nevertheless, the novel maps the eclectic hybridity and incorporates itself into ancient, medieval and modern Indian values and conventions. The text resists and asserts the polyglotish and hybrid Indian culture. In the story, the personal becomes quite national and continental.

As mentioned in the beginning that the world of story (text) has fabulistic and folkloric Indian tradition called *nautanki* or something what Bakhtine calls Carnivalesque wherein Rushdie represents polyphonic Voices centering all the motives to the character called Saleem. The text also gives a nihilistic, absurdist and existential account to its readers. It seems to be a plea for an idealistic Indian culture. All the local, national, historical, religious, political codes seem to be broken. This is observed at this point that the novel exposes Indira Gandhi's and Congresses Party's betrayal of all secular, social, democratic and constitutional values including the repression against public during the emergency in 1976. The two poignant aspects are supposed to be the seeds and motivation factor for the novel's birth. Critics and readers both observe that there is a novel within the novel – both in the content and the technique.

Rushdie's *Fictory* (hi-story, *faction*) and his narrative formation of *Midnight's Children* strive to constitute the national identity and the poly-vocal Indian hybrid culture. Thus, Rushdie's attitude towards history, religion and culture seems to be the humanistic and the deconstructive one. The novel indicates a great deal of intersexuality – first of all it reminds us of the influence of *Arabian Nights (Alph-Lailah) "1001 Nights* as it is told in the novel that at the stroke of midnight 1001 children were born. By employing the technique of magic-realism which is quite akin to the "willing suspension of disbelief" technique or machinery in literature remind us ST Coleridge and Gabriel Garcia Marquez. Since the production period of the text was the second last decade of the last century, it employs most of the postmodern techniques of narration which are well adjusted in the novel. Rushdie uses magic realism technique as an analysing tool to catch out the eternal experiences and spots of time which appear slippery in a normal way of linear narrative technique for a commentary on time. The technique encircles the vast, wide and large realities, truths and meanings of life. *Midnight's Children* is supposed to be Rushdie's "Whale" that is too much and too big when it is taken as a family chronicle, neo-historiography through magic realism, literary fantasy, family history, parody, allegory, black humor and an autobiography. The text is a saga written in a controlled and well managed anger, a master piece of third world narrativity against the discrimination of the country's minorities.

Being a landmark, *Midnight's Children* marks a new beginning in Indian English literature, it sets a new period of Indian English writing amalgamating many tastes together in an alien technique. The text provides a 3D effect of midnight time – the divided and undivided India with family-nation interface using all possible myths in a first-person narration taking an account of diasporic dislocation, transnational space along with the age-old sexual practices between old and modern couples.

The text has been weaved in past tense as a mode of narration using compound words and deliberate mis-spellings for depicting amorphous and messy Indian reality. In most of his native expressions Rushdie uses the so-called Hindustani/Rekhta/Rekhti or what now we call Urdu-Hindi in Roman script. Rushdie also brings in use the mongrel-cheap-Bombay-street-expressions – may be a *tapori* touch in his deep and typical linguistic expression. Rushdie projects the orthodoxical stereo type stagnant Islamic culture from Kashmir, decaying British Bombay to the so-called liberal and humanistic moderate world view.

The space and time of every kind in the text are sharply in focus. The nature of narrative and artistic mode reveals the influence of narrative technique of *Arabian Nights,* the great *Mahabharata* and to some extent the echoes of *Katha Sarit.* The story of Saleem told by Rushdie creates a constant suspense for its readers. Saleem's telepathic and telephonic powers are representative of human transcendence in a justified way.

Midnight's Children represents a Neo-Avant Guard Production and its representation. There are leaps of faith and an Abyss of doubt in Neil Ten Kortenaross' words. The novel is a surrealistic "comic zeugma of synchronicity" of a third world space. The narrator openly admits that the novel is an account of Saleem Sinai's version, a version – therefore the gravity for the hermeneutics of suspicion to the novel, narrator or whatever happens in the novel would always remain open for justful discourse with a hermeneutic labour. The novel does not deal with a passage to India but all about India as a whole.

The technique of the novel, once again, defeats the plot that is something that Ricoeur has already talked about in his *Time and Narrative* with special reference to 17th, 18th, and 19th century novels with all narrative techniques and innovation in the narrative modes. The technique of 'magic-realism,' too, proved that the birth of life-time (concordance-discordance) and the character declares the death of plot that was once mistakenly supposed to be the soul of drama and novel as well. Here it is witnessed that the novel remains quite a novel without losing its identity in the absence of a plot as a soul of the novel. It does not affect its function, life events, and time do not stop – they go on… and the novel with all its comprehensive depth is experienced and identified – the big game of life continues.

Mr. Trivedi may be partially right in judging Salman Rushdie, the person as Funtoosh, but his flack on *Midnight's Children* and his "sovereign author-ity" seems to be unnecessary. It can rather be said metaphorically that the novel is "a tale, told by an idiot, full of sound and fury, signifying" and re-signifying many things, a tale which initially talked about the undivided Indian 'Tiranga'. Leaving a couple of lapses, the novel is found as one of the finest literary works in English – in fact a landmark in Indian English fiction. Critics are calling the text as a postmodern chutney in Indian tin drum. Rushdie's [mis]representation or [well] representation of history, historiography, family and nation will always remain an attraction for a justful hermeneutics. He should be given the due credit for his *fictory*, *faction* or if we better call it *hiterature* – a fine *hiterary* commentary on time and tense, a prism on a single *subject.*

Waqt ke saath hai mitti ka safar sadio – n se
Kisko maaloom hai, kahan ke hain kidhr ke hum hain…

(With time, dust has been travelling for centuries,
Who knows, of where we are, and are headed to what end….)

Nida Fazli

CHAPTER 7

A Turn towards the Hermeneutics of Suspicion

In the preceding chapters of the present book, an attempt has been made to analyse, explore and investigate Paul Ricoeur's philosophy of language and literary hermeneutics. After having proved language as a vitally/entirely metaphorical phenomenon, the book explored the ancient, medieval and modern conventions of hermeneutics. In the end, a very useful framework for literary interpretation has been incorporated. It has appeared that the narrative agencies of human life strive to create metaphors to narrate events, imprints, history, ideology and identity.

The dead and live metaphors constitute the empire of language. The metaphors which become so automatised that they lose the gravitational attraction of being a charged metaphor so much so that they fail to narrate the infinite richness and the freshness of fresh human reflections – they in a way, exhaust their users. Thus, new metaphors which are charged enough are required for the work. Language, being in a constant flux, has to be in this way – it has to beget novel metaphors to a valid cyclic period of time to serve the purposes to man and beyond. Language has to open the gates of semantic innovations and pertinences to enlarge, validate, and enrich the human discourse.

It has been noted that hermeneutics and interpretation theory in the 20th century gradually and strongly manifested itself as one of the predicaments of philosophical traditions, conventions, theoretical, critical and practical status on the intellectual stage. Paul Ricoeur, with the framework of his extensive and exhaustive network and references, has always been found in progression and flux too. He keeps himself engaged and involved in writing and rewriting his own ideas. Modern hermeneutics is inevitably associated with German intellectual think-tank and philosophy. From the traditional hermeneutics, reaching to Schleiermacher and William Dilthey – Ricoeur is not only acknowledged as one of the prominent representatives of present hermeneutic philosophy but also as a thinker who challenges every founding structure of the traditional hermeneutics by reshaping and redefining the status and position of hermeneutic tradition.

In the present, the hermeneutic discipline seems to have dramatic changes as a combined outcome of fundamental, intellectual, economics and cross-cultural communication and open dialog nationally, internationally, globally or Glocally. It might have carried on – or brought on by the revolution in technology – the fiber optics, the greatest historical change where in all narrative modes have seen a shift from page to picture or from page to screen or virtual narratives. In today's time, it seems that narratives are more seen rather than read as earlier were heard. Ricoeur has, therefore, been worried in his *Time and Narrative* about the death of the art of narrating and story-telling. It is seen that in today's times, novels, stories, and fictional work are more watched than read with the help of audio-visual aids. The screen narratives have occupied the minds of people and have changed the perspectives of life. The self is constructed through the screen narratives rather than the real cultural screen culture. Thus, to understand the self, it is the screen that rewrites life – or rather re-shapes life and brings the subject in a very colorful and impressive ink. The page that was only in black and white has now the most attractive devices for fancy and imagination to create special effects from 2D to 5D world experiences.

The greatest challenge, in today's time seems to be the screen narratives as an object of hermeneutic labor. There emerged new areas of problem – i. e. film as text or text as film – or screen as a text or text as screen. Man in real life, man in real life, men from real life to reel narratives and life from reel narratives to real life which gives rise to another hermeneutic circularity. Nevertheless, narratives whatsoever show the true virtual spaces where we see our actual faces, practices, ideologies, life realities and all the action texts. There are hidden voices entwined with metaphors in all human narratives, therefore, all identities are narrative identities.

"Perspectives on Hermeneutics" has been an attempt to reflect on the problems mentioned above leaving the screen narratives. The book comes to the whole convention of hermeneutics starting from Indian, Jewish, Chinese, Christian and Islamic traditions of interpretive philosophy. The introduction attempts to question the whole notion of the nature of language. The primary concern in this modest attempt was to understand the nature of language as if it was entirely metaphorical which Ricoeur impressively proves through his concepts of semantic innovation and new semantic pertinences being generated naturally in language.

Language appears to be metaphorical in every sense of the term. Thus appears the requirement of hermeneutics and the principles or the ways of interpretation of linguistic or nonlinguistic expressions and human actions as well. It also includes a general methodology of understanding the phenomenology of Dasein and Cogito. It is observed that during the Renaissance period, hermeneutics was given a new currency. After Martin Luther's thesis hermeneutics enters different and distinct directions: ontological, phenomenological and transcendental spheres. It has been noted that it was Schleiermacher who for the first time tried to free hermeneutics from the religious domain and defined it as *an art of avoiding misunderstanding.* He concentrated on physiological or divinatory aspects. He based his phenomenological dualism on ego and non-ego. For him the ego has a body and a soul both. Man has some organisation and his intellect is organic. There is nothing like pure mind and pure soul. He believes that the author himself functions in language. Schleiermacher associates divinatory or psychological aspects with feminine forces and grammatical and linguistic with masculine forces. Dilthey later redevelops Schleiermacher's understandings of hermeneutics as *general theory of understanding* in his great and revolutionary essay "The Rise of Hermeneutics." (1900) Dilthey goes from textual expressions to the life expressions and thinks that it takes place in *objective mind* and for him understanding is always in the *totality of man himself.* He believes that the prime source of human understanding arises from language, literature, moral norms and religion. His hermeneutics has three aspects: *experience, expressions and understanding.* In conclusion, Dilthey's *objective mind* and *man as totality in himself* seem to be quite similar to that of Schleiermacher's division between linguistic and psychological aspects.

Heidegger incorporates the act of interpretation into an existential philosophy of understanding called Dasein by making an impressive and influential analysis of B/being in his *Being and Time.* He concludes that man is a time bound being. He tries to recover the ontology of textual being which is only found within the metaphoricity of human discourse. For him, metaphorical can only exist in the metaphysical and metaphors are produced when physics and metaphysics clash….!

He brings understanding of the event in intentional, phenomenological, historical existential, ontological and linguistic context. For him, understanding is something which was *laying there* but has been appropriated *in now* – the *now* is always temporal. In his opinion, there are three kinds of awareness: *fore-having, fore-sight and fore conception. Fore-having* is what is out there, *fore-seeing* is the conscious interacting grasp and linking it to *fore-having* which has been foreign till *now*, till *then.* This is something that has now become conceivable and graspable, something home like. *Fore conception* is pre-creation – as the writer consciously gets into the hidden semantic meanings, it is a pre-reflective faculty or agency which transmits and transforms the present of the present. According to him, language which is the house of B/being – *speaks*. Thus, Heidegger takes a sacred turn in saying that all being is in Being.

Gadamer in his *Truth and Method* presents a hermeneutics of tradition. He rejects the hermeneutics of *being* and considers it only a tool for interpretation. He names it as a *universal method*, a method of dialogue and fusion. Gadamer ponders over the historicity of language and revises the validity of tradition for better human understanding. For him interpretation of a text generally involves the application in the sense of an assimilation or appropriation to a new life-context of a work as the text slips away from its author and escapes from its original zone and as it builds a career of its own.

Paul Ricoeur seems to be questioning and suspecting Gadamer's historicity, traditionality and contextuality of the text. Ricoeur exemplifies his theory of epoché on Marx, Freud and Nietzsche. Ricoeur moves from text to action. He seriously dips deep in Kierkegaard's principle of *cogito ergo sum*, Heidegger's *Dasein* or B/being, Schleiermacher's *general hermeneutics*, Dilthey's concepts of *explanation and understanding*, Bette's concepts of *explanation*, Habermas' hermeneutics of *explanatory understanding* and his idea of *depth-hermeneutics*, Freud's theory of *psychoanalysis*, Gadamer's idea of *historicity, tradition, application and fusion of horizons*. Ricoeur also criticizes Saussure's understanding of language as a system of signs. The other half of the introduction deals with Ricoeur's understandings of metaphor, language, time and narrative – which are discussed in detail in the following chapters.

Hermeneutics of Metaphor and the Nature of Language, as promised in the introduction seriously deals with the hermeneutics of metaphor and the evolution of language being metaphoric. The first half of the chapter discusses metaphor and language prior to Paul Ricoeur and in the second half evaluates and critically analyses his *La Metaphore vive (The Rule of Metaphor)*. Metaphor, throughout the ages has been a bone of contention for linguists, philosophers, literary critics and many others in ancient, medieval and modern discourses. The chapter explores the above said problem from Roman Quintilian's *Institute of Oratory* to Paul Ricoeur's *The Rule of Metaphor*. Roman Quintilian concludes metaphor in three different aspects: necessity, to gain increased significance, force; and to ornament. Although it was Giambattista Vico who is credited for being the first to identify Metaphor, Metonymy, Synecdoche and Irony – as four basic tropes to which all others are reducible. This reduction was popularised in the 20th century by Kenneth Burke – he called these tropes as *four master tropes of literature*. He equates metaphor with perspective; Metonymy with reduction; Synecdoche with representation and Irony with dialectics. Burke seems more interested with the truth value rather than being all of them figures.

I. A. Richards strongly refuses Aristotle's understanding of the same. Richards formulates – or happens to formulate one of the most impressive *frames* for metaphor's explanation and understanding that is: tenor and vehicle. He separates the original idea and the borrowed one from each other or what is being said and to what the thing is compared with. Richards grounds metaphor on some common association in language. His metaphor seems to be more rhetoric than semantic or semiotic. Although, to some extent he seems to be having the same notion that language by nature is entirely metaphorical. For him there is nothing like the genius part that cannot be imported to one another in metaphor. He mentions in his definition that everyday language too is equally metaphorical.

Max Black twenty years later, in his essay "Metaphor" propagates the theory of substitution and modifies Richard's metaphorical frame. He proceeds from word metaphor to statement metaphors. He distinguishes between interaction and the substitution view of metaphor. Metaphorical statements have two distinct subjects: *the principal* and *the subsidiary* one. For him these subjects are *systems* than things. The metaphor works through application of the *principal subject* to a system of associated implications characterised by the subsidiary *subject.* He talks of metaphorical transfers or a shift in meaning as well. Max Black appears to be against the hegemony of words.

Donald Davidson opposes Max Black's substitution views. He associates it with an emotive notion of language. In his understanding metaphor nudges its reader with a similarity view. Beardsley claims metaphor to be elliptical similes, which has *self-contradictory* attribution in which one is not able to find connoted meaning. If the *self-contradiction* seems to be directly significant, then it gets named – oxymoron (as cruel kindness). But if it is indirectly significant – then it becomes paradoxical (as female male). Thus, for Davidson, the *self-contradiction* is the basis of all metaphors.

Paul Ricoeur criticises all the above English language critics saying them common language philosophers – especially English language critics. Ricoeur, too, thinks that metaphor destroys one old order only to re-create or invent another one which belongs to the heuristics of thought. Ricoeur slightly refutes Aristotle in saying that *to metaphorise well* has to do something with verbs rather than to a noun figure (For Aristotle metaphor was to name thus – a noun). According to Ricoeur metaphor ceases to be arbitrary and trivial. He associates metaphor with poetics especially with a theory of mimetic structures which subordinate muthos. There is a double tension in it – first is the submission to reality and second the fabulative invention which proceeds with enabling elevation. The double tension creates a referential function. He thinks that metaphor is at work of *saying and poeticizing.* He associates figure and catachresis with metaphor mentioning that the ideas lack proper sign – similar is the case with that of catachresis which stands for a situation which is with a sign already having one idea that is made available to the idea on an ad hoc basis. Thus, metaphor resembles catachresis and becomes quite a part of the function of language. Ricoeur further associates word metaphors with semiotics and statement metaphors with semantics of discourse. At this point he indicates the limitations of Saussure's understanding of language as a system of signs. He observes that the semantic of discourse constitutes half of the language part – and the other half has been ignored by Saussure as sign leaves out the order of discourse. Thus, innovation of a new meaning must also be equally a linguistic creation. He also mentions polysemy as a part of linguistic impetus to become a common meaning adding to the lexical entices which adds to the history of language as code or system. Thus, metaphors increase polysemy at the time when they are dead and all the living metaphors are at work to evolve and create new language.

Under another debate – the monism of sign and primacy of word, Ricoeur reflects that there is a metaphorical crisis found in the context of word, there is an abyss, a constant ignorance as the message always remains with sentence. The word is at the mercy of being connected – the connecting layer between *phonema* and *syntagma.*

Mentioning polysemy, synonymy and homonymy, Ricoeur talks of two principal aspects of language that they add and satisfy – that is *congruence* and *plentitude.* Polysemy adds *same-senses relation*; and synonymy and homonymy add *productive vagueness* in a generic sense as a constant demand of more and further discrimination made on the actual context. Thus, synonymy at once, simultaneously plays two distinct roles – *the stylistic and emphasis or reinforcement.* He calls polysemy a *lexical ambiguity*. Thus, metaphors serve all these purposes or all these functions which are found together as a whole in the structure of metaphor which create and add to the empire of language. Ricoeur believes that metaphor is a trope *of resemblance par excellence* in classical rhetoric. It is primarily connected with naming or denomination. In model, the point of resemblance gets closely united with those of borrowing deviation, substitution and exhaustive paraphrases. Resemblance, in his words, motivates borrowing.

For Ricoeur, metaphor and metonymy do not primarily define figures and tropes but they strongly define the general process of language. Metaphor has *iconic moments*; the *resemblance* and *fictive aspects* of metaphor also add to some new situations and contexts to function in language. They add to the ways in which we perceive and – this becomes the poetic function of metaphor. Metaphor bears a semantic challenge – something he calls semantic new impertinences and semantic innovations. Metaphor appears to be *self-contradictory and self-destructive* and it reveals the logical structure of the similar. Resemblance corresponds to the predicative operation in which approximation carries close to the resistance of being distant. Metaphor serves to bring closer – something that was earlier distant. Thus, the difference shares something to add to language. Metaphor gets associated with the *copula* – that connects the links between the subject and the predicate of a proposition. Metaphor moves from saying to *saying as*. The similarity and resemblance also add an imaginary *and illusionary* dimension to it. Metaphor has a *schematic structure* which invokes images – and thus, there is an *epoché* required – that is the suspension proper to the imaginary or illusory (meaning).

Metaphor has a sense and a reference, a sense that has to do something with meaning and reference to reality out there. In this way metaphors *describe and re-describe* reality. This description and redescription add to language. The poetic language to become deviation in it, is too productive by nature – it results in the very essence of creativity and making structure. Ricoeur adds a novel idea that metaphor has a *split-reference*, therefore, for him, the expansion for the real reference becomes the condition of access to virtual mode of reference. The epoché of natural reality becomes important. In the metaphorical discourse the referential power in Ricoeur's words, is linked to the eclipse of the ordinary reference. In this way, the creation of heuristic functions opens the road to rediscription. There, in metaphorical expression or metaphoric truth is speculation which joins the same job of catachresis and vagueness. The splitting of reference and description of reality gets attached with the imaginative variation of fiction. Thus, it requires an epoché – a suspension proper!

"Hermeneutics of Time: Threefold *Mimesis* and the Aporetics of Temporality in the Poetics of Narrativity" critically explores and analyses Ricoeur's *Time and Narrative* which is in three volumes. Herein, he seriously develops and interests into the aporetics of temporality in the poetics of narrativity. The work reveals the three-fold mimetic structure in the narrative constructs. The chapter concludes that metaphor, time and narrative configuration have a productive circularity. Narratives and metaphors add to language equally – narratives by their circularity and fabulative inventions and metaphors by their – productive and re-descriptive function. Thus, time appears to be of three different kinds: *prefigured time*, that is stage one of mimesis as is life and its narrative pre-understanding – that is original which precedes to the second stage – that is the *configured time* – something like a meditation on textual configuration – a meditation on text which composes a narrative. After that comes a third part the *refigured time, a third* stage of mimesis which is the application of narratives into one's own life – AND this continues as prefiguring, configuring and refiguring of time etc.....

Ricoeur seems to be re-interpreting Aristotle as plot was considered a soul part. He thinks that the interpreters were mistaken; he mentions that Aristotle did talk of it, but he also talked about the *concordance and discordance* process of continuation of things around us – the basic structure and function of time which puts everything together. The events, incidents and actions are joined together in the plot. Thus, it is the concordance and discordance mechanism of temporality which constitutes the plot – the temporality makes the plot – a well-knit plot!

For Ricoeur, symbols contain important information in the narrative anchorage. They contain temporality therein with them. Time for Ricoeur has no division, there is only one time-and that is present. Thus, there is the present of past things, present of present things and present of future things. Heidegger, Ricoeur and Einstein – all three seem to have a similar opinion. Ricoeur re-declares the death of plot, he openly admits that in modern narratives characters have superseded plot. He makes a remarkable and an impressive analysis of English (mostly), and French narratives to prove and strengthen his argument. The English narratives from the 17th century till now – the modern narratives have proven and shown how plot has been replaced by character and the techniques of concordance and discordance representation in the narratives. Thus, narratives give form to the unformed. In conclusion, the poetics of narrativity bears temporality. The narratives require an epoché to re-configure the narrative reality and the truth value of the things projected within. The world of the text and the world of the reader have to face hermeneutic challenges in reading a novel. The reading becomes a task and act – quite comprehensive to understand the affairs of the textual functions and the reader's subjective and linguistic play with and within the play. Thus, through this process directly or indirectly narrative identity gets constituted which must be submitted to an epoché.

"'Exigesis,' Hermeneutics and the Textuality of Text" talks of exegesis, existence and hermeneutics of text in relation with the understanding of the changed subject through the textual and configurative temporal experience of the world of the text. The chapter sheds light on the subjects' authenticity of consciousness – the so-called *cogito*. This is something that Ricoeur too agrees to be a product of false consciousness; therefore, it must be submitted to epoché or a justful hermeneutics which explores the existential changes with the subjects. Ricoeur calls it the *problematic of cogito*. Critiquing the symbol and symbolic expression, Ricoeur reflects that it is a *technique of night* and this psychoanalysis can-not go beyond symbols. Therefore, it is within a limit of symbolic anchorage. Focusing on the textuality of text and the textual discourse, Ricoeur extends the nature of the text; text for him, always has a gravity of hermeneutic question. A text to Ricoeur is a discourse fixed by writing. Writing thus bears a distanciation from its subject to the linguistic domain. The dialectic of appropriation and distanciation gets created. Appropriation becomes the understanding through distances, it corresponds to the senses. Writing always calls and invites desperately for reading, thereafter, the fixation in writing becomes one of the central problematic. The reader and the text fall in a dialectical process. The world of the text and the world of the reader happen to meet in the reading process. The reading enlightens the darkness in the text that is there without any reading. The reader loses his/herself and lands in the textual territory and privileges the textual world over his/her own. The two worlds, nevertheless, have to be properly appropriated.

Ricoeur refutes Dilthey's division of the two concepts – *explanation* and *interpretation* as one for natural sciences and other for human sciences. For Ricoeur, *explanation*, too, is related to linguistic sciences – he gives examples from structural and formalistic approaches of linguistic understanding of the text as they too, appear to be explanatory sciences. Thus, the *interpretation-appropriation dialectic* becomes responsible for the understanding of oneself. The fulfilling of text becomes the real aim of reading the text-as writing awaits calls for reading similarly as life demands to be narrated.

Thus, the self-understanding and the understanding of self goes across the detour of the understanding of signs. The self becomes contemporaneous in the emerging process or constituent process of meaning. The text becomes his/her own which before was unknown territory. The reading process throws the reader in *the heaven of the here and the now moments*. Therefore, any current understanding of any text should also be put to epoché – because it comes through the distanciation and appreciation dialectic, because there is no single interpretation or understanding valid for all the times. Because all understanding takes place within one's self which lives in a language house. Humans are inscribed with writing – thus the cogito and Dasein with the attached ideologies are required to be put to a justful hermeneutics of suspension!

"From Sacred Scripture to the "Secular Scripture" (Literature): A Framework for Literary Hermeneutics" If after introduction, the following study is the brain, then this one may surely be considered the heart and the soul of the book. It presents a conclusion before conclusion. This only consists of the analysis of Ricoeur's hermeneutics and also submits the proposed framework. It is an analysis of hermeneutic convention from sacred text to secular scripture. It starts with the problem of writing and the convention of fixing dogmatism in human discourse. Writing makes humans soulless and barren beings. It traps people in dependence syndrome which creates emptiness. Rousseau too, mentions Ricoeur, considered writing one of the main evils that plunged civilisations to havoc. Ricoeur writes that with writing comes the separation of soul, from the message as the message gets disguised in writing. Thus begins the tyranny and inequality – it started the rules of priesthood rather than the word of God. Writing caused a break-up of the speaking community and the separation of soul – it propagated dogmatisation and annihilation as – most of the evils were born with writing.

Hermeneutics in modern times, with the changes in the world, has had a long journey from sacred to secular discourse. From the fall of Ottoman empire or the fall of Constantinople – it was the time of renaissance, reformation, spread of democracy and people's political rights, the impact of constitutions in different other institutions, saw a transformation from Godly laws to the earthly laws – in other words it went from Theo-centric to Geo-centric world as a whole.

In English, throughout the 17th, 18th and 19th centuries – namely the age of Dryden, Pope, Dr. Johnson, Coleridge, Wordsworth, and Arnold etc. scholars were more interested in producing good literature only. AND – no emphasis was given on interpretation. The main interest was in analysis, appreciation, satirizing, narrating or glorifying. But after the publication of the great work "The Rise of Hermeneutics" by Dilthey gave a challenge to the act of reading and understanding. But why do we need hermeneutics in literature after all? Literature in English was meant only to amuse, please, delight, or to entertain. Writing simply did not require any interpretation because most of the narrators and playwrights used to write prologues to the obscure and ambiguous aspects of their works. All of them condemned obscurity in literature. Language was just a matter of rhetoric; the interpretive principles were neither required nor studied nor taught.

At the time of Romantic Revival in the 19th century, the notion of genius got associated with creative writing; Coleridge privileges secondary imagination over primary imagination – this much used to be discussed in English Department classes. Nevertheless, literature became something manufactured by and created by a genius. Wordsworth falls divine after his escape from France, he starts creating spiritual insight into the natural phenomena – he weaves natural divinity into his writing. Swift gets declared a genius of his age and time. Thus, the importance of genius with literature becomes a general association – the creator gets equated with the divine Creator on the basis of his creation through his/her imaginative faculty. Observing these changes and paradigm shifts in general notions, after the Romantic Revival, Northrop Frye describes Romantic literature as *secular scripture* – herein the meaning becomes subjective. Thus, it was Eliot all alone who, having been influenced by Gadamer and other critics, pondered over the problem of interpretation. One of the major influences on reader-response-theory seems to be that of Wilhelm Dilthey – and thus a road goes from phenomenology to hermeneutics – the hermeneutics of suspension!

The chapter also sheds light on the relation between metaphor, language and time relation, transposition and the appropriation of the text, the play of heuristic fiction, the necessity and justly required criticism of the subject and ideology. One of the most outstanding contributions of Ricoeur – the narrative identity and oneself as another phenomenon is also brought into consideration. For Ricoeur, identity is always narrative – and it is not ethnic, political or historical etc. *Freud and Philosophy* for the justification of Ricoeur's epoché is referred to partially but enough to cover the topic. The three master's – Marx, Nietzsche, and Freud dominate Ricoeur's philosophy of epoché. All of them show a common opposition to the phenomenology of the sacred. Marx relegates economics and absurd theory of reflex consciousness; Nietzsche towards bilogism and perspectivism – incapable of expression without contradiction. Freud seems to be fixed only with psychology and decked out with a simplistic panasexulism. All agree on the notion of false consciousness but in a different way. Ricoeur mentions Descartes' and other philosophers' 'doubts' as they think that – *things are not as they appear.* Ricoeur's suspicion is not skepticism; it is for a new foundation, a new reign of truth and not by any destruction but by the invention of an art of interpretation – and understanding is hermeneutics. Thus, the suspension can be shown in three different ways and on three different levels, (a) economic, political or social level, (b) psychological level and (c) on the level of faith, value, truth or religion. Hermeneutics includes all *suspension of all presuppositions* of all the texts. Ricoeur, through his subjective analysis of text appears to be an individual thinker – living in *Lebenswelt*. His hermeneutics ruins the Husserlian idealism in the phenomenology of meaning and interpretation.

One of the most important parts of the findings of this research is presented at the end of this chapter-which is a strong stand against theory in the post-theory time for a final proposal and submission of the framework (hermeneutic) for literary analysis. It discloses the fashionable none/Sense of THEORY – especially the hypocrisy of theory in English Departments and many other Departments of Humanities. Ours is the time of the post-theory period where a justful hermeneutics and practice of epoché seems to be most needed in the pluri-vocal empire of language. In our time, Ricoeur's hermeneutics of suspicion are required more than ever before – because today there is always a powerful and panoptic gatekeeper at every door of the textual domain in every sphere of the modern communication system. They appear to be as strong as commandos at national borders and danger zones which may threaten the disguised authority. Most of them have the anxiety of influence syndrome – may be because of an inferiority complex or victim of their own ignorance. Hermeneutics of suspension has to free *text* from stagnant literary authorities, from the territory of modern day textual lalas, mullas and neo-Shylockeans for the textual economy, values, presentations, and perspectives including all sorts of voices – human or holy, all have to be free from all other background sounds and music.

The chapter ends with the hermeneutic framework (*Voice (human or holy) IMPACTS)*. The framework also shows Ricoeur's channel of hermeneutics – the hermeneutics of suspension and the third structure – cum model shows Ricoeur's subversion of Jakobson's model of linguistic communication into a channel of overall human hermeneutics.

"Fictory, Faction, or Hiterature?: Rushdie's Metaphor of Midnight and His '[Re] Configuration' of Time – the Mystery Called Maya" finally deals with practical aspects of the proposed framework with Rushdie's *Midnight's Children.* The framework *Voice IMPACTS* is applied as an experimentation keeping the channel of Ricoeur's hermeneutics. The analysis is made on the configuration of time interpreting the metaphor of midnight which goes from text to metaphor and from metaphor to the text. In conclusion, it appears that Ricoeur's claim for true configuration of time which was half historical and half fictional gets proved and fulfilled in the text. Thus, the text of *Midnight's Children* appears to be *half of the time* and *half about the time*. The technique, too, defeats the conventional notion of plot. It truly shows the concordance and discordance mechanism of time in a very remarkable way – in a way of magic-realism.

It has been observed that fascination towards history in modern fiction may be because of the prophecy made in the 1980s about the intervention or better called cultural intrusion in the literary domain. Literary discourse should not reflect only the past with the present – but rather the literary narratives should transcend time – they should go beyond time. There is a crisis of pure literary discourse in present times. Rushdie strives to create his fictional text only after the distortion or destruction of historical facts, religious faith, political and cultural differences. This is the reason that in modern day theologians` language; Rushdie is considered a mighty genus and – diabolically inspired. It is observed that history is being concretised excessively in literary discourse because of the intrusion of the cultural studies into literary discipline. Fictory or fiction may thus be given an emerging trend or genre of postmodern literature. History should not eclipse the true and pure literature. History fetches a cultural color to literary text – which limits the validity of the literary text and relevance. There should not be any confusion between literary studies and cultural studies, there should be a clear distinction as the similar problem can also be observed between Feminism and Women's Studies – Theater Studies and Film Studies etc.

Ricoeur's theory offers a broader framework and canvas other than only literary interpretation; it can well be used for freshness of the *all old and new narratives, secular and sacred both*. The epoché provides a parameter for the possibility of positive and productive changes. Ricoeur has appeared a truly and extremely positivist thinker – who brings life – the practical life and narratives together in reverse – and talks of narrative identity impressively. Ricoeur's framework has all the potential to understand the workmanship in a text – the artistic hard-work through hermeneutic labor. The organisation of language appears to be the genesis of men deep in metaphors. Hermeneutics in the modern world seems to be the last and final solution for all the problems that humans have!

Ricoeur has been constantly ignored only because he possesses a very strong notion to dismantle the propaganda or the functioning vicious ideologies or the obsolete and invalid meanings and amalgamated faith, wrong practices and conventions. He has been largely ignored because he seems to have all the potentiality to challenge the capitalists – to challenge the status quo of the capitalist empire/vampire!

The further areas of research generated by the book for the future researchers may be the following as they did not fall in the ambit of current research: Paul Ricoeur and the hermeneutics of 21st century narratives, Ricoeur's understanding of the text and a subjective turn, the clash of (civilisation) text and Ricoeur's third world: a better world, the text in digital and screen narratives, hermeneutics of world narratives, hermeneutics beyond time and space: communication beyond – a comparative study of Butler Bakhtin and Ricoeur, the hermeneutics of digital turn, hermeneutics of 9/11 literature, the narrative self and identity in Diaspora literature, a comparative study of Ricoeur and Baudrillard, a comparative study of Derrida, Lacan, and Ricoeur, language and narratives in the age of artificial intelligence, hermeneutics in *Inter-Networking* in the age *E-kranti*, Ricoeur's epoché: a paradigm shift, Hermeneutics in the age of *gate-keeping and panopticism* as the most commonly read 200 newspapers print the same headlines in their news items on certain topics and issues in the age of democracy and diverse cultures. Thus, words on page, sounds, images, actions and speeches on screen should equally be subjected and submitted to a justful hermeneutics of suspicion!

Works Cited and Consulted

Abrams, M. H. *The Mirror and the Lamp: Romantic Theory and Critical Tradition.* New York: OUP, 1953. Web.

Abrams, M. H. and Geoffrey Harpham. *A Glossary of Literary Terms.* 9th Edition. USA, Delhi, Boston: Cengage Learning, April 24, 2008. Web.

Abulad, Romualdo E., SVD. "What is Hermeneutics?" *The Literary – Theoretical Influence on the Thought of Hans Wilhelm Frei and Paul Ricoeur with Reference to Narrative Identity.* Kritike Volume One. Number Two. December 2007.11. Retrieved in January, 2013. Web.

Alexis, Deodato S. Itao. "Introduction." *Paul Ricoeur and Philosophy in the Twentieth Century.* Marcelino Agís Villaverde, Universidad de Santiago de Compostela. 2010. Web.

Amaladas, Anand. *Indian Exegesis: Hindu Buddhist Hermeneutics.* Chennai: Satya Nilayam Publications, 2003. Print.

Aristotle. *Poetics.* Ed. Amlan Das Gupt. India: Longman Study Edition, 2007. Web.

Aristotle. *Poetics.* USA: Penguin Classic. S. Paperback, Revised edition September 1996. Print, Web.

Authors on Writing Metaphors and Intellectual Labor. California: Barbar Thompson University of California San Diego, 2005. Web.

Bergmann, Albert. *The Philosophy of Language: Historical Foundations and Contemporary Issues.* Netherlands: Mustiness Hijholff / The Hague, 1974, Print. Web.

Black, Max. "Metaphor." *Proceedings of the Aristotelian Society. Ed.* Daniele Gioda (1954) 55, pp. 273-294. Web.

Bleicher, J. "Contemporary Hermeneutics-Hermeneutics as method, Philosophy and Critique." *Routledge* & *Kegan Paul,* 1980. Print.

Bloom, Harold. *A Map of Misreading.* USA, London: Oxford University Press, 1975. 2003. Web.

Blundell, Boyd. *Paul Ricoeur between Theology and Philosophy: Detour and Return.* Bloomington: Indiana University Press, 2010. Print.

Burke, Kenneth. *A Grammar of Motives.* USA, California: University of California Press, 1945, 1969. Web.

Bruns, G.L. *Hermeneutics Ancient and Modern.* New Heaven: Yale University Press, 1992. Print.

Chandler, Daneil. *Semiotic: The Basics.* 2nd addition. USA: Rutledge, 2007. Web.

Cand, Geir Amdal. "Explanation and Understanding: The Hermeneutic Arc Paul Ricoeur's Theory of Interpretation." *PhD Thesis*, May 2001. University of Oslo. Depart. of Philosophy. Web.

Clarke, Richard L. W., Kurt Mueller-Vollmer. Ed. *Friedrich Schleiermacher Outline of the 1819 Lectures: Compendium of 1819 – The Hermeneutics Reader.* London: Continuum, 1989. 72-97. World Applied Sciences Journal 15 (11): 1623-1629, IDOSI Publications, 2011. Web.

Clark S. H., *Paul Ricoeur.* London and New York: Routledge, 1990. Print.

Cohen, Richard A. and James. *Ricoeur As Another: The ethics of Subjectivity.* I Edition. New York: State University of New York, 2003. Web.

Coming to Terms with Barth's "Third Thing": Hans Frei, Paul Ricoeur, and the Possibility of Postliberal Homiletics. Lance B. Pape Granville and Erline Walker Assistant Professor of Homiletics, *Brite Divinity School III Ibero-American Conference on Paul Ricoeur`s thought* "Recognition, Social Justice and the Good Life." (Santiago de Chile, March 20-22, 2013). Web.

Crotty, M. *The Foundation of Social Research: Meaning and Perspective in the Research Process.* Ed. Sydney: Allen &Unwin, 1998. Web.

Caputo, John D. *Radical Hermeneutics, Studies in Phenomenology and Existential Philosophy.* Bloomington: Indiana University Press, 1987. Print.

Dauenhauer, Bernard P. *Paul Ricoeur: The Promise and Risk of Politics.* Lanham, Md.: Rowman and Littlefield, 1998. Print.

Davidson, Donald. "What Metaphors Mean." *Critical Inquiry.* Vol. 5, No. 1, Special Issue on Metaphor (Autumn, 1978), pp. 31-47. Print, Web.

Danesi, Marcel. *Vivo, Metaphor and the Origin of Language.* USA: Indiana University Press, 1993. Web.

Darsch, T. S. *Classical Literary Criticism. England: Penguin Books*, 1977. Print. Web.

Davit, Michael and Richard Hanley. Ed. *The Blackwell Guide to the Philosophy of Language.* USA: Blackwell Publications, 2006. Print.

Derrida, Jacques. "The White Mythology: Metaphor in the Text of Philosophy." *New Literary History* 6.1 (1974). Web.

Devidson, Donald. "What Metaphors Mean." Stockholm: Spark Tank Oche Handling, 2004. Web.

Flym, Thomas R. *Existentialism: A Very Short Introduction.* New York: OUP, 2006. Print.

F, Kermode. *The Sense of Ending: Studies in the Theory of Fiction.* New York: Oxford University Press, 1966. Print.

Gadamer, Hanse George. *Hermeneutics, Religion and Ethics.* Trans. Joel. Weinsheimer. Yale University Press, 1999. Print.

Gadamer, Hanse George. *Hermeneutics, Religion and Ethics.* Trans. Joel. Weinsheimer. Yale University Press, 1999. Print.

Ghaseani, M. Taghinead, A. Kabiri and M. Imani. "Ricoeur's Theory of Interpretation: A Method for Understanding Text" (Course Text). *A World Applied Science Journal* 15(11): 1623-1629, IDOSI Publications, 2011. Web.

Ghaseani, M. Taghinead, A. Kabiri and M. Imani. "Ricoeur's Theory of Interpretation: A Method for Understanding Text" (Course Text). *A World Applied Science Journal.* 15(11): 1623-1629, IDOSI Publications, 2011. Web.

Gutting, Gary. *French Philosophy in the Twentieth Century.* Cambridge: Cambridge University Press, 2001. Print.

Gu, Ming Dong. *Chinese Theories of Reading and Writing: A Route to Hermeneutics and Open Poetics.* SUNY series in Chinese Philosophy and Culture Albany: State University of New York Press, 2005. Web.

Husky, Rebecca K. *Paul Ricoeur on Hope: Expecting God.* Phenomenology and Literature (Book 6). New York: Peter Lang Publishing Inc, First printing edition, 2009. Web.

Hall, W David. *Paul Ricoeur and the Poetic Imperative: The Creative Tension Between Love and Justice.* New York Press: State University of New York Press, Sunny Series in Theory, 2008. Web.

Hahn, Lewis E. Ed. *The Philosophy of Paul Ricoeur.* Chicago and La Salle: Open Court, 1995. Print.

Hall, W. David. *Paul Ricoeur and the Poetic Imperative: The Creative Tension between Love and Justice.* Albany: State University of New York Press, 2007. Print.

Habeeb, M. A. R. "Reader-Response and Reception Theory." *Modern Literary Criticism and Theory: A History.* USA: Blackwell Publishing 2005, Web.

Hodge, Joanna. *Derrida on Time.* New York: Rutledge, 2007. Web.

Hengel, John Van Den, S.C.J. "Paul Ricoeur's *Oneself as Another* and Practical Theology. *Ricoeur and Foucault Between Ontology and Critique Patrick Gamez.* University of Notre Dame. *Études Ricoeuriennes / Ricoeur Studies,* Vol 4, No 2 (2013), pp. 90-107. 2013.160. Web.

Itao, Alexis Deodato. "Paul Ricoeur's Hermeneutics of Symbolism: A Critical Dialectic of Suspicion and Faith." December 2010. Volume 4, 2. December 2010-17. Retrieved on December 17, 2013. Web.

Ihde, Don. *Hermeneutic Phenomenology: The Philosophy of Paul Ricoeur.* Evanston: Northwestern University Press, 1971. Print.

III Ibero-American Conference on Paul Ricoeur`s Thought "Recognition, Social Justice and the Good Life" (Santiago de Chile, March 20-22, 2013). *Kritike* Volume Four Number Two (December 2010). 1-17. Web.

Introduction to Literary Hermeneutics. Peter Szandi Tran Trans Medha Moodmanser Cax Western Reserve 1995, Print.

Jervolino, D. *The Cogito and Hermeneutics: The Question of the Subject in Ricoeur.* Dordrecht: Kluwer, 1990. Print.

Jha, Dr. Shefali. "Hermeneutics." *Research Methodology and Methods.* Ed. Professor Yogendra Singh. New Delhi: IGNOU, 2005. 120-30. Print.

Joy, Morny. Ed. *Paul Ricoeur and Narrative.* Calgary: University of Calgary Press, 1997. Print.

Kant, Immanuel. Level III, Lecture 3. "'The *Transcendental Aesthetic*: A Priori Intuitions". *The Critique of Pure Reason.* Translation and Comments by. Philip McPherson Rudisill, 2012. Web.

Kaufmann, Sebastian. "The Attestation of the Self as a Bridge Between Hermeneutics and Ontology in the Philosophy of Paul Ricoeur." Marquette University Dissertation 2009. PhD. Milwaukee, Wiscounism. Web.

Kenzo, Mabiata Justin Robert. *Dialectic of Sedimentation and Innovation: Paul Ricoeur on Creativity after the Subject.* USA: Peter Lang Publishing Inc., 2009. Web.

Kerning, Richard. Ed. *Poetics of Modernity Towards: A Hermeneutic Imagination.* Humanity Book, 1999. Print.

Kaplan, David M. Ed. *Reading Ricoeur.* Albany: SUNY Press, 2008. Print.

Ricoeur's Critical Theory. Albany: State University of New York Press, 2003. Print.

Kearney, Richard. Ed. *Paul Ricoeur: The Hermeneutics of Action.* London: Sage, 1996. Print.

On Paul Ricoeur: The Owl of Minerva. Aldershot: Ashgate Publishing, 2004. Print.

Kemp, T. P. and D. Rasmussen Eds. *The Narrative Path: The Later Works of Paul Ricoeur.* Cambridge, MA: The MIT Press, 1989. Print.

Klemm, David E., William Schweiker. Eds. *Meaning in Texts and Action: Questioning Paul Ricoeur.* Charlottesville: University Press of Virginia, 1993. Print.

Kirby, John T. "Aristotle on Metaphor." *The American Journal of Philology* 118.4 (1997): 517-54. Web.

Laverty, Susann M. Laverty, S. M. "Hermeneutic Phenomenology and Phenomenology: A Comparison of Historical and Methodological Considerations." *International Journal of Qualitative Methods.*2. September 2003. Retrieved in January, 2013. Web.

Lafont, Cristina. Trans. Jose Medina. "The Linguistic Turn in Hermeneutic Philosophy." *Hermeneutics, Religion and Ethics. Hanse – George – Gadamer.* Trans. Joel. Weinsheimer. Yale University Press, 1999. Print.

Lawler, Leonard. *Imagination and chance: The Difference Between the Thought of Ricoeur and Derrida.* New York: State University of New York Press, 1993. Web.

Lycan, William J. *Philosophy of Language: A Contemporary Introduction.* 2nd Ed. USA: Rutledge Taylor and Francis Group New York and London, 2000. Web.

McCarthy, Joan. Dennett and Ricoeur on the Narrative Self. philpapers.org, 2007. Web.

Metaphor and Conditional Philosophy from Kant to Derrida. New York and London: Rutledge Taylor and Francis Graph, 2007. Print.

Moore, Gregory. *Nietzsche, Biology and Metaphor.* Cambridge: Cambridge University Press. 2012. Web.

Miller, Alexander. Ed. *Philosophy of Language.* USA: Rutledge, 2007. Print.

Markey, Richard. *Introduction to Literary Hermeneutics.* USA: John Hopkins University and Michael Sprinkler State University of New York, 2010. Web.

Ritivor. Andrew Deciv. *Paul Ricoeur: Tradition and Innovation in Rhetorical Theory.* 4-6 Brand Southern: Illinois University Press. 2006. Web.

Muldoon, Mark S. *Tricks of Time: Bergson, Merleau-Ponty and Ricoeur in Search of Time, Self and Meaning.* Duquesne: Duquesne University Press, 2006. Web.

Nietzsche, *Biology and Metaphor Gregory Moore Cambridge*, Cambridge University Press 2007, Print.

Ott, Walter. *Locke's Philosophy of Language.* Cambridge: Cambridge University Press. 2004. Print.

"The Philosophy of Paul Ricoeur." *Paul Ricoeur.* Ed. Levis Edwin Hahu. Vol. 22. Paperback. USA: Library of Living Philosophies. 1998. Web.

Paul Ricoeur and Contemporary Thought Ed. John Walt, William Schweker, and W. David Hall. USA: Routledge, 2006. Web.

Paul Ricoeur: The Hermeneutics of Action: Philosophy and Social Criticism series.

Ed. Richard Kearney. New York: SAGE Publications Ltd, 1996. Web.

Putti, Joseph. *Theology As Hermeneutics: Paul Ricoeur's Theory of Text Interpretation and Method in Theology.* USA: International Scholars Publications. 1994. Web.

Pirovolakis, Eftichic. Reading Derrida and Ricoeur: Improbable Encounters Between Deconstruction and Hermeneutics. New York: SUNYP, 2010. Web.

Pandikattu, Kuruvilla. *Between Before and Beyond: An Exploration of the Human Condition Inspired by Paul Ricoeur.* Pune: Creative Ventures, 2013. Print.

Pellauer, David. *Ricoeur: A Guide for the Perplexed.* New York: Continuum, 2007. Print.

Quintilian, Roman. *Institute of Oratory.* England: Lee Honeycutt, January 4, 2010. Web.

Radical Hermeneutics: Studies in Phenomenology and Existential Philosophy. Ed. John D. Caputo. Bloomington: Indiana University Press, 1987. Print.

Ramberg, Bjørn and Gjesdal, Kristin. "Hermeneutics." *The Stanford Encyclopedia of Philosophy.* Edward N. Zalta. ed. Summer 2013 Edition. First Published on Wed Nov 9, 2005. Retrieved in January, 2013. Web.

Rasmussen, David. "Rethinking Subjectivity: Narrative Identity and the Self." *Philosophy and Social Criticism* 21. (5): 159–72, 1995. Print.

Reading Ricoeur. Ed. David M. Kaplan. New York: Phil-Papers, State University of New York Press, 2008. Web.

Reagan, Charles E. Ed. *Studies in the Philosophy of Paul Ricoeur.* Athens: Ohio University Press, 1979. Print.

---. *Paul Ricoeur: His Life and Work.* Chicago: University of Chicago Press, 1996. Print.

Richards, Ivor Arms Troy. *The Philosophy of Rhetoric.* New York and Condon: Oxford University Press, 1936. Print.

Ricoeur, Paul. "Explanation and Understanding: On Same Remarkable Connections Among the Theory of the Text, Theory of Action and Theory of History." Eds. C. E. Reagan and D. Stewart. *The Philosophy of Paul Ricoeur: An Anthology of His Work.* Boston: Beacon Press, 1978. Print.

----. *Editors Lectures on Ideology, and Utopia.* New York, USA Columbia: Columbia University Press, 1986. Web.

----. *From Text to Action: Essays in Hermeneutics II.* Trans. Kathleen Blamey, John B. Thompson. *Evaston: Northwestern* University Press, 1991. Print.

----. Fallible Man. Trans. Charles A. Kelbley. Rev. Ed. New York: Fordham University Press,1986. Print.

----. *Freud and Philosophy: An Essay on Interpretation.* Trans. Edward G. Ballard and Lester E. Embree. Evanston: Northwestern University Press, 1970. Print.

----. *Freedom and Nature: The Voluntary and the Involuntary.* Trans. Erazin Kohak. Evanston: Northwestern University Press, 1966. Print.

----. *Hermeneutics and Human Sciences: Essays on Language, Action and Interpretation.* Trans. Ed. John B. Thompson. Cambridge: Cambridge. University of Chicago Press, 1988. Print.

----. *History and Truth.* Trans. Charles A. Kehbley. Evanston: Northwestern University Press, 1965. Print.

----. "Inaugural Lecture: Imagination in Discourse in Action." *Analecta Husserliana: The yearbook of phenomenological Research: The Human Being in Action.* Ed. Anna-Terresa Tymmieniecka Springer Science, Business Media, B. V. Tymieniecka, *Anna-Teresa* (Ed.) Vol. 7. (pp. 3-22). 1978. "International Phenomenology Conference," 5th 1975. Published in 1978. Web.

----. *Interpretation Theory: Discourse and the Surplus of Meaning.* Fort Worth: Texas Christian University Press, 1976. Print.

----. *Memory, History, Forgetting.* Trans. Kathleen Blamey, David Pellaver. Chicago: University of Chicago Press, 2004. Print.

----. *Oneself as Another.* Trans. Kathleen Blamey. Chicago: University of Chicago Press, 1992. Print.

----. *On Translation.* Trans. Eileen Brennan. New York: Routledge, 2006. Print.

----. *The Conflict of Interpretations: Essays in Hermeneutics.* Northwestern University Studies in Phenomenology and Existential Philosophy. Evanston: Northwestern University Press, 1974. Print.

----. *The Course of Recognition.* Trans. David Pullovers. Cambridge: Harward University, 2005. Print.

---. *The Just.* Trans. David Pellauer. Chicago: University of Chicago Press, 2000. Print.

----. *The Philosophy of Paul Ricoeur: An Anthology of his Works.* Ed. Charles E. Reagan, David Stewart. Boston: Beacon Press, 1978. Print.

----. *The Rule of Metaphor: Multi-Disciplinary Studies in the Creation of Meaning in Language.* Trans. Robert Czerny, Kathleen McLaughlin, John Costello, S.J. Toronto: University of Toronto Press, 1978. Print.

----. *The Symbolism of Evil.* Trans. Emerson Buchanan. New York: Harper and Row, 1967. Print.

----. *Time and Narrative. The Creation of Meaning in Language.* Vol.I, III. Trans. Kathleen McLaughlin and David Pellauer. London: Chicago University Press, 1984-1988. Print.

Russell D. A. Michael, Winter Bottom. *Classical Literary Criticism.* India: Worlds Classics OUP, 2010. Print.

Roark, Toni. *Aristotle on Time: A Study of Physics.* Cambridge: Cambridge University Press, 2011. Print.

Ricoeur's Theory of Interpretation: A Method for Understanding Text (Course Text) *Ghasemi, M. Taghinejad A. Kabiri and 1M. Imani.* Theological Studies, 55. (1994). Web.

Scott, Alison. "Baumann, Ricoeur and the Hermeneutics of Suspicion." *Conlinum International Publishing Group*, New York, 2009. Print.

Schrift, Alan D. *Twentieth Century French Philosophy: Key Terms and Thinkers.* Blackwell Publisher, 2006. Print.

Stiver, Dan R. *Theology after Ricoeur: New Direction in Hermeneutical Theology.* 1st Edition. USA: Westminster John Knox Press, 2001. Web.

Seikkula, Aura. *On the Notion of Culture and Identity: A Study of Paul Ricoeur's Narrative Identity.* Germany: VDM Verlag, 2008. Web.

Soskie, Janet. *Metaphor and Religious Language.* Oxford: OUP, 1985. Web.

Searle. John. *Expression and Meaning.* London, USA: Cambridge University Press. 1979. Web.

Source, T Kirby "Aristotle on Metaphor." *The American Journal of Philosophy.* Vol.

118, No. 4. Winter. 1997. P.517-554. Johns Hopkins University Press. Web.

Stahl, Gerry "Marxian Hermeneutics and Heideggerian Theory: Interpreting and Transforming our World" Phd. Dess. Illinois, 1975. Web.

Simms, Karl. *Paul Ricoeur.* London and New York: Rutledge, 2003. Web.

Scott, Alison. "Baumann, Ricoeur and the Hermeneutics of Suspicion." *Continuum International Publishing Group*: New York, 2009. Print.

Sainsbury, RM. *Departing from Frege, Essays in the Philosophy of Language.* London, New York: Rutledge, 2002. Print.

Soames, Scott *Philosophy of Language.* Oxford: Princeton and Oxford University Press, 2010. Print.

Schrift, Alan D. *Twentieth Century French Philosophy: Key Terms and Thinkers.* Blackwell Publisher, 2006. Print.

Simms, Karl. *Paul Ricœur.* Routledge Critical Thinkers. New York: Routledge, 2002. Print.

Schrift, Alan D. *Twentieth Century French Philosophy: Key Terms and Thinkers.* USA: Blackwell Publishers, 2006. Print.

Simms, Karl. *Paul Ricoeur.* London and New York: Rutledge, 2003. Web. *The Narrative Path: The Later works of Paul Ricoeur.* Ed. T. Peter and David Rousseau. USA, Cambridge: The MIT Press, 1 Edition, November 1989. Web.

Thompson, John B. *Critical Hermeneutics: A Study in the Thought of Paul Ricoeur and Jürgen Habermas.* Cambridge: Cambridge University Press, 1981. Print.

The Convergence of Ricoeur's and Von Wright's Complex Models of History. Linda L. Cox Austin Community College Études Ricoeuriennes / Ricoeur Studies, Vol 5, No 1 (2014), pp. 95-1. Web.

Tomlinson, Barbara. "Authors on Writing Metaphors and Intellectual Labor" University of California. San Diego, 2005. Web.

Uggla, Bengt Kristensson. *Ricoeur Hermeneutics and Globalization.* USA: Continuum International Group. 2010. Print.

Uggla, Bengt Kristensson. *Ricoeur, Hermeneutics and Globalization.* New York: Continuum Studies, 2010. Web.

Venena, Henry Isaac. *Identifying Selfhood: Imagination, Narrative, and Hermeneutics in the Thought of Paul Ricoeur.* Albany: State University of New York Press, 2000. Print.

Venema, Henry Isaac. *Identifying Selfhood: Imagination, Narrative, and Hermeneutics in the Thought of Paul Ricoeur.* Suny Series, McGill Studies in the History of Religions. Paperback. New York: State University of New York Press, 2000. Web.

Verene, Donald Phillip. *The New Art of Autobiography: An Essay on the Life of Giambattista Vico.* Oxford: Clarendon Press, 1991. Web.

Vico, Giambattista. *On the Study Methods of Our Time.* Translated by Elio Gianturco. Reissued with a Preface by Donald Phillip Verene, and including "The Academies and the Relation between Philosophy and Eloquence," Translated by Donald Phillip Verene. Ithaca, N.Y.: Cornell University Press, 1990. Web.

Vanhhaoger, Kevin J. *Biblical Narratives in the Philosophy of Paul Ricoeur: A Study in Hermeneutics and Theology.* USA: Trinity Evangelical Divinity School, 2007. Web.

Valdes, M. Ed. "Life: A Story in Search of a Narrator." *A Ricoeur Reader: Reflection and Imagination.* Hemel Hempstead: Harvester Wheatsheaf, 1991. Web.

Williams, Caroline. *Contemporary French Philosophy: Modernity and Persistence of Subject.* London and New York: The Athlone Press, 2001. Print.

Wall, John. *Moral Creativity: Paul Ricoeur and the Poetics of Possibility.* New York: Oxford University Press, 2005. Print.

Williams, Caroline. *Contemporary French Philosophy: Modernity and Persistence of Subject.* London and New York: The Athlone Press, 2001. Print.

Wiecinski, Andrzej. Ed. *Between Description and Interpretation: The Hermeneutic Turn in Phenomenology.* Hermeneutic Press, 2005. Print.

Williams, Caroline. *Contemporary French Philosophy: Modernity and Persistence of Subject.* London and New York: The Athlone Press, 2001. Print.

Direct Web Sources

http://www.kritike.org/journal/issue_8/itao_december2010.pdf

http://www.biography.com/people/paul-ricoeur-9458208

http://en.wikiped.ia.org/wiki/Paul_Ric%C5%93ur

http://www.iep.utm.edu/ricoeur/

http://www.amazon.com/Paul-Ricoeur/e/B000APSDRC

http://ricoeur.pitt.edu

http://www.kritike.org/journal/issue_2/abulad_december2007.pdf

http://www.amazon.com/Paul-Ricoeur/e/B000APSDRC

http://www.fondsricoeur.fr/photo/Paul%20Ricoeur%20and%20philosophy

http://www.biography.com/people/paul-ricoeur-9458208

http://www.youtube.com/watch?v=6iwc_VW26PU

http://www.egs.edu/library/paul-ricoeur/biography/

http://www.loc.gov/loc/kluge/prize/ricoeur.html

http://books.google.co.in/books/about/Oneself_as_Another.html?id

http://www.gongfa.com/robinsonlike.htm

http://www.giffordlectures.org/Author.asp?AuthorID=218

http://www.bu.edu/wcp/Papers/Soci/SociTura.htm

http://web.ed.ntnu.edu.tw/~t04008/frontpage/online/ideology/ricoeur1.doc

http://www3.undpress.nd.edu/excerpts/P01504-ex.pdf

http://www.revuedumauss.com.fr/media/BlancRic0307.pdf

http://idosi.org/wasj/wasj15(11)11/22.pdf

http://www.sunypress.edu/pdf/61659.pdf

http://www.talmidim.cz/filosofie/Paul%20Ricoeur%20(Routledge

http://web.ics.purdue.edu/~smith132/French_Philosophy/Win91/paulr.pdf

http://www.lse.ac.uk/europeanInstitute/research/forumForEuropeanPhilosophy/pdf/paulricoe

http://www.unipune.ac.in/snc/cssh/ipq/english/IPQ/.pdf

http://www.rgpost.com/media/Ricoeur.pdf

http://www.arsdisputandi.org/publish/articles/000217/article.pdf

http://www.452f.com/pdf/numero01/01_452f-misc-xamist-en.pdf

http://www.janushead.org/8-1/ricoeur.pdf

https://www.youtube.com/watch?v=K1WhOICr1bEThe Motive for Metaphor

https://www.youtube.com/watch?v=r3pFfcBSxhE Hidden Metaphors in Gesture, Sign, and Spoken Language-Haun Saussy

https://www.youtube.com/watch?v=Rp7nxAiC-Pg Metaphor, Narrative and Subjective Cultural Consciousness

http://plato.stanford.edu/entries/vico/

http://www.freud-sigmund.com/ Paul-Ricoeur-Time-and-Narrative-vol1.pdf

http://ricoeur.pitt.edu/ojs/index.php/ricoeurSome Edia journal. Ricoeur Studies.

http://www.kritike.org/journal/issue_2/abulad_december2007.pdf

http:// www. Kritike. Org/ournal/issue8/itao.

http://www.ualberta.ca / ~ iiqm/backissues/2_3final/pdf/laverty.pdf.

http://plato.stanford.edu/archives/sum2013/entries/hermeneutics/.

http://plato.stanford.edu/archives/sum2013/entries/hermeneutics/.

http://www.ualberta.ca/~iiqm/backissues/2_3final/pdf/laverty.pdf.

http://ricoeur.pitt.edu.

https://www.youtube.com/watch?v=DauVUMGAbIY

http:// www. Kritike. Org/ournal/issue8/itao

Index

E

F

G

H

I

J

K

L